TRADING
Psychology

TRADING
Psychology
The Bible for Traders

ANIRUDH SETHI

Notion Press

Old No. 38, New No. 6
McNichols Road, Chetpet
Chennai - 600 031

First Published by Notion Press 2017
Copyright © Anirudh Sethi 2017
All Rights Reserved.

ISBN 978-1-948230-80-3

This book has been published with all reasonable efforts taken to make the material error-free after the consent of the author. No part of this book shall be used, reproduced in any manner whatsoever without written permission from the author, except in the case of brief quotations embodied in critical articles and reviews.

The Author of this book is solely responsible and liable for its content including but not limited to the views, representations, descriptions, statements, information, opinions and references ["Content"]. The Content of this book shall not constitute or be construed or deemed to reflect the opinion or expression of the Publisher or Editor. Neither the Publisher nor Editor endorse or approve the Content of this book or guarantee the reliability, accuracy or completeness of the Content published herein and do not make any representations or warranties of any kind, express or implied, including but not limited to the implied warranties of merchantability, fitness for a particular purpose. The Publisher and Editor shall not be liable whatsoever for any errors, omissions, whether such errors or omissions result from negligence, accident, or any other cause or claims for loss or damages of any kind, including without limitation, indirect or consequential loss or damage arising out of use, inability to use, or about the reliability, accuracy or sufficiency of the information contained in this book.

Contents

1. Trading Psychology — 1
2. Applying Trading Psychology to Enhance Trading Success — 17
3. Conquering the Psychology of Trading — 26
4. 10 Psychological Stock Trading Principles — 41
5. Top Ten Trading Psychology Myths — 50
6. Developing your Mind for Trading: Building the Inner Team for Consistent Profitability — 58
7. Trading Psychology and Attitude — 66
8. Trading Psychology Diagnosis: Identifying the Root of Trading Problems — 74
9. A Powerful Technique for Changing Your Trading Psychology — 83
10. Trading Psychology and Trade Management — 92
11. Mind Shift: A Different View of Trading Psychology — 101
12. Psychometrics and Trading Psychology — 110
13. Five Guiding Principles of Trading Psychology — 118
14. Managing Trading Psychological Risks — 124
15. Price Action Trading Psychology for Consistent Result and Profit — 132
16. Healthy Psychological Profile for Successful Trading — 140
17. 3 Keys to Mastering your Trading Psychology — 149
18. Developing Your Mind for Trading: Building the Inner Team for Consistent Profitability — 157

19. Managing the Mind That Trades:
    Micro Management of a Trader's Psychology   163
20. A Psychology Checklist for Trader   171
21. Mastering Fear and Impulse   175
22. The Brain's Role in Trading Performance   184
23. The Psychology of Taking Losses   193
24. Why Stock Traders Fail (And Others Succeed)   202
25. Which Trading Personality Are You: Warrior, Nomad or Settler? 207
26. Why Is Trading Failure In Our DNA and How to Fix It? 214
27. The Psychology Behind "Harmonic" Trading   221
28. Trading Psychology: Coping with Losing Trades   227
29. 18 Biases That Explain Why Traders Make Mistakes   234
30. 4 Trading Metrics to Boost Your Trading Performance 242
31. Goals: Improve Profitability by Setting Goals   249
32. Luck vs. Skill for Trade Success   253
33. Neuroeconomics: Losing Money? Here's Why   257
34. Why 95% of Traders Lack Self Awareness   266
35. Why Your Mind Will Forever Keep You a Losing Trader 271
36. Trading Behaviour – Emotion vs. Logic   276
37. How to Remove Doubts, Uncertainty, and Fears   285
38. Risk Intelligence: The Dirty Little Secret at
    The Heart of All Successful Trading   290
39. Neuroplasticity: Your Brain and Your Trading   299
40. Intelligence, Overconfidence and Trading   305
41. The Journey of Self-Development   311
42. Testosterone, Cortisol, Predict Risky Trading   316
43. Attribution and Cognitive Bias   322
44. Optimistic Pessimism is Good for the Trader   326
45. Dealing with Loss Aversion in Trade is
    Indispensable for Profit   333
46. Trading Psychology Quotes: 337

Trading Psychology

Trading psychology alludes to the mental and passionate angles that direct a trader's choice and is an imperative factor in deciding his prosperity or disappointment in the trading procedure. Certain feelings like insatiability, fear and dissatisfaction assume vital parts in the trading procedure. Greed is characterised as extreme yearning to gather more riches. It can be either gainful or destructive, contingent upon how a trader uses it in various circumstances. It has positive outcomes in the buyer advertise. The more extended a trader remains on the amusement, the more prominent riches he can assemble. In any case, it is dangerous when, all of a sudden, a bear advertise strikes in. Fear, then again, is the correct inverse of ravenousness. It keeps down a trader from making strides in the trading procedure. What's more, like insatiability, it can be both dangerous and valuable, depending upon the circumstance of the market. Lament is another feeling a trader must be cautious of. There are numerous traders who bounced into the trading procedure in light of disappointment, winding up losing more money all the while. A sound psychology in trading is an unquestionable requirement if one wishes to wind up a fruitful trader. There are numerous qualities and aptitudes required by traders with the goal to be effective in the money related markets. The capacity to comprehend the internal workings of an organisation, its basics and the capacity to decide the heading of the pattern are a couple of the key qualities required, yet none of these is as critical as the capacity to contain feelings and look after the train.

Common Sense of Psychology

The psychology of trading is critical, and the purpose behind that is genuinely basic. A trader who frequently dashes through all the stocks, without prior warning, is compelled to settle on speedy choices. To finish this, they require common sense. They additionally, by expansion, require train. So, they stay with beforehand settled trading plans and know when to book benefits and losses. Feelings can't act as a burden. Best traders will concur that trading is as much about psychology as it is about a decent methodology. Without the mental grit to adhere to a system, the best methodology on the planet won't do much good. Effective traders do not just ace a methodology, they ace their own psychology, creating characteristics (for example, train and persistence) which enable them to actualise their systems. Trading, to me, is the best individual attempt a man can go up against in his life. I say this because of how troublesome it can be now and again and how all-devouring it can be as well. It is one of the last callings that your identity and what you consider 'yourself' are reflected to you in view of your value bend. The field of dynamic trading is a testing, quick paced condition with almost boundless potential outcomes and entanglements. The chances are apparently stacked against dynamic traders in the commercial centre, with thinks about recommending that upwards of 80% reliably lose money and just 1% accomplishes unsurprising long-haul productivity. With four out of five traders demonstrating customary loss, it is questionable if anybody will seek a profession in the trading business. All things considered, it's not regular for a person to put time and money into a business that has an 80% shot of falling flat, things being what they are, so what is the reason behind the appreciation for dynamic trading as a calling? The appropriate response lies in the advantages that achievement in the commercial centre can give to prosperous traders. Monetary autonomy, self-strengthening and an escape from a subpar vocation are a couple of advantages delighted in by the individuals who beat the chances and handle the metal ring.

Assessment Paralysis

Most traders begin by drenching up data. This data will come as stock picks, books, courses, trading mentors, masters and so on. Your own convictions, foundation and identity attributes will then take that data and process it into what I call your establishment for trading. Next, you will take this recently discovered data into the universe of the market. This can be energising and somewhat startling in the meantime. On the off chance that you are fortunate, you will put on a couple of trades and things will go easily. The money will simply stream in. On the off chance that you are unfortunate, you will rapidly acknowledge why 90%+ of traders fail during the initial couple of years. Regardless of how you begin, you will definitely face a loss that will hit you in the gut. This loss will look like the first time a young lady broke your heart or the mistrust you had when you heard at school that Santa didn't exist, after your folks helped you draft your Christmas list of things to get and forgetting treats for quite a long time. You will feel a sense of absolute uniqueness as your trading world unwinds substantially speedier than the time you spent to develop it. This is the stage where most traders will spend their whole professions. In any business, investigation of the organisation's execution to drive and facilitate development is foremost. Trading is the same. The main issue is, you need to disentangle when it's a great opportunity to change your model versus when comes about are simply clamour from the market. Consider it, on the off chance that you have quite recently put in hours, weeks or months exploring a framework. This framework, on all fronts, appears as though it will give you an edge over the market about 60% of the time. Notwithstanding this edge, it likewise gives you 2-to-1 regarding the measure of champs and washouts. In every way, this would be viewed as a framework worth testing in this present reality. Obviously, since the market is irregular, assume that out of your initial 6 trades, just 1 works. The prepared trader will realise that it's a matter of setting a sufficiently substantial specimen set of trades for things to get out. The lesser trader or the trader stuck in the examination loss of motion stage will unmistakably. Change this framework before it has sufficient energy to sprout.

Challenge of Trading

Dynamic trading as a calling presents many difficulties to an individual entering the commercial centre. Insights are not empowering, with most observational proof recommending that a person's trading vocation will be brief and costly. Life span in the commercial centre, among new traders, is overwhelmingly short-lived. Scholarly investigations concentrated on the period of time new traders stay dynamic to demonstrate that almost 40% most recent one month in the market and just 7% stay dynamic the following five years. Notwithstanding the short trading profession, a tenderfoot trader's passage into the budgetary markets can likewise prove to be costly. The measure of money related loss maintained by another trader amid his or her presentation into the commercial centre can change fiercely and is at last ward upon how much capital is at the trader's transfer. Likewise, foolhardy execution of use by an unpractised trader can quickly transform a sensible draw down into calamity. While dynamic trading produces a greater number of failures than champs, the likelihood of accomplishment exists. Individual accounts of monetary profit, the noteworthy track records of renowned financial specialists and profiles of informal investors who took little measures of funding, and in this manner, assembled quick fortunes are effortlessly found through some attributes of the psychology of the trading business. Maybe the most convincing confirmation that trading achievement is conceivable is the insights encompassing the trading practices of gainful traders. Studies have demonstrated that the 1–2% of traders who accomplish long haul productivity represent 12% of throughout the day-trading activity. This relationship delineates that fruitful traders have discovered a strategy for directing trade that makes an "edge" that can be connected over and again to the commercial centre. Through reliable and computed activity, these traders can consistently flourish.

Trading Randomness

Understanding that the market is irregular is most likely the key fundamental aspect of being plainly gainful. I have done everything regarding anticipating the following activity of the market. Elliott Wave, symphonious trading, point and figure, great break out gauges, so on and so forth. On occasion, the market would hold fast to my investigation, which would make me feel like I was responsible for the circumstance. Be that as it may, there were times when the market would go through my key level as though it didn't exist. Since I've been doing this for a long time, I now understand that my investigation does not exist any place else but in my mind. The main reason the market would react to my investigation depends on regardless of whether the other dynamic traders who can impact the development of my stock are on an indistinguishable stage from me. It just takes one trader with enough money to totally nullify your examination. It doesn't take a crowd of individuals hollering and shouting on the floor or setting a huge number of trades over the web. It just takes one individual, some place on planet earth, to choose that the stock ought to go higher or lower. All in all, where does this abandon you? I will never instruct you to not play out some level of examination, since I put stock in the specialised investigation. What I am stating is, you should expel any passionate connection for what the market can or will do next. You need to trust that the market will and can do anything. Until the point that you result in these present circumstances acknowledgment, you will constantly stop benefits or get halted out shy of the breakout move, in light of the fact that your examination has disclosed to you that if x happens then y is ideal around the bend.

Trading Enthusiasm

The mental cosmetics of every trader have a huge bearing on regardless of whether accomplishment in the commercial centre is accomplished or even remotely conceivable. Dealing with one's feelings when going up against with advertise instigated difficulty presents many difficulties to the dynamic trader and is a basic part of the execution. Fear and greed are the two feelings that apply the most impact upon a person's execution in the commercial centre. In programmed enthusiastic reactions, for example, these two have been logically appeared to "hamper" more perplexing basic leadership forms engaged with dynamic trading. Unless legitimately tended to, fear and greed can be drivers of passionate basic leadership and straightforwardly in charge of keeping the steady use of sound trading philosophy.

Fear

At the point when a trader's screen is throbbing red (a sign that stocks are down) and awful news comes to fruition regarding a specific stock or the general market, it's normal for the trader to get frightened. At the point when this happens, they may blow up and feel forced to trade their property and go to money or to shun going out on a limb. Presently, in the event that they do that, they may stay away from the specific loss. However, they likewise will pass up a major opportunity for the increases. Fear capacities as a security gadget and is an essential piece of survival. On the other hand, in the trading condition, fear turns out to be an execution inhibitor. In the region of dynamic trading, there are two characterisations of fear, each with special negative effects after trading execution

Fear of disappointment: Fear of disappointment related to individual self-esteem, with the aftereffect of a losing trade and loss of capital. Subsequently, expanded weight expedited by hair-splitting notwithstanding the unwillingness to execute trades misgiving of loss are regular issues identified with a trader's fear of disappointment.

Fear of progress: Fear of accomplishment is harder to fathom, as it runs unreasonably to a great many people's perspectives toward accomplishment. Self-harm and giving back benefits, known as "giving" to the market, are execution depreciators that emerge from a trader's fear of accomplishment. Without an instrument by which to oversee fear and the subsequent nerves, a trader is probably going to encounter high anxiety, inward clash and a general negative involvement in the commercial centre.

Traders need to comprehend what fear is; essentially a characteristic response to what they see as a danger (for this situation, maybe to their benefit or money-making potential). Evaluating the fear may offer assistance. Or, then again, they might have the capacity to better manage fear by considering what they fear and why they fear it. Likewise, by considering this issue early and knowing how they may naturally respond to or see certain things, a trader could disconnect from and distinguish those sentiments amid a trading session, and after that, endeavour to concentrate on moving past the feeling. Obviously, this may not be simple and may take rehearsing, but it's important to the well-being of a speculator's portfolio.

Greed

In the realm of trading, achievement is measured through the amount of money in one's trading account. The score is kept in dollars and pennies; accordingly, greed in dynamic trading is fixated on the collection of hard money. Covetousness is a determinant of a wide assortment of practices that are unfavourable to productive trading. A couple of the most widely recognised entanglements are:

Overtrading: Overtrading can be credited to covetousness in the longing to profit empowers taking trades that are outside of the embraced system. Imprudent trading is regularly the outcome, with the trader overlooking pre-set decides for pursuing benefit or compensating for the loss.

Forceful hazard taking: With a specific end goal to profit and fulfil insatiability, a trader may embrace chance parameters that surpass accessible assets. Taking strangely extensive positions and taking part in foolhardy money administration are basic issues related to greed.

Failure to characterise benefit and loss: Profit and loss are key components of money administration that must be characterised before each trade is taken. Covetousness makes this troublesome, on the grounds that the benefit targets are regularly irrational and the acknowledgment of a loss defers the moment of delight that a triumphant trade gives. The outcome is the inclination to display uncertainty when taking benefits and hesitance in existing losing trades. Greed is difficult to overcome, that is because inside a number of us there is an impulse to consistently attempt to improve, to endeavour to get only somewhat more. A trader ought to perceive this nature in the event that it is available and create trade designs in view of balanced business choices, not on what adds up to an enthusiastic impulse or conceivably unsafe intuition. If greed is left unmanaged and remains a considerable piece of a trader's mind, times of managed achievement can prompt sentiment trade related happiness, as sentiments of arrogance can prompt forceful hazard taking and hyper-forceful trade choice. The impact that insatiability and happiness have upon a trader's mind can be considerable and destructive to a solid trading attitude. The errand of dealing with these issues must be sincerely tended to, keeping in mind the end goal to conquer the difficulties them a chance to benefit.

Equity Curve of Trading

Individuals invest a considerable measure of energy in dissecting their individual victories and losses in trade, searching for some kind of knowledge that will enable them to decipher the code possibly in the event that I pick an alternate moving normal or on the off chance that I cut my loss before. These are useful things when taking a gander at a couple trades, yet how might this affect the greater part of your trades? Have you sincerely kept up a similar framework sufficiently long to try and investigate how minor changes could offer assistance? For me, checking on singular trades is basic. However, much more imperative is the survey of your value bend. This enables you to have an elevated perspective of your trading execution. The insane thing is, if you plot your value bend, you will see a portion of similar examples that you find in value diagrams. As we represent the time of 2013, I have a fourfold best at 70% return. I am presently sitting appropriately around half. In the course of the most recent 3 months, each time I hit 70%, I would have a garbage trade that backs me off my high and afterward, I rapidly move down there again just to be denied. What hit me only this previous week is that each time I approach the high, my craving for chance decreases. I am worried that I will, in some way or another, lose the money. So, I start to trade so moderately that I gradually disintegrate any increases until I pull far from my record top. I realise that I am losing my craving for a chance, because when I back off my record highs, it is a moderate procedure. Be that as it may, in the wake of sponsorship off I will run ideal move down to my record top in 20% or less of the time. This is simply because, after the pullback, I backpedal to trading freely and with certainty. My point, in disclosing to you this story, is that when you survey your value bend, you can mentally consider how you are handling the data exhibited to you by the market. It is better on the off chance that you begin your survey of your record first by taking a gander at the value bend before you go into every individual trade.

This will fill you in regarding whether it's truly your framework or if it's you attacking yourself.

Creating a Trading Plan

Traders should try to learn about their area of interest as much as possible. For example, if the trader deals heavily and is interested in telecommunications stocks, it makes sense for him or her to become knowledgeable about that business. Similarly, if he or she trades heavily in energy stocks, it's fairly logical to want to become well versed in that arena. To do this, start by formulating a plan to educate yourself. If possible, go to trading seminars and attend sell-side conferences. Also, it makes sense to plan and devote as much time as possible to the research process. That means studying charts, speaking with management (if applicable), reading trade journals or doing other background work (such as macroeconomic analysis or industry analysis), so that when the trading session starts the trader is up to speed. A wealth of knowledge could help the trader overcome fear issues in it, so it's a handy tool. In addition, it's important that the trader consider experimenting with new things from time to time. For example, consider using options to mitigate risk or set stop losses at a different place. One of the best ways a trader can learn is by experimenting - within reason. This experience may also help reduce emotional influences. Finally, traders should periodically review and assess their performance. This means, not only should they review their returns and their individual positions, but also how they prepared for a trading session, how up-to-date they are on the markets and how they're progressing in terms of ongoing education, among other things. This periodic assessment can help the trader correct mistakes, which may help enhance their overall returns. It may also help them to maintain the right mindset and help them to be psychologically prepared to do business.

Trading Mistakes and Remedies

There are a few normal slip-ups made over and over by new traders, each demonstration contrary to the accomplishment of progress and productivity. Nevertheless, given the correct time and consideration, each blame can be helped. Recorded beneath are a couple of normal mix-ups made by new (and some veteran) traders:

The absence of a far-reaching trading plan: The commercial centre is a dynamic field, with boundless potential outcomes confronting a dynamic trader. Without an obviously characterised trading plan to use as a perspective, a trader will work inside the market from a reactionary stance and battle to remain available "lead lap."

No characterised money administration methodology: Money administration might be the most vital aspect of trading. In the event that central standards of money administration aren't utilised, an undue hazard may endanger the dissolvability of the trading account.

Following up on 'tips' or 'guidance': Making trading choices on the basis of 'hot tip' or 'inside data' can be a frequent result of passionate trading. Chances are that the hot tip is talk, prattle or something more terrible regardless of the possibility that valid, there is a solid plausibility that the tip has been broadly coursed and is, as of now, valued in the market.

Fulfilling the craving to be 'ideal' rather than profit: The primary objective of effective trading depends on monetary securities, as it is considered the most efficient in terms of making a benefit. At the end of the day, the market is constantly right, and traders are regularly off-base. The acknowledgment that one cannot be right about numerous things and still make a profit is a troublesome thought to acknowledge. However, it is a key piece of a sound trading outlook.

Each of the previously mentioned botches acts as a potential boundary to a trader's prosperity and benefit. Be that as it may, through committing satisfactory time and exertion, the recurrence of these oversights can be decreased or dealt with. Participating in the accompanying exercises and applying them to trading operations can make a mental situation that is helpful in the cure of trading related difficulties:

Objective Defining

Goals can be an enabling technique for measuring trader development and assume a vital part in building certainty. Defining practical occasional objectives in light of execution and result is fundamental to precisely gauge the relative accomplishment of a trading operation. Defining the trading objectives, and that too from diverse perceptions, distinguishes the successful traders from the rests.

Creating trading rules: An arrangement of obvious likelihood based trading rules is an essential piece of characterising the discourse amongst trader and market. For example, rules administering trade section and leave, time of day in which to trade and length of trading session give the commercial centre characterised limits. Amid unstable periods, a definite arrangement of trading principles can fill in as a perspective and give a genuinely necessary setting to the tumult.

Actualising money management procedure: As expressed before, money management is the most efficient key of profit. A thorough money administration methodology relates hazard to compensate and unmistakably characterises the correct cost of a losing trade and the pickup of a triumphant trade. Legitimate money administration decreases the tension encompassing the money move engaged with a given trade and puts the monetary effect in context.

Objective setting is instrumental in encouraging a positive, sure mental state of mind and in giving a gauge to trader advancement. A control driven trading plan wipes out happiness, as the standards represent all connections with the commercial centre, including both productive and losing trades. Through the usage of an exhaustive money administration technique, nerves identified with capital loss are significantly lessened.

Risk Acceptance

Some of you perusing this will state that you generally put your stop and lose the money. While you may state this, you truly would prefer not to lose the money. You'll put your stop out there, which could be quite distant from your entrance cost. Throughout the following couple of hours or days, relying upon your time span, you will gradually move the stop up on the grounds that the stock is not "acting" legitimately. Beyond any doubt, sooner or later, your new stop arrange is activated just before the market takes off. In the event that this has transpired, it is a standout amongst the most baffling occasions that can happen in the market. Your examination was correct, the market, at last, gave you what you expected; be that as it may, you were not willing to acknowledge the arbitrariness of the market, and the reality is, you could lose money. Until the point when you acknowledge the hazard, you will translate the commotion of the market as a potential danger and will discover some method for supporting your idea that you should leave the trade now.

Knowing When to Take Profits

What is your trigger for leaving a trade as a victor? Kindly don't give me some hogwash about either key level. Unless you are naturally trading for benefits, which are presumably under 1% of the trading populace, how precisely do you book benefits? Again, this idea sounds sufficiently basic, yet when you factor in that most traders have a desire of what the market will do next, it makes this just about an inconceivable assignment. For instance, back in March of 2003, my business accomplice and I were, for some time, put alternatives on the DIAs. We had about Rs. 200k in benefits. As yet, we had executed our trading plan perfectly. At the time, we anticipated that the Dow would hit the 6k – 7k level which it, at last, did in '09. However, for this battle, they did not have enough vitality. Rather than tuning in to what the market was letting us know as far as the revision was finished, we hung on for what we anticipated would happen. This pivotal oversight implied that as opposed to turning out marginally north of 1M, we would lose the 200k. Subsequently, we were discussing this awful experience, and the two of us had a similar feeling that the time had come to take benefits, but since we didn't have a reasonable trigger, we simply hung on for what the market would do next. Do you wind up hanging on for what your examination says the market ought to do next? You should make sense of when it's a great opportunity to leave with the money to proceed onward to your next victory.

Error Recognition

Perceiving when you are incorrect does not mean the stock veered off from how your examination expressed things ought to go. Keep in mind, the market is totally irregular. Understanding when you are incorrect is something you have to characterise. For me, it's how much a position conflicts with me before I see a benefit. When this happens, things will go one of two routes for me. In the first place, the market will give me the benevolence of an opportunity to leave and will close the position with a minor loss or slight pickup. Also, the market will proceed the other way, and I will scrub down. Kindly don't become involved with my particular principles, concentrate on the way that you have to know when you are incorrect. Tolerating that, you won't generally hit the nail on the head will spare all of you sorts of time and money. All the more imperatively, you will start to think about the market as far as midpoints. You will have an x level of champs and x level of washouts. There is no getting away from this reality. Demonstrate to me a trader that dependably should be correct, and I will demonstrate to you a negative value bend.

Market Limit Recognition

In the event that you haven't perused the market wizard's books, kindly do; particularly the first, it's a work of art. As you read these stories of effective traders, you will see that they have huge increases. I'm talking about taking a couple of thousand rupees to a huge number of rupees. Notwithstanding the span of their additions, the consistency of their wins practically appears to be unrealistic. The reason their increases seem to have no restrictions is that these best traders don't think as far as yearly targets or desires for their trades. They have their framework, and they take whatever the market presents to them. On the off chance that this implies a fortune benefit, they don't hope to justify the business sector's developments or leave the trade rashly. They just take after their guidelines and let the market go wherever it must. I mysteriously concocted the splendid thought to make a 100% in the market for 2013. To date, I am at the half mark. The distinction now is that I never again have any desires for picks up. I should turn a benefit, other than that, I'm finished with agonising over such things. On the off chance that you set an objective, you will either fall marginally beneath it or above it. By putting this keep on your trading, you will definitely hit the objective.

Self-Reflection on Trading Psychology

Never be excessively glad that you are unwilling, making it impossible to call attention to your blemishes. As you read this book, you will see various cases where I have called out blemishes in my trading. This is both restorative and furthermore compels me to understand that my issues have little to do with my framework and more around how I rationally approach the market. On the off chance that you approach the market from a negative point of view, you will lose money. Negative does not mean you hope to lose, but rather, you may have a considerable measure of fear in your trading or have not completely acknowledged the hazard. Looking into your value bend and keeping a trading diary will enable you to explore the times when you tumble off the rails.

Keeping in mind the end goal to effectively stay away from the numerous entanglements exhibited by dynamic trading, sufficient time and exertion must be given to the fair appraisal of one's enthusiastic and mental condition of being. Accomplishing a perspective that cultivates fruitful trading is a full-time attempt and a discipline the majority of its own. The improvement of an exhaustive trading plan and the capacity to execute that arrangement with no wavering or predisposition is a key part of endeavouring to accomplish long haul gainfulness.

Applying Trading Psychology to Enhance Trading Success

Much has been composed, as of late, about the significance of trading psychology, yet next to nothing has been offered on the most proficient method to apply the standards in trading practice. In this book, we will survey key standards of trading psychology. We might investigate how you can apply trading psychology in the mix with the trading frameworks you have learned, created or picked up, to improve your trading execution. For the most part, in western societies, individuals are presented with next to no data or preparation on how to deal with their psychology. What's more, many individuals have no clue about how their feelings work or how to function with them to deal with their conduct and lives. This is similarly valid for the particular territory of money related trading. The requirement for powerful self-administration in the trading setting is plainly evident when the learner traders start their adventure towards turning into a viable and fruitful trader. They experience the passionate changes of extravagance, fear, freezing, faltering, insatiability and lament. They may understand that their feelings influence their trading execution. Sadly, some amateur traders come to trust that only if they could be separated from their feelings, their trading execution would make strides. That is a terrible misconception. Feelings, when comprehended and used, can make the edge to performing great in the market. Our feelings are refined types of subjective procedures. They are a piece of our transformative improvement and have, utilising a term found in developmental psychology, "versatile advantage" for our species. Feelings can be used, overseen and can be of extraordinary advantage for trading achievement.

Meditation Enhances Chances of Trading Success

New advances in psychology pertinent to trading psychology incorporate care as a powerful system in helping traders roll out vital behavioural improvements. Meditation originates from the Eastern Yogic and Buddhist customs, whose experts have examined the psyche and its workings for a great many years. Care and the utilisation of careful mindfulness are, as of now, changing the scene of psychology in the West. Research bolsters the utilisation of care in an extensive variety of points. Some of these include: expanding centre and focus, lessening stress, helping people beat critical mental difficulties and improving execution based exercises, for example, game and trading. Traders ought to be particularly intrigued by building up the ability of care as an approach to build up their trading execution and decrease push. We want to utilise a more extensive term than 'feelings.' We allude to 'states.' A state is just a mix of a man's manners of thinking, stance and breathing example, consideration and the psychological connection that they are encountering at a specific minute in time. We are dependable, in some perspective. If you somehow managed to audit your trading encounters, you will discover times where you are performing great and in that effective experience, you have a specific state. You will likewise have encounters where you were in a specific state that was not helpful for your trading. We have discovered that high performing traders, despite having a very much tried trading framework, deal with their states while trading so they have an ideal state for their trading circumstance. You can't profit over a time of continuous months on the off chance that you are not in the best possible trading outlook. There are numerous things that go into accomplishing the best possible trading attitude, and I have expounded on this subject widely. In any case, if there is one overall topic that you have to comprehend concerning your trading outlook, it is poise.

Keeping Transparent Ideas on Trading Success

The majority of the trading can come down to your capacity or failure to control yourself, notwithstanding the close consistent impulse to trade, in view of more often than not, doing as such means you will exact damage on yourself. As a trader, hypothesising in the business sectors, an attempt that is clearly extremely unsafe, it is dependent upon you to control yourself, and this capacity begins with the mental comprehension of what you are doing, what is conceivable and what you are gambling. My recommendation is that you contemplate the way that it's anything but difficult to lose money trading, instead of the way that you MIGHT hit a major champ on any given trade. It's tied in with understanding and tolerating the hazard and afterward carrying on in accordance with this acknowledgment, which implies essentially that you shouldn't be trading a ton since high-likelihood trading openings are not as regular as the same number of traders thinks they are (or trade as in the event that they seem to be). Building up the ability of care can enable traders to enhance centre and focus. Like tennis players who frequently report 'seeing the ball better' when carefully mindful, the trader applying careful mindfulness may start to "see the market better" alongside the directional signs it gives. In such manner, the act of care is much similar to what competitors call 'being in the zone.' Mindfulness advances more elevated amounts of fixation and an expanded ability to end up plainly assimilated with the market. Things being what they are, what are the qualities of master traders? They have a tried trading framework, a tried trading plan and amazing execution of their trading plan inside the edge of the sorted-out hazard and money administration. To do all that well, they oversee themselves and their states – their trading psychology.

Focus on Victorious Attitude

In this book, we will look into psychology, particularly a sub-train inside subjective psychology that reviews aptitude and master execution. We will likewise draw on the creating comprehension of the connection between mental process and changes in individuals' neurology; a region of psychology known as neuro-cognitive psychology. We will interface this data to how our feelings work, propensity arrangement, the improvement of mastery and how this applies to creating oneself as a fruitful and master showcase trader. A major test numerous traders confront is to keep their brains right now as opposed to remembering past occasions or anticipating what they may accept what's to come. For instance, a trader may neglect to enter a trade on the grounds that as the section point is drawn nearer, the trader's brain remembers the earlier loss. Instead of hazarding another loss, the trader evades the trade despite the fact that it was a sound set up. A trader who concentrates on the future or the past as opposed to the present may miss imperative market prompts and signs that flag an adjustment in course. The trader may clutch the trade due to his or her market predisposition. Care is of extraordinary advantage to the trader since it can help the trader remain present as well as enhance the capacity to see when he or she ends up noticeably diverted and disappears from a present concentrate available. Maybe the best advantage of care is that it is an ability that can help the trader to trade the market as opposed to trading their feelings. For some traders, trading can be very unpleasant. At the point when a trader ends up plainly focused on the longing to get away from that anxiety, it can turn out to be great to the point that the attention on the trade is lost. The trader's consideration shifts from the market's activity to the trader's inside condition of distressing sentiments and contemplations. Therefore, the trader may lose his or her capacity to deal with the trade and poor outcomes are generally the result. Care can enable the trader to figure out how to venture outside his or her considerations and emotions as well as focus on what is most critical for their trade. Clinicians call this 'capacity defusing.'

Enhance Attention on Mental Capacity

Care is turning into an essential piece of trading psychology since care encourages us to see our inside state (counting what the psyche is letting us know and our emotions) from a more disconnected viewpoint. Specialists are discovering that the more we battle with our musings and sentiments, the more trapped with them we can progress towards. Tip top competitors, for instance, have troublesome considerations and emotions amid rivalry. They have adapted to keep up their attention on their play as opposed to taking care of their inner state. Through the ability of care, we start to see our considerations and affections for what they are – ordinary passing occasions – and not something that requests a quick reaction. Along these lines, care is a mental capacity that helps keep the trader's mind cantered on the trade. Care is a beneficial expertise to create. Notwithstanding the particular advantages applicable to the trading plot here, looking into it has demonstrated that care can help advance unwinding, diminish stretch, enhance invulnerable capacity, lessen torment and elevate the inclination. Care can enable traders to keep up concentration on their objectives and on what is important most to them in their trading and their lives. Care aptitudes are so critical to traders that I have composed a book called *Trade Mindfully*. Over the past 15 years, there has been a development in the investigation of ability and master execution. This has prompted a creating comprehension of the examples of conduct drew in by individuals who turn into the master in their specific space. The principal design that I need to investigate is the utilisation of training to shape a propensity. As an animal variety, we have a superb capacity to computerise any example of conduct and an accumulation of conduct examples to make ability. Mechanism of conduct enables us to do complex aptitudes without conscious exertion and liberates our constrained consideration for different issues. Free consideration can be moved to other data and factors that might be helpful for our execution and achievement.

Money Management Psychology for Trading Success

Getting your money administration down is vigorously subject to having the best possible trading mentality and in addition, having a firm comprehension of what money administration really implies. Here is the thing that it implies basically:

- You generally consider hazard before remunerating.
- You realise what your per trade hazard sum is, and you never surpass that sum. This ought to be a dollar sum that you are rationally and fiscally ready to securely lose on any given trade.
- You see how to put a stop to loss legitimately and how to deal with your position sizes.
- You have an unmistakable comprehension of how to put benefit targets and a general procedure for leaving trades.
- You see how to compute the hazard compensate on a trade and this additionally implies you know that a trade won't be worth going for a broke reward, and it doesn't bode well.

At the point when traders consider trading psychology, they consider the negative things like fear, avarice and other undesirable feelings that disable trading or restricting convictions that conflict with achieving objectives. Positively, trading psychology manages unconstructive feelings and contemplations. There is another side to trading psychology, the positive psychology that can enable traders to build up the mental abilities required for trading. This is the thing that I call High-Value activities. Comprehend that capital protection is truly the way to money administration. Capital protection implies dealing with your trading capital so you are not utilising excessively of it on any one trade and that you are not utilising it too as often as possible. Basically, you need to just utilise your trading capital when an extremely evident/high-likelihood trade goes along in light of the fact that then you have more money-flow to use on better trades. Try not to pass up finished trading.

Consideration of Critical Components of Trading

When we have computerised driving, our consideration is allowed to take care of the critical variables of the conditions and the conduct of different drivers (the unique situation). Note that I have stressed on the word 'relationship' in the past sentence, each snippet of data that we have to go to and every connection between those snippets of data take up a considerable measure of consideration. The points of confinement and engagement of conscious consideration when gaining some new useful knowledge are a region of subjective psychology called psychological load hypothesis. This is a piece of a more extensive territory of research called human intellectual design, which is the investigation of conscious consideration, oblivious preparing and the connection between the two. I would trust that as a trader or somebody inspired by trading, your considerations have swung to the experience of figuring out how to trade. Like any ability that takes mastery, there are various examples of consideration and conduct associated with trading. When adopting new abilities, those various examples can assess your accessible consideration making an unnecessary subjective load (a lot to recall without a moment's delay). High Values Actions (or HVAs) are activities that convey high esteems to traders. HVAs are activities that:

- are under the trader's control
- identify with the way toward trading
- assist the growth of the trader's capacity to peruse and trade the market
- put the chances of making fruitful trades with the trader's support
- help realise trading certainty and more positive feelings to traders

More or less, HVAs enable the trader to keep consideration and centre where it should be – on the activities most essential to trading, not on the negative feelings and contemplations that fly up at times naturally when making a trade. By knowing and focusing on the activities that have high incentives, traders can enhance their capacity to trade well and inevitably achieve new levels of accomplishment. Awfully regularly, a trader's concentration is lost. When consideration is put on troubling contemplations and awkward feelings, traders are diverted and trading turns into a battle with feelings.

Strategies for Trading Instruments

As we are in the matter of creating or upgrading aptitude in trading in the business sectors, the time has come to expound on psychological load hypothesis. For a great many people, our conscious consideration is restricted to in the vicinity of five and nine "lumps" of data for the novel material itself and the connections between partitioned components of it. This uses our transient memory. These days alluded to as working memory, to hold the new data, as there is minimal pertinent material in past experience to draw on. A lump is the biggest important unit that a man perceives in the learning setting. As data and examples of conduct are disguised, when the data goes into long haul memory, it can be attracted upon and used to increase what is in working memory. This is when conscious consideration is arranged for new data. The least complex approach to judge, regardless of whether your trading strategy is compelling, is to demo trade it for two or three months and see what sort of results you get. The benefit is seen as a measure of gifted example acknowledgment, self-administration and administration of the trading procedure. We prescribe that traders take a stock of their aims and their convictions. Having that mindfulness is the initial step to testing and changing intolerable convictions.

Conquering the Psychology of Trading

Psychology is the most imperative factor in trading and the greatest obstacle. In any case, why do a couple of individuals effectively take a shot at it? It's basic, as the majority of them don't know how to overcome it. Making trades is unpleasant. Each trader has triumphs and disappointments, losses and slip-ups. Mental mistakes are quite often stretch based, implying that because of the worry of the trading circumstance itself, traders settle on ineffectively considered or hasty decisions that create frenzy or fear. The least complex approach to avoid mental trading blunders is to oversee push and avert freeze, by finding a sensible market clarification for any given trading circumstance. In the event that you are set up to focus on doing a couple of little customs consistently, you can see effective positive changes to your trading comes about. As enthusiastic speculators, we can have the steady clash between what we intentionally need and what our subliminal personality needs. Feelings have no place in an informal investor, swing trader or even a long-haul trader's attitude towards their speculations. When we attempt and shield ourselves from fear, we wind up turning to our frequent impulses to go into a position of solace, regardless of whether that place is a reality. We quit assuming liability for our own particular feelings of fear and begin pointing the finger at others for our issues. Towards the end, we attempt and locate a simple way out via hunting down enchantment pointers or Holy Grail arrangements. Genuine change occurs at the subliminal level, so by following little customs consistently, these progressions can happen speedier than through some other procedures that manage just the cognizant personality.

Avoid Poor Planning Preparation

Basic mistakes that prompt anxiety and frenzy incorporate poor planning and preparing. You can keep this circumstance by doing your examination through gatherings and at work instruction. Different emphasize focuses incorporate being excessively passionate about money or foreseeing benefits. Attempt to understand that nobody can know everything in trade circumstances and don't under gauge the capacity to short stocks. Realise what you are trading and the significance of trade timing. It's critical to compute the hazard and reward proportion of stock trades through current stock value, benefit and leaves value destinations. What's more, enter the market with as nonpartisan an approach as could be expected under the circumstances. You will confront solid resistance inside from yourself when you venture out making a bigger vision for your stock trading. This implies you should relinquish your negative behaviour patterns and go out on a limb and do what is required to achieve your objectives. I have seen numerous traders who mind themselves and briefly take after their stock trading vision. The issue emerges when traders experience the feelings of losing; many tend to bring down their desires and backpedal into their shell, backpedalling to what they are used to. They begin returning to old propensities and backpedalling to the starting point once more. Alongside push-caused poor choices or frenzy, traders can likewise make the mental blunder of pie in the sky considering. As such, they come to trust their own view of the commercial centre as totally exact and that the inclinations of the commercial centre won't influence them. This, as well, can prompt trading mistakes. This can be avoided by understanding that the market is not controlled by a trader's understanding or forecast of it. Some traders have a go at psyching themselves up by shouting, yelling, talking positive considerations, working more and so on. Beyond any doubt, you should be sure that by exclusively making these strides, you are intuitively fortifying and you are lacking in some part of trading that is keeping you from achieving that genuine level of dominance. They cover the hidden issues that you have to confront in advance and focus.

Keeping Negative Aspirations Away from Trading

Whenever you roll out improvements, you will confront inside resistance from fear, weakness, uncertainty and even restriction from relatives or friends. You will, in all probability, even get negative vitality from everyone around you who are undermined by what you are doing. Change does not occur without any forethought, and you need to stay with your feelings despite self-questioning. Be understanding and permit yourself an opportunity to accomplish the objectives that you set out to reach. Try not to enable yourself to end up as a casualty of these negative contemplations. They will just serve to distract you from focusing on what should be finished. Once more, we need to assault the base of the issue which is the manner by which you decipher these emotions. You won't really have the capacity to free yourself of them; be that as it may, you can quit concentrating on them. Concentrate on the future and on what you need out of it. It is key that you change your point of view with regards to cynicism.

Regular Gratitude

Be thankful for what is working in your life at the present time and not on what isn't working right now. Consider every aspect of your life and record what you must be thankful for. Value the great things about your well-being, connections, trading/vocation and riches and some other zones that are important to you. You could likewise remove time from your day when you may be feeling not as protected and offer thanks for something in your life. This will dependably lift your mindset. The hard-remorseless truth is that the vast majority don't profit in the share trading system. Terrance Odean, a collaborator teacher at the University of California, did an entrancing investigation of speculator achievement rates back in the 1990's. Odean assembled the trading history of more than 60,000 online money market funds and utilised the information to ponder the trading practices of speculators. Doing this examination amid the season of a positively trending market, half of the financial specialists in his investigation really lost money. A bulk of them basically made a little or lost a bit. Supposed experts improved, as the greater part of them neglects to beat the S&P 500 in any given year. Odean found that a little minority of people create exceptional returns in the market. Around 33% of the speculators in his study beat the market and out of the majority of the 60,000 records, he analysed just a little world class 5% delivered stupendous additions of more than 2.41% a month while a minor 1% of traders produced using 4.86% a month. As such, a securities trade is a place where a couple of first class traders profit off of every other person. This mirrors some other aggressive action, where it truly is just a couple of people who ascend to the best. To put it another way - for each five individuals who get in the share trading system and end up noticeably ridiculously wealthy, fifty individuals lose money, even in a positively trending market. Furthermore, for each one hundred individuals in the market, thirty individuals beat the market reliably year in and year out while every other person either wastes their time or loses money. In the wake of assembling the information, Odean presumed that one reason a great many people have such a great amount of inconvenience in money markets is on the grounds that they are pompous in their capacities. They are essentially hallucinating about their speculations. They are unadulterated Gulla-bulls.

Contributing Affirmations

Work out a couple of assertions particular to your contributing exercises that will reinforce what you, as of now, accept or change a portion of the old convictions that might be waiting at the intuitive level and can be keeping you away from accomplishing the outcomes that you need. Sooner or later, they may begin to consider psychology. They'll understand that they are fearful the greater part of the time in the market – anxious of losing or passing up a major opportunity for picks up. So, they begin to consider their very own psychology a tad bit. They'll consider their identity and trust they have to discover a system that will coordinate their identity. In the event that they endeavoured to purchase and hold, they'll begin to think, 'well I like activity, so I have to locate a transient procedure.' They may then fiddle with day trading or on the off chance that they were already day trading, they'll think they have to locate a more drawn out time allotment to trade. In any case, whatever the case the key is, they are searching for a system that will go about as an enchantment shot for them. Actually, what they truly need to comprehend is themselves. They have to comprehend being a performing artist in the stock trade and how that really impacts their conduct with regards to their positions. They have to know themselves and burrow deep to find their own particular inspirations before they will have the capacity to adhere to any procedure reliably. Here are a couple of speedy illustrations you are allowed to utilise:

- 'It is anything but difficult to remain engaged and submitted in every aspect of my trading.'
- 'I trust that I have what it takes to be effective with choices.'
- 'Know your probabilities and hazards before entering another trade.'
- 'Comprehend that sitting on the sidelines is a position.'

This is the thing that understanding the structure of the share trading system implies. It doesn't mean finding the correct procedure that will profit in the market. It implies seeing how an individual cooperates with the stock trade and how the share trading system impacts their conduct. It implies having comprehension of your own individual psychology with regards to taking a position in the money related markets. Without knowing this, you will never profit in the stock trade after some time, regardless of what system you utilise. Also, to take this in will mean going on a trip of self-disclosure.

Intuitive Visualization

Close your eyes and find a photo of the effective trader that you know you can be, in your psyche. Envision what you will be doing when you have accomplished the outcomes you need. See what you will be wearing, the spots that you will go to and the general population that you will connect with. Hear what you will be stating and what others will be stating to you. Feel the sentiments of progress, satisfaction and bliss. Go about as though you have accomplished your goals and feel the sentiments of every last bit of it. Research demonstrates that this has substantially more effect if the vision is wrapped in feeling and positive feeling. Another mental blunder is trader vulnerability, which can relate specifically to the absence of experience and furthermore cause fear in the trader and loss in the commercial centre. From imprudent choices to negative self-esteem because of loss, traders frequently discover advertise developments significantly agitating as well as stunning. An ideal route for traders to manage these mental issues and the blunders they cause is to rapidly see the potential for loss recuperation and figure out how to assimilate the feeling of astonishment made by the loss. Trading is not tied in with accomplishing a huge win but rather by taking care of and adjusting losses and wins after some time. By venturing far from an individual feeling of loss or disappointment, traders would be able to effectively and smoothly watch showcase variances, settle on more educated choices and just lessen mental worry after some time. Loss and the fear of losing regularly and adversely impact a trader's basic leadership abilities and their failure to control feelings. To deal with your hazard and feelings, you need to acknowledge the negative sentiments that you endeavour to smother. As opposed to disregarding them, confront them and give no noteworthiness or importance to these sentiments. In the long run, we will progress toward becoming what we oppose, like the way we say that we will never wind up like our folks. The vast majority of us do. Along these lines, by demonstrating no significance or imperviousness to your negative emotions, you enable yourself to concentrate on your positive objectives.

Contemplation or Quiet-Time

The research, additionally, demonstrates that contemplation or times of calm time during the day can be the most effective way to accomplishing your objectives and getting the outcomes you fancy. There are various sorts of contemplation that can be achieved, so do your examination and find what works best for you. You can develop a collection of contemplation systems that you utilise, depending upon how you are feeling at the time. I'm very little of great contemplation, so I close my eyes for 15 minutes and simply think. What you need to accomplish is only a quieting approach to transcend the market commotion and think clearly. In any case, even the vast majority of the general population, who do invests energy into the market and understand that individual psychology is a major segment of what appears like slippery achievement, doesn't go on the way of self-revelation and develop enough to profit in the share trading system. The vast majority of those that realise that psychology is critical don't know how to fit it into the bewildered. So, they keep it aside and endeavour to pursue the bogus arrangement of finding the correct trading procedure, PC program or the one master who is constantly right. They never get the accomplishment out of the business sectors that they need. It resembles somebody attempting to become an extraordinary baseball player by figuring out how to bat, without having a clue at all on how to keep track of who's winning. They might have the capacity to hit the ball, but if they don't recognise what an out or a run is, they won't have the capacity to run the bases and will simply remain there after they hit the ball. You should know how the amusement is organised to have the capacity to win. You can put forth a couple of inquiries to see how much your past influences your reasoning. Make sense of what the conclusions of others intend to you:

- 'Do you intensely depend on others?'
- 'It is safe to say that you are reluctant to talk before others because of fear of sounding moronic?'
- 'Do you seek others for endorsement before you resolve to activity?'
- 'Do you continually talk about your past achievements?'
- 'Do you require a contribution from others in your basic leadership process?'

For those of you who reply "yes" to a majority of these inquiries, you are frightful to act or focus on an arrangement of activity without outer endorsement. Consider how this influences your stock trading exercises, you will rapidly acknowledge how fear keeps you from turning into the trader that you know you are or can be. Be straightforward with yourself, and you will then push ahead.

Managing Stress Effect

Traders should isolate basic leadership conduct from individual fear, unrealistic considering or control issues. Rather than depending on self-investigation of a circumstance, take a gander at showcase motions in a philosophical example. Trade deliberately in light of market changes and past examples. Recall that being a beneficial and capable trader isn't about enormous wins, it is about little reliable wins which balance typical market change loss. Stay away from passionate interest in the market, and consider the market's variances as a virtual drive of monetary nature instead of something which can be controlled unequivocally by singular information. You don't have to deny your feelings or attempt the unthinkable undertaking of shutting them out to prevail in the share trading system. You should simply observe and comprehend the structure of money markets for what it is and adjust to it. When you do that, the considerable bulk of the feelings of fear and enthusiastic anxiety the stock trade may make you feel will vanish. This is all it takes to become an effective world class trader. All it does is adjusting you to reality, nothing more. It truly isn't as hard as it sounds. However, so few ever fulfil this. We will travel together in this book to find the reasons why this is so by looking at the keys to effectively doing this in the share trading system and the reasons why individuals don't do this. By looking at progress as well as disappointment, we will have the capacity to comprehend our own practices better and keep away from the traps of others. The prizes can be enormous. The share trading system offers a chance to make a boundless measure of money for those that can climb into the positions of the trading world class. I am aware of no such open door. In any case, exploiting the monetary markets requires you to comprehend the truth of the market. Maybe a couple of people can do this. There is a basic clash between what you may expect of the share trading system and what it truly is. We will look into this soon.

Managing Critical Perceptions of Trading

Stock trading brings a decent amount of worry, as all of you know. The inquiry spins around how you handle the anxiety. Some become physically ill, some go into a frenzy and some even go into misery because of the rough swings that money markets can create. Contingent upon the circumstance and the individual, the anxiety response might be minor or extremely serious. Your physical reaction to push is debilitating. As you keep on experiencing distressing circumstances, the more usual you move toward becoming to the possibility of the negative emotions that are related with stretch. These negative emotions transform conviction into uncertainty and apprehension. Practice yoga, ponder, play sports, work out, invest energy in your friends and family, chip away at your otherworldly development. You have to de-push your psyche and clear your brain. Fixating on your trades will do only consume you and cause you to be tense constantly. There is a whole other world to live than trading stocks. Try not to give trading a chance to get you too high or low. The way to bringing stress levels is down to be grounded and to be sure that you can settle on the correct choice when the time comes. That accompanies encounter, so be understanding. At the end of the day, in this present reality, we are continually working under an arrangement of principles that guide our conduct. These tenets are so instilled in us that more often than not we don't consider them by any means. We realise what side of the street to drive, the most proficient method to answer the telephone, et cetera. In the event that drivers did not learn and obey movement controls, there would be confusion on the streets. Be that as it may, with regards to the share trading system, individuals are not given any genuine arrangement of guidelines to pass by. Anybody can purchase or offer a position on an impulse. What's more, with each position, a financial specialist takes the risk of raking in huge profits or losing everything. Nevertheless, the share trading system has a structure to it that makes it so that a speculator who makes choices in light of an arrangement of tenets can profit in the market. The issue is, there is no compelling factor outside of the individual trader to constrain him to take in the standards and ensure he obeys them. Thus, the share trading system is, as a result, a Goliath roadway framework in which the drivers are controlling their autos with no ability to know east from west. Most of them drive off the street and crash. A couple of them arrive securely at their goal. To do so, they should assume the liability to isolate themselves from all of the alternate drivers and follow the street signs to get to where they need to go.

Assessing Uniqueness of Trading

Individuals begin in the stock trade without understanding that the share trading system is unique in relation to whatever else they have ever gotten into. Accordingly, they have a tendency to do what they regularly do somewhere else when they feel doubtful or are in question. They take a gander at a specialist to take after or else simply do what every other person does. This works in almost everything else we do and as such, it appears to be normal to do it in money markets. For example, have you gotten off of a plane and followed every other person to get to the baggage carousel without looking at a single sign? It is anything but difficult to do on the off chance that you have been on an arrangement for quite a long time and are extremely drained. This sort of crowd conduct is absolutely normal in numerous social circumstances. When individuals are in the share trading system, they take part in a comparable kind of crowd conduct by purchasing and holding stocks with the reasoning that they can do so perpetually to profit, since it is the thing that every other person they know is doing. In actuality, it is the thing that they are advised to do by the divider road deals constraint that needs individuals to purchase and hold common finances everlastingly so they can benefit from the administration charges. The issue is, the share trading system requires that individuals create and stay with an arrangement of standards that incorporates a strict money administration arrangement of when to cut loss so they don't turn out to be a huge loss. Nothing goes up everlastingly, and most stocks and organisations really wind up going under sooner or later. That is the idea of free enterprise. There is rivalry consistently and that implies change. Only a few stocks go up for a long time despite the possibility that money markets and economy thrive because of consistent development and rivalry in the economy. New divisions rise in the economy constantly and in bear markets, most stocks go down. Like clockwork or so there is no less than one bear advertise that brings loss of no less than 30%, with the supplies of frail organisations going down to zero. To put resources into a wicker container of individual stocks in the share trading system, with the thought you will purchase and hold them always, would resemble opening up a business and assuming you are never going to change a single thing about it. You will open it up and keep it precisely the way it is until the end of time. Obviously, that would be ridiculous. However, that is the sort of thing individuals do when they get into the share trading system.

Overcoming Anger in Trade

Outrage is another passionate reaction that has no place in a stock trader's heart. Make sense of what is alarming you inside and figure out how to manage it promptly, before it shows up as repressed outrage, which will show its terrible head as soon as possible. Outrage makes you vindictive and invites terrible basic leadership in the expectations of "getting back" at the market or driving trades because of the dissatisfaction of losing. I can't reveal to you how frequently this has transpired when I was a lesser trader, and I never observed anything besides loss coming from it. Verbalising and communicating your outrage in suitable ways will enable you to drop the famous "things." You will detect a sentiment opportunity inside from not covering up your past passionate encounters which have kept sorrow, frenzy and uneasiness alive. For the vast majority, money markets are basically a hallucination that they share with the majority of financial specialists like them. They get tied up with it, imagining that they need to only stay there to get rich. When the market, in the long run, conflicts with them, they enter the domain of mutilated considering and nonsensicalness. They begin to sift through proof that they are situated mistakenly in the share trading system and are in peril of losing money and concentrate on data that supports their latent conduct. They tune in to and concentrate on gathered specialists who reveal to them what they need to hear. In a merciless bear showcase, they hang on and watch their positions lose esteem and simply stay there and decline to confront reality until it is past the point of no return. At that point, they offer out in dismay. Furthermore, since they have been following the group the whole time, they can offer out in a frenzy-like condition when every other person offers immediately. At that point, they'll stay there and accuse their loss on another person. It may be a non-existent securities trade controller who, they believe, covertly controls everything, their stock representative or some gathered market master they had been tuning into an urgency that they find to blame.

Develop Trading Understandability Gradually

When you initially begin day trading, you will probably encounter the surge that originates from a triumphant trade. To be completely forthright with you, there are a couple of things which can contrast in this existence with a grand slam trade. All things considered, as you pick up understanding, you will rapidly understand that not having control of your feelings can cause monetary demolition. The capacity to remain totally level-headed and enable yourself to execute your trading plan with no feeling will enable you to dependably think plainly and unbiased. When you never again relate the adrenaline surge with trading, you have quite recently traversed from the betting domain into the business domain. Kindly don't interpret this to mean you can't be amped up for trading and accomplishing your life's dream. You can't be amped up for profiting, as it doesn't exist as time goes on. Try not to pummel on yourself on the off chance that you have had a huge loss in the market. You see, most Gullabulls had no clue that they needed to assume individual liability for their speculations and just took after the group, since they had no clue the stock trade required that of them, and that is the thing that every other person does. Like I stated, that is the thing that makes the share trading system not quite the same as everything else. You may do so on the off chance that you have been following the pack in the market, it isn't your blame. You didn't know any better. Nonetheless, you do now. All Gulla-bulls, in the long run, are confronted with a decision after they endure a difficulty in the money markets, of either proceeding to take after the group and to keep on getting similar outcomes again and again or to split far from the group and assume individual liability for their choices. The latter is the best way to profit in the share trading system after some time, without depending on basic blind luck.

Stop Loss in Trading and Earn Benefit

If somebody, somehow, happened to request that you name five numbers off the top of your head, it is improbable you would name the five numbers recorded here: 10,000, 26, 25, 20 and 30. You'd most likely pick an entire cluster of arbitrary numbers, not knowing the significance of your choice. In any case, when traders venture into their trading, they experience numbers that are more critical than others. For instance, if a trader goes to set a stop loss and take the benefit, in light of present circumstances, he or she is substantially more likely to enter in Rs. 25 for a take benefit and Rs. 15 for a stop loss than he or she is to enter Rs. 24.92 and Rs. 14.92. Human brains normally round up or round down numbers. As a result, our characteristic goals have a tendency to be exemplified in business sectors where our subliminal picks uniformly round numbers to stamp as essential focuses on a diagram. Other than basic numbers, the aggregate awareness of all traders, examiners and speculators tends to place an incentive in occasions like record-breaking highs and/or lows. Moreover, inside one securities trade, two organisations may react contrastingly to a 10-week moving normal or a 20-week moving normal, contingent upon the historical backdrop of the reaction of the stock to the marker. Next time you open an outline, watch out mentally for help and resistance lines. If there isn't an officially settled pattern at a specific esteem, it is likely that the help or resistance level is weaker since the main market activity at the specific level is because of adjusting. In the event that there is support or resistance at that level, the expansion of adjusted stop loss and take benefit requests will just remain to build the power of the help and resistance. For a few stocks or securities, this impact might be best seen on a fleeting skyline, where even a little measure of requests can enormously impact quick value changes. Finding and understanding the significance of mental help won't just improve you as a trader but as a more gainful trader. Similarly, as with most outlines, there is normally something else under the surface.

Screen commercial centre changes from the stance of the trading framework, rather than from an individual perspective. Everybody needs to be free of oversights and mistakes, yet that sort of hair-splitting isn't conceivable in any condition, surely not in the market driven variances of the share trading system. When making trades, perceive any mistakes made and quickly move to cut the loss. Attempt to evade the slant or make loss back instantly with one major score. Concentrate on the little strides and shake away the moral duty that can cause a freeze, indiscreet decisions or unrealistic speculation to undermine your abilities and cause mental mistakes.

10 Psychological Stock Trading Principles

The psychological stock trading guideline implies that once value begins drifting, there is a decent possibility that the pattern will proceed. Novice traders endeavour to call tops and bottoms and enter trades contrary to the progressing pattern, in spite of the fact that riding the current pattern would frequently yield much better outcomes. A year ago, when I had the benefit of talking to cycle forecaster Charles Nenner, I inquired as to whether there was one book he would prescribe for all traders to read. Decisively, he alluded to *The Investor's Quotient* by Jake Bernstein. Since that meeting, I have perused Mr. Bernstein's book and have observed it be an abundance of data on the brain science of fruitful contributing. Marty Schwartz has been my most loved trader from the *Market Wizards* book and me as of late read his own particular book. In the accompanying book, I might want to examine and return to 11 of his own trading tenets and standards, which I use, to some degree, in my own particular trading. It could enable different traders to enhance their own trading and give a few bits of knowledge on how an expert trader approaches trading. In this book, we examine the 10 most significant psychological stock trading standards from the world's well-known trade scientists.

1. Trading Is an Execution Movement:

This is the central thought behind my latest book. Like the playing of a show instrument or the playing of a game, trading involves the use of information and abilities to continuous exhibitions. Accomplishment at trading, as with different exhibitions, relies on a formative procedure in which concentrated, organised practice and experience over a broadened time yield ability and aptitude. Many trading issues are inferable from endeavours to prevail at trading, before experiencing this learning procedure. My research suggests that expert traders represent more than 75% of all offering and prospective contracts. It is difficult to manage accomplishment against these experts without sharpening one's execution and by ensuring that, you don't lose your capital in the learning procedure. Trust in one's trading originates from the dominance presented by one's learning and improvement, not from psychological activities or bits of knowledge. In the event that you are particular, sorted out and follow up on plans, you will stay away from expensive endeavours regularly caused by unconstrained choices.

2. Achievement in Trading Is an Element of Gifts and Abilities:

Trading is the same as chess, Olympic Games or acting. Natural capacities (gifts) and created capabilities (abilities) decide one's level of accomplishment. From shake groups to ballet performers and golfers, just a few members in any execution movement are adequate to support a living from their exhibitions. The way to progress is to find a consistent fit between one's abilities/aptitudes and the open doors accessible in an execution field. For traders, this implies finding an unrivalled fit between your capacities and the markets and systems you will be trading. Numerous execution issues are the aftereffect of a problematic fit between what the trader is great at and how the trader is trading psychologically and that which is in your pocket or the record of the two sorts of capital. The psychological one is the more imperative and costly of the two. Holding to losing positions costs quantifiable wholes of genuine capital. However, it costs limitless sums of psychological capital! By assuming aggregate liability for your trading results, great or awful, and not accusing companions, traders, showcase letters and so on, you will be predictable and honest to your trading framework. Furthermore, consistency is the most profitable key to progress.

3. Red Light/Green Light:

Marty Schwartz utilises a 10-period exponential moving normal (Ema) to recognise bullish and bearish situations and as a channel. At whatever point cost is over the 10-time frame EMA he searches for purchase trades and when the cost is underneath the 10 time frames Ema, he is searching for short open doors. This approach and standard can be particularly useful when utilised as channel criteria. For instance, a trader could utilise a 10 period Ema on the day by day or week after week time span to decide the heading of his trades. At that point, he can go to the lower time spans where he executes his trades and search for trades with the heading which the Ema recommends. With the past standards, a trader could make a modern arrangement of tenets and channel criteria for his own particular trading. In positively trending markets, you must be long or impartial, and in bear markets, you must be short or unbiased. It might appear to be obvious. It is not, and it is a lesson adapted past the point of no return by a long shot! Illogic frequently rules and markets are hugely wasteful regardless of what the scholastics accept! Once in a trade, you have definitely no power over its inevitable heading, regardless of the number of supplications or petitions advertised. Expectation and fear are two of the best foes of the examiner, cultivating just false observations. You should evade these emotions no matter what. The more inflexible you can be in your execution of trades, the more gainful will be your outcomes.

4. Do Not Put Stops Underneath the Low or More the High in Range:

Moving midpoints and the 10-time frame EMA are powerless in extended bond markets when cost, as a rule, does not regard the moving midpoints adequately well and keeps on breaking above or beneath the moving normal commonly. This is the point at which his stop loss tip could enable you to abstain from whipsawing. Novice and unpractised traders regularly utilise fund psychologically as ways to deal with their stop loss situation, which makes it simple to "figure" where the larger part of stop loss orders are (in another book, we talked about this wonder as to round numbers). Along these lines, if you see that your stop loss arranges frequently get hit, and then the value turns around the other way, it might be an ideal opportunity to re-examine your approach. No, it is typically not your trader chasing stops, but simply the way you utilise "excessively self-evident" and extremely normal procedures for stop position. To trade effectively, take on a similar mindset as a fundamental psychologist and trade like a professional. It is basic to comprehend the essentials driving a trade and to comprehend the market's technical. When you do, at that point, and at exactly that point, you can or should you, trade. Screen your execution input for results. The main input a trader can rely on is the composed record of trade comes about and the recorded contemplations encompassing each trade execution. You should know how well or how ineffectively you are getting along. You should also know whether poor outcomes are caused by your powerlessness or of your trading framework. The comprehension of mass brain science is regularly more essential than the comprehension of financial aspects. Markets are driven by people making human mistakes and making super-human bits of knowledge!

5. The Core Skill of Trading Is Pattern Recognition:

Regardless of whether the trader is outwardly investigating diagrams or dissecting signals, design acknowledgment lies at the core of trading. The trader endeavours to recognise moves sought after and supply continuously and reacts to designs that are demonstrative of such moves. The greater part of the distinctive ways to deal with trading - specialised and major examination, cycles, econometrics, quantitative recorded investigation, market profile- are basic strategies for conceptualising designs at various time spans. Traders will profit most from those strategies that fit well with their subjective styles and qualities. A man capable of visual handling, with prevalent visual memory, may profit by the utilisation of graphs. Somebody who is exceedingly expository may profit by measurable investigations and mechanical signs. Trading can be a forlorn diversion and one of like pulls in like, it is imperative for us to develop and keep up a solid relationship. If we connect with individuals who are exceptionally energetic, who look to accomplish, who have goal-oriented objectives and who will move forward paying little respect to snags, we will get comparable drives.

6. Comprehend the Scenario

With regards to news and basic information, most traders simply concentrate on the real numbers and then ask why the business sectors are not carrying on as indicated by the news discharge. Marty Schwartz utilises value response to news discharges and essential information to comprehend the quality and market notion.

You don't usually trade the real number, yet this is how traders and speculators see the numbers:

1. Astonishments and huge deviations from desires can move the business sectors. Information which comes in not surprisingly, as a rule, does not have an impact any longer since showcase members expected it, and it has been evaluated.
2. It might be conceivable to peruse advertise quality and assumption from the response to the news. For instance, when value energies after a negative number, it could disclose to you that financial specialists are generally extremely bullish and the other way around. On the other hand, in the event that you don't see a solid response to a particularly terrible or uplifting news, markets may have effectively expected something like that and the value activity changing before the occasion, and estimated it in.
3. Hence, it is imperative to place everything in setting with regards to understanding value responses to the central information. We give a rundown of news instruments, sites and assets to keep up with what is going on every day.

7. Pattern Recognition Is Based on Implicit Learning:

Verifiable learning happens when individuals are presented with complex examples more than once and in the end disguise those, despite the fact that they can't verbalise the basic principles of those examples. This is the way kids learn dialect and punctuation, and it is the means by which we figure out how to explore our way through complex social connections. Verifiable learning shows itself as a "vibe" for an executive action and encourages a quickness of example acknowledgment that would not be conceivable through standard examination. Indeed, even framework designers, who depend upon unequivocal signs for trading, report that their regular introduction to information gives them a vibe for which factors will be promising and which won't, in their testing. Research discloses to us that certain adapting just happens after we have experienced a large number of learning trials. This is the reason trading fitness, like ability at other execution exercises, for example, guiding a contender fly and chess, requires extensive practice and presentation for sensible situations. Without such immersive introduction, traders never really disguise the examples in their business sectors and time allotments.

8. Associate with Charts and Work Ethics:

The hard working attitude of Marty Schwartz is inconceivable, and it features the discipline a trader needs. For instance, he draws every one of his diagrams by hand and uses paper for his diagrams. He says that it encourages him to "interface" with his instruments better and in spite of the fact that it requires significantly more time, the advantages are gigantic. Most traders haphazardly flip through many instruments, self-assertively include some flat lines and play around with pointers until they unintentionally discover something that may resemble a passage flag. A smidgen more care and a more thoroughly considered trading procedure would enable traders to accomplish a more expert approach. Marty Schwartz' training, hardworking attitude and routine are the principle explanations behind his remarkable achievement, and it underlines the distinction between the approach of the normal losing trader and the reliably winning trader. Inspiration is equivalent to an effective trading procedure. The positive emotions you can involve from obtaining things because of trading endeavours can be used as encouraging feedback for future trading choices. Make it a consistent practice to expel benefits from the market. Spend some of them and spare some of them.

9. Passionate, Cognitive, and Physical Factors Disrupt Access to Patterns Acquired Implicitly:

Once an entertainer has created abilities and moved along the way toward fitness and aptitude, brain science ends up noticeably vital in supporting consistency of execution. Numerous execution disturbances are caused when moves in our subjective, passionate as well as physical states cloud the inclinations and instincts that lie at the core of understood learning. This most usually happens because of execution nervousness - our feelings of trepidation about the result of our execution meddle with the entrance of the information and aptitudes that are expected to encourage that execution. Such executional disturbances normally happen when traders trade positions that are too expensive for their records and don't keep up sound hazard administration with their positions. The expansive P/L swings cause moves in enthusiastic states that meddle with the (verifiable) preparing of market information. Subjective, behavioural and biofeedback strategies can be extremely helpful in showing traders abilities for keeping up the "Yoda state" of quiet focus that is expected to get to the verifiable information.

10. Utilise Checklist and Trade Plan:

With regards to settling on trading choices, Marty Schwarz has extraordinary tips. A physical agenda which expresses all your entrance criteria can enable you to maintain a strategic distance from hasty and sincerely determined trading choices (botches). If you can really observe that the trade that you are going to take conflicts with our tenets, you will probably stay away from that trade or you need to settle on a dynamic and cognisant choice to break your guidelines. A trader ought to set up a trading plan before the market opens, examine his instruments and record potential trade situations. A trading plan can help diminish worry in the open market hours and give direction during the trading procedure. If you are uncertain about a trade, survey your arrangement, see what your underlying considerations were and then settle on a choice, whether the trade agrees with your criteria or not. When you have acquired a goal, verify that your next test is set. If you have met a beneficial target at that point, set another one so that you have made another test, another mountain to climb.

If you don't begin to deal with climbing another mountain, you will tumble off the present one, giving back all that you have achieved.

The vast majority of these are genuinely normal and understood stock trading standards, but like in life, the straightforward and clear ways are frequently neglected while we invest energy in looking for the uncommon and the confused, despite the fact that a trader needs certainty and trust in his capacities and his technique. He needs to comprehend that he can't control the result. The market manages what will happen and a trader's occupation is to respond in a similar manner. On the off chance that you face a loss and need to win, it typically results in a calamity. Along these lines, think process-situated, acknowledge loss quickly and proceed to the next trade.

Top Ten Trading Psychology Myths

Trading stages have been around for quite a while and this has prompted many people to figure out some rightful presumptions about the entire procedure. The following passage is a rundown of the most known things that are not really honest. Regardless of whether you're a prepared trader or you're new to the Forex showcase, the myths about Forex trading are continually twirling around you. These myths can influence anybody, regardless of the extent of their trade. My work as a trading analyst has given me an insight into the components that can affect unsuccessful traders over an assortment of settings, from exclusive firms, to speculation banks and flexible investments. Having met and worked with more than 100 expert traders in the past couple of years, the primary conclusion I've come to is that a large portion of the speculations about trading achievement is just not genuine. In this book, I thought I'd expose three of the unavoidable myths about trading accomplishment out there and offer my own points of view. By identifying the myths, traders can stay away from superfluous disappointments. While there are many trading myths, we'll take a gander at 10 that surface frequently and influence each phase of advancement, from why individuals get associated with Forex to creating procedures. Forex is a market where the trading of money for the expense. It's the market which gives availability and liquidity to the traders to purchase and offer one outside money in return of another. Forex traders look for the benefit in purchasing monetary forms low and offering them high. This sort of trading turned out to be more mainstream, across the board, for online Forex representatives. There is a great deal of data accessible about Forex on the web. However, there are numerous myths encompassing the remote trade showcase:

1. Trading Is Easy:

Many individuals that need to jump into the universe of the remote trade showcase trust that Forex trading is simple. They assume that all you need to do is read a book or two and, you will have the capacity to acquire the day by day benefits with only 2–3 hours of trading every day. Others imagine that they can purchase a beneficial methodology, and it will make them rich in Forex. Truly, that is only a myth. Prevailing in Forex isn't less demanding than mastering any other calling. It requires some serious energy, money and a considerable measure of training. Anybody can get the stage and the data, but making beneficial trades take a great deal of time and ability.

2. Get Rich Quick:

Promoting has quickly extended to the retail advertiser in Forex. This has brought many individuals into the territory, and they are on a mission to get rich speedily (or with little exertion). This, sadly, is exceptionally uncommon. Trading takes persistence, and there is no last goal. Traders don't just profit and then leave after that. They make a great many trades, regardless of the possibility of time holes in the middle. Trading requires consistency, not a betting mindset where you toss it all at two or three trades. Traders can't benefit at whatever point they need, even if Forex advertise is open 24 hours per day. You won't be sitting in front of your computer the entire day to have the capacity to trade 24 hours. You'll need to create computerised trading programming to get the benefit of a 24 hours a day working timetable. Accomplishment in the share trading system doesn't suggest that you will get achievement in Forex showcase. There are numerous contrasts between trading stocks and the spot monetary standards. As a matter of first importance, Forex showcase requires a considerable measure of diligent work and devotion, as this market is open for 24 hours every day. You can't simply sit before your COMPUTER for the entire day and night, so an ideal way to do it is to should locate the most reasonable eras for trading. "Buy hold" methodology won't work in Forex advertise. You won't have as much data about monetary forms as you can get from the organisations' reports and measurements.

3. Feelings Are at the Root of Trading Problems:

Yes, feelings can meddle with focus and execution, but that doesn't imply that they are an essential driver. Without a doubt, passionate misery is as regularly the consequence of poor trading as it is the reason. When traders neglect to oversee chance legitimately, a trading size that is too substantial for their records, they welcome outsized passionate reactions to their swings in P/L. Similarly, when traders trade untested examples that have no target edge in the commercial centre, they will lose money after some time and experience a justifiable level of dissatisfaction. I know numerous effective traders who are furiously aggressive and exceptionally passionate. I also know numerous fruitful traders who are exceptionally explanatory and not enthusiastic, in any manner. Trading is an execution field, though not as much as games or the performing arts. Achievement is a component of gifts (inalienable capacities) and abilities (obtained capabilities). No measure of passionate poise can transform a man into a fruitful artist, football player or trader. When people have the essential abilities and aptitudes for progress, the mental elements end up plainly imperative. Psychology manages how steady you are with the aptitudes and abilities you have, it can't supplant those aptitudes and gifts.

4. The Main Cause of Trading Failure Is a Loss of Discipline:

These are the myths perpetuated by the "trading mentor" and the "master."

a) They don't trade themselves and b) they have a personal stake in your conviction that their administrations are for the most part what stands between you and achievement. The primary driver of trading disappointment is an absence of a target edge in the commercial centre, trading arbitrary examples that have never been tried out for progress. We could never consider purchasing an auto just by looking at it. We'd need to explore it, test-drive it and associate in the engine. Nonetheless, numerous traders will hazard money trading designs that they never research or test-drive. Commonly, the reason they stray from those techniques is that, instinctively, they understand that those strategies are not working. In any execution field, we locate an immovable truth: the colossal entertainers invest more energy rehearsing their exhibitions than really performing. That is as valid for the Broadway character as is for the Olympic competitor. Numerous traders surmise that, at work, preparing will be sufficient. Sadly, their records regularly don't survive their expectations to absorb information. An official in a trading firm told me, a year ago, that the normal time it takes a normal trader to blow through their whole record is seven months. That is the reason financier firms are consistent in their chase for new clients. It isn't so much that these traders are for the most part inadequate in the discipline, they haven't occupied with adequate practice to make sense of the correct markets and trading styles for them and to sharpen their aptitudes. In other execution fields, you can discover moderately simple levels of rivalry. You can join a group theatre, play rounds of golf at the standard 3 course or set the test level on your chess computer. There is no simple level of rivalry in trading. When you put a trade on a noteworthy trade, you are up against the aces from the very beginning. No big surprise, it is so hard to succeed! Discipline is vital for trading achievement. However, there is substantially more to progress than just discipline. It takes purposeful practice and the development of aptitudes at perusing and following up on advertising designs.

5. Trading Is Just for Short-Term Profits:

High use has made here and now Forex trading well known. However, this is not the way it must be. Long haul money patterns are driven by essential components, and these long haul patterns are tradable. Long haul traders concentrate on the bigger pattern and are not worried about ordinary gyrations. It is doubtful that taking a more extended time period might be gainful to a few traders as it will lessen the quantity of spreads paid (the likeness a commission), and traders will probably maintain a strategic distance from here and now drive trades. Monetary forms can be utilised, as a venture, to differentiate or support purchase and hold portfolios. Many starting traders get signed by the visually impaired flag following. That resembles handing over the entire obligation of your activities to another person. That may sound cool. However, you wind up with the tremendous loss. Figure out how to depend on without anyone else's information and aptitudes. Keep in mind that there were no extraordinary flag adherents in any monetary market.

6. Anybody Can Trade for a Living with Dedicated Effort:

That is drivel. How many individuals make their living from acting or melodic execution? What extent of individuals playing games can really make money from games? Many individuals play chess or poker. However, how many of them can support a living from it? To bring home the bacon, from any execution movement, implies that you are reliably great at what you do. Not every person has the ability, aptitude or drive to be that effective, in any field. Among the numerous traders I've met in different settings, from locally established, autonomous traders to proficient ones in firms, the best indicators of trading achievement have been the measure of the trader's record and the assets accessible to the trader. If a man makes 30%, every year, on his records for quite a long time, he would be one of the world's best money administrators. Most money directors of common assets, mutual funds and annuity reserves can't support such execution. Assuming a trader starts with Rs. 60,000 of capital, he or she may not be content with Rs. 18,000 of benefit. This leads the trader to acknowledge immense use and court a danger of destruction when an unavoidable string of losing trades occurs. Indeed, such overabundance use is the primary driver of passionate misery in trading. Let us investigate how the Turtles profited. They took in a trading technique, figured out how to be reliable with that strategy and were sufficiently given money by Richard Dennis, so that they could trade numerous business sectors, with enough size to scale into positions in each.

7. The Market Is Rigged:

Losing traders frequently point to a fixed market or a degenerate intermediary as the purpose behind their disappointment. While it is a simple presumption to make, Forex is not a trick. The Forex advertise is, by a wide margin, the biggest on the planet. It is influenced by a huge number of trades and possibly a large number of data sources every day. This implies that if somebody adopts a non-efficient strategy to their trading, one of the other smart members will generally rapidly see it. This is the method for all business sectors. (Forex tricks are more typical than you may understand. Know the signs before you discard your money. There is no logical strategy to know something ahead of time in the market with a 100% assurance. There would be no Forex showcase if you could know the correct money rates beforehand. Trading is not the round of convictions, it's a session of chances. One of the principal things that new traders learn is to think in terms of probabilities and hazards, to compensate proportions.

8. Traders Need Complex Strategies:

It's a prevalent misconception, which numerous online vendors would need you to accept. The primary necessity to be fruitful in Forex is self-restraint and money administration. There are numerous traders that make steady benefits with rather straightforward and old methodologies. A few cynics and disillusioned traders surmise that Forex is quite recently some new prevailing fashion to trick individuals to part with their hard-earned money. In spite of the fact that there are many tricks that are taking cover behind the "brand" of Forex, it doesn't imply that the Forex itself is a trick. There are numerous institutional Forex agents, controlled Forex account chiefs and other strong organisations in the market which you can trust.

9. More Trades with More Pairs Is Better:

While it is decent to surmise that if a trader profits from trading once every day, then they can make 10 fold the amount of trading 10 times each day. This is, by and large, not the situation. Trading less and concentrating on a couple of money matches that the trader comprehends will be valuable to traders. Unless a trader is gifted and concentrates on scalping procedures, the dominant part of traders will profit by being tolerant, concentrating on something they know and sitting tight for the best open doors, even if there are only a few. Loss happens and endeavouring to discover a methodology that is correct each time will either leave the trader on the sidelines inconclusively or will carry the trader into the market with an over-streamlined technique that won't adjust to new conditions. Tolerating that loss happens and finding a system that gives a slight edge in the economic situations that are traded is sufficient to get positive returns.

10. Money Management Means Placing a Stop:
Money administration (MM) is seemingly the most vital factor in deciding achievement once the trader has built up some aptitude in getting steady returns. MM is not just putting in a stop request on a trade, it incorporates the amount of the aggregate record that will be gambled on each trade. This ought to, for the most part, be under 1%. It will look at what number of trades can be open at a solitary time, and if numerous positions are open do so, they have to fence each other or they would be able to be very connected. By concentrating on money administration, a trader takes their trading to next level. Overlooking money administration implies unavoidable disappointment, even with the best technique. Along these lines, since it is the trader's money in question, they should endeavour to build up their own particular aptitudes and arrive at their own decisions, rather than absolutely depending on the counsel of others. Experienced experts can enormously help new (or other experienced) traders. However, all data ought to be sifted and investigated before the data is followed up on.

Achievement is conceivable in trading, as it is in any execution field. In the event that anybody lets you know that the way to trading achievement is not quite the same as it is for the specialist or Olympian, you realise that you're hearing a myth. In the event that you pick the way of the first class entertainer, trading can be brilliantly testing and fulfilling. On the off chance that trading is not your optimal way for self-advancement, you are obviously better off finding your enthusiasm somewhere else and dealing with your money judiciously. The objective is to build up the best inside you, regardless of whether that is as a trader or as something else. Your life merits nothing less.

Developing your Mind for Trading: Building the Inner Team for Consistent Profitability

It's an unavoidable reality that your Forex trading achievement or disappointment will, to a great extent, rely upon your mentality. At the end of the day, if your Forex trading psychology is wrong, you wouldn't profit! Shockingly, most traders disregard this vital reality or are unconscious of how basic having the correct mentality is to Forex trading achievement. On the off chance that you don't have the right trading attitude, it doesn't make a difference how great your trading system is, on the grounds that no procedure will ever profit if it's utilised by a trader with the wrong psychology. Regardless of whether you are another trader or have years of experience overseeing other individuals' money, like Jeffrey, whether you are reliably productive or reliably battling. Your trading outlook is the basic factor in your execution. It's valid for competitors (you definitely know this on the off chance that you contend in a game), and it's particularly valid for traders. You have presumably done what's coming to you of perusing about trading psychology. It's turned into a prevalent field. Be that as it may, perusing about mental traps is just helpful to a limited degree. The genuinely constraining issues we each face as traders are typically hard to distinguish and change in 'the warmth existing apart from everything else' when it truly matters.

Developing Trade Propensities

Many individuals appear to be ignorant of the way that they are trading with a mentality that is repressing them from profiting in the business sectors. They feel that in the event that they simply locate the correct marker or framework, they will mystically begin printing money from their computers. Trading achievement is the final product of building up the correct trading propensities, and propensities are the final product of having the best possible trading psychology. The present lesson will give you the understanding you have to build up a productive trading outlook, so read this lesson deliberately and don't reject any of it. I guarantee you that the reason you are battling in the business sectors now is because your attitude is conflicting with you, rather than for you. When he puts money on hold, the trader rapidly gets some answers concerning the qualities and shortcomings of the mind that he or she conveys to trading. Regardless of whether you need to think about your shortcomings or not does not make a difference. Abruptly, the hazard is genuine, and the trader's most profound inwardly loaded convictions surface all of a sudden and commandeer the reasoning personality. Trading has a method for compelling the trader to recognise his passionate and mental shortcomings. Truth be told, most traders, until the point that they start trading life, have made an extraordinary showing of keeping away from familiarity with their self-restricting convictions. In any case, in that constrained snapshot of grasping equivocalness called "live trading," your genuine convictions about your ability to oversee instability turn into the submarine that torpedoes an impeccably fine trading arrangement. What's more, here's a gender related issue for you. Men arrange and explore uniquely, in contrast to ladies in another condition. Men and ladies have diverse personality maps. Men have the tendency to depend on their premonitions, while ladies explore more by seeing and recalling subtle elements. Therefore, men get muddled when the geometry of the earth changes. That is an issue for male traders, in light of the fact that a value graph is a geometric grid that is continually in flux. What was quite recently the floor is presently the roof or the other way around! No big surprise, men get somewhat befuddled by constant value activity, but we don't have the tendency to let it out to ourselves.

Have Practical Desires

The principal thing you have to do to build up the best possible Forex trading outlook has sensible assumptions about trading. What I mean is this, don't believe you will leave your place of employment and begin making a million rupees per year, after 2 months of trading live with your Rs. 5,000 account. That is not how it functions, and the sooner you ground your desires in all actuality, the sooner you will start to profit reliably. You have to acknowledge that you can't over-trade and over-use your approach to trading achievement. In the event that you do those two things, you may profit incidentally. However, you will soon lose it all, and that's just the beginning. Acknowledge the truth of how much money you have in your trading record and the amount that you will lose per trade. Here are some different focuses to consider:

Trade with dispensable "risk" capital: Disposable capital is money you don't require for any everyday costs, including retirement or other long haul things. In the event that you don't have any expendable or hazard capital, keep demo trading until you do, or quit trading by and large. No matte what you do, don't trade with money. You will wind up plainly passionate about losing. Continuously expect that you could lose whatever money you have in your record or in a trade. If you're genuinely OK with that, you're ready. Simply ensure you don't mislead yourself. Truly be "alright" with it. Trading with "terrified" (money you can't bear to lose) will prompt extreme passionate weight and cause continuous loss.

Ensure you can at present rest around evening time: This is identified with the above point about dispensable capital. However, the distinction is that you have to ask yourself before every trade you take if you are 100% unbiased or OK with possibly losing the money you are going to chance. If you can't rest during the evening because you're pondering about your trade, you've gambled excessively. Nobody can disclose to you the amount to hazard per trade, it relies upon what you're alright with. In the event that you trade 4 times each month, you can clearly hazard somewhat more per trade than somebody who trades 30 times each month. It's depends on your trade recurrence, your abilities as a trader and your own hazard resistance.

See each trade is autonomous of the past one: This point is vital in light of the fact that I realise that numerous traders are far too affected by their past trade. The truth is, your last trade has ZERO to do with your next trade. You have to abstain from being euphoric or presumptuous after a triumphant trade or vindictive after a losing trade. The truth is, each time you trade, it should simply be viewed as another execution of your trading edge. On the off chance that you simply had 3 continuous victories, you have to abstain from gambling more than expected on your next trade, since you are feeling exceptionally sure. Similarly, you have to abstain from hopping again into the market immediately after a losing trade, just to attempt to "make back" what you lost. When you do these things, you are working 100% on feeling as opposed to working on rationale and objectivity.

Try not to get joined to your trades: If you take after the 3 focuses we just talked about, you ought to have minimal possibility of winding up excessively appended, making it impossible to your trades. Try not to think about any trade literally. If you lose on a couple of trades a line, it doesn't mean you suck at trading. Similarly, if you win on 3 trades a column, it doesn't mean you are a trading "God" who is insusceptible to losing. On the off chance that you don't hazard excessively per trade and you aren't trading with money you require for different things throughout your life, you likely won't get excessively appended, making it impossible to your trades.

Assuming responsibility of the Mind: Just as there are damaging components of the self, there are productive and engaging parts of the self as well. This is basically the idea of our humanness. Be that as it may, they must be stirred, sustained, supported and created for them to end up a dynamic (and vocal) portion of the council of the brain. As you create care and apply it to trading, what you find is that you, as an executive of the leading body of the trading panel of the psyche, have been sleeping. You have not been watching out for the matter of building up the brain as a trader. Furthermore, in light of the fact that you, as an onlooker of the brain, have been snoozing (not conscious), the trading board of trustees of the psyche has floated without authority and is not obviously. In awakening the observer of the mind through mindfulness, the trader finds effective and productive components of the self. He finds intrinsic indwelling assets that have been sitting tight for him to wake up and create. These are what Carl Jung called the enabled side of the paradigms. These prime examples offer a frame to the different passionate powers at work, in the mind's trading board of trustees.

Comprehend the Power of Patience

One of the greatest acknowledgments that enabled traders to hand the corner over their own trading was that they didn't need to trade a considerable measure to make a good month to month return. Consider it, a great many people consider a 6% yearly return useful for a bank account, and if you get 12% a year on your retirement support, you are quite cheerful. So, how can it be that most traders hope to make 100% a month or some other implausible return? What's the issue with making 5 or 10% a month? That is, as yet, extraordinary through the span of one year. While I can't suggest you will make a specific rate each month, if you simply comprehend that slower and more reliable increases are the best approach to long haul accomplishment in the business sectors, you will obviously be better off towards the finish of each trading year. Here are some different focuses to consider about tolerance:

Figure out how to trade on the everyday diagrams first: By figuring out how to trade on the day by day outline time spans to start with, you will normally adopt a greater picture strategy to the business sectors, and you'll stay away from the majority of the compulsion to over-trade that the lower time allotments prompt. Starting traders particularly need to back off and figure out how to trade off the everyday graphs first. Day by day outlines give the most applicable and viable perspective of the market.

Quality over amount: I see myself as an "expert sharpshooter" of the market; I hold up, and I hold up, and I hold up, at times, for a considerable length of time. I hold up for even 1 week without trading, when I see a value activity setup that triggers my "this one is an easy decision" alert.

Client your "shots" shrewdly: To truly pound home the energy of tolerance in building up the best possible trading outlook, you have to comprehend that being patient will work to impart positive trading propensities inside you. Tolerance fortifies positive trading propensities, while enthusiastic trading strengthens negative ones. When you start to trade persistently, you will observe how utilising your "projectiles" carefully functions. You just need a couple of good trades a month to make a respectable return in the business sectors. After you accomplish this through tolerance, you will figure out how to appreciate not being in the business sectors, since it's then that you are "chasing your prey." This, rather than the fatigued and disappointed trader who remains up throughout the night, gazing at the diagrams like a trading zombie and simply won't acknowledge that they have to trade less regularly.

Be Sorted Out in Your Way to Deal with Business Sectors

Traders need a business trading plan and a trading diary. You have to design out a large portion of your activities in the market before you enter. The more you design before you enter, the higher likelihood you will have of profiting long haul. You are continually going to decipher the market all the more precisely while you're not in a trade, so pre-arranging everything expands your chances of profiting, since you will be working more on rationale than feeling.

Keeps an Expert Trading Diary

Traders require a reputation. This is a basic part of manufacturing the correct Forex trading outlook, since it gives you a substantial report that you can take a gander at and in a flash, get crude criticism on your trading execution. When you begin keeping a diary of your trades, it will end up being a propensity, and you won't have any desire to see passionate outcomes gazing back at you in your trade diary. In the long run, you will look at your trading diary as something of a show-stopper that demonstrates your capacity to trade with teach and also your capacity to take after your trading plan. This is something any genuine financial specialist will need to check if you anticipate trading other individuals' money.

Think before you 'Shoot,' Not afterward

The greater part of the arranging and acquisition that I just talked about closely resembles your intuition before you shoot. A firearm is an intense weapon, we as a whole realise that we have to think before we shoot, regardless of the possibility that we are simply chasing or shooting at a firearm go. Moreover, the business sectors can be intense "weapons" with respect to profiting. Along these lines, you need have as much intuition before you enter a trade as you can, in light of the fact that after you enter, you are going to be more passionate, and you would prefer not to set yourself in a place of always entering deplorable trades. On the off chance that you design your activities before you enter, you ought not to lament your trades, notwithstanding when you have losing trades.

The Mind Is Developed, Not Found

Left to its own devices, the psyche will float in the verifiable adjustment to which it was conceived. This is the place most traders remain stuck. They never deal with the idea of building up the potential that exists inside each of us. In their visual impairment, they continue looking "out there" for answers to their trading burdens. They search for an outer group to connect to, as opposed to building up the interior group of the self. In any case, by conveying an alternate observer to the trading advisory group of the brain, you locate a different potential for what the trading psyche can resemble. We, as a whole, exist as the potential that is restricted just by the observer that we are. Figuring out how to build up the observer of the thoughts in the brain that travel all around and perceiving that we are not our musings, enables you to deconstruct the old board of trustees of the mind appearing in your trading as self-restricting convictions and to reconstruct it into a psyche for reliable gainfulness in trading. This is the test that must be overcome. It is your mind that trades. Its potential can be created. Furthermore, trading makes improvement unavoidable in the event that you are reliably productive. It is your life, and you, and only you, are in charge of the mind you control to develop of your life. Grasp it.

Trading Psychology and Attitude

Most of the traders realise that each of us has our own "attitudes" to things, and our states of mind may even be remarked on by others with articulations, for example, "I like your mentality" or "You have an uplifting disposition." For some odd reason, despite the fact that we as a whole have states of mind to things, we may not really be completely and intentionally mindful of precisely what those dispositions are or how they are affecting our practices. The same applies to trading. Numerous traders may not understand that their trading achievement (or absence of) is being impacted by the fundamental states of mind living in the oblivious personality. It is useful to better comprehend your own states of mind, so you can know about how they might be affecting your trading. The Forex trader's attitude is a critical component that must not be ignored. For a trader to expand a trading style that matches his mentality, he should recognise his key identity characteristics (the two qualities and shortcomings). Many traders surmise that gainful trading is simply an issue of having a decent trading framework. This perspective of trading misses the mark concerning what is true should it have been fruitful. A quality trading approach consolidated with appropriate hazard control and great money administration is vital. However, the greatest factor deciding your prosperity will originate from building up the trader inside you. The trader inside you is the aftereffect of numerous things, such as your convictions, your identity, your attitude or outlook, your character and your well-being. You can't purchase these things at the trading store! Rather, you should distinguish and know yourself and then make whatever alterations are important.

Confidence and Disposition for Trading

You can have the best procedures and methods but if you don't trust that you will make extraordinary progress, then you are likely right. You need great confidence, an awesome disposition and trust in what you are doing, and you also need to appreciate it. In the event that you find trading truly grinding and exhausting or on the off chance that you are overwhelmed with extraordinary fear and your pulse goes more than 130 bpm each time you trade, then these are solid markers that you are not in good shape. When you begin getting on edge and anxious, it's best to make a stride over from the PC and accomplish something that returns you to your upbeat, casual and certain perspective. Make yourself some tea, go for a walk, ponder, tune into your most loved music – whatever works for you. When trading in a depressed state, you're just going to burrow yourself a deeper hole, as you will probably settle on terrible choices driven by the freeze. Not very many of us are normally certain and have an awesome self-conviction. Whatever is left of us can get it by raising our mindfulness and adopting more of ourselves and our conduct. Keeping in mind the end goal to land at a "settled attitude and feeling," we apply our interior assessment procedures to things with a specific end goal to make a considered appraisal. The assessment procedure and result enables us to make a judgment about the thing under investigation, so we can accomplish that "settled attitude and feeling." It is this 'assessment and judgment' process that is the outcome of the attitude we embrace toward the question. You should first discover or build up a trading framework that matches your identity and trading style. Numerous traders fizzle since they pick a trading framework that is not lined up with their conviction framework. For instance, odds are that if you're a maverick and don't care for swarms, you won't be a decent pattern trader, who would be required to take after the horde of traders, to profit by being with this jam in the pattern. Know yourself enough to recognise what your convictions are, so you can trade by understanding them.

Possessing Positive Feeling Is Winner Attitude

It is imperative that traders feel positive and effective when they are trading. Preferably, you ought to expect a large portion of your trades to end in the money. However, acknowledge that there will be losses and don't give them a chance to divert you from your course. Concentrate on the final product, which is to finish the day in benefit. In case you're into the law of fascination or positive pie in the sky considering or non-existent imaginative kind of thing then extraordinary – concentrate on that. If not, look at it along these lines – if you don't expect most, if not the greater part, of your trades to complete in-the-money and feel negative about it, you will presumably have a wide range of negative feelings like fear, outrage and impatience. They can influence your judgment when trading. Strikingly, it doesn't make a difference whether the "thing" being surveyed is a genuine question, a man or a conceptual idea. We can assess and judge it, and thus build up an attitude toward it. As we regularly find in our general surroundings, a man's dispositions can change form to a great degree of positive to amazingly negative. This can result in practices that 'normally mirror the hidden attitude.' How positive or negative an attitude is will decide the sort and power of the feelings and ensuing practices identified with it. The level of enthusiastic force and the practices related to the attitude may likewise change, contingent upon conditions. For instance, a trade benefit may build the inspiration of your attitude toward the trade, trading and even yourself, and as long as that benefit proceeds with the energy, emotions may proceed. In any case, if that same trade all of a sudden betrays the setup and goes into a loss, those past positive sentiments may rapidly turn and end up noticeably negative. They may then draw out a less uplifting mentality and result in undesirable trading practices.

Imperative Techniques Assessment for Successful Trading Attitude

Traders can develop your certainty by honing on a demo account (most double choices specialists give you one after you make a store). When you rehearse a technique repetitively and see awesome achievement, it will develop your certainty and faith in the framework and in yourself. This will help you when trading without a doubt. Honing is crucial on the grounds that reiteration will prepare you to perceive circumstances that finished well for you. If a technique doesn't work for you, locate an alternate one. Each trader is unique, and diverse things work for various individuals. In case you're not happy with the methodology you're utilising, you're likely not going to be exceptionally fruitful at it at any rate. It is also a smart thought to examine the feelings that beat you in various circumstances when trading, that way you can begin to comprehend what settled on you to settle on those choices and how to stay away from them later on. You should sharpen your trading aptitudes through instruction, trading and more trading. You should practice or "paper trade" until you build up a beneficial trading approach. It might take years to create both the "science" of trading, which speaks to your trading aptitudes and the "workmanship" of trading, which speaks to your judgment and attitude. Most new traders flop around there because they don't have the teaching to take a shot at their trading approach until it is profitable. In the event that you consider playing golf or tennis, you would not go after money until you turn into a decent player. Furthermore, you don't turn into a decent player until you have honed your skill for a considerable length of time. The same is valid for trading! Think how silly it would be for you to play against master golfers or tennis players if you were only a tenderfoot. However, this is precisely what numerous new traders endeavour to do. Each time you effectively trade the monetary markets, you are contending with different traders, some of which are the best on the planet. You should, in this manner, recognise that all business sectors are title fields and that you are going up against the best traders in any money related market. Consider how stupid it would be for a tenderfoot trader to enter a market and expect a positive result while going up against traders that are specialists. This is why new traders need to rehearse until their aptitudes are produced enough to have the capacity to effectively contend.

Enthusiasm for Trading Success

It is generally said that an enthusiastic trader is not an especially decent one. Already, achievement has been connected to training and controlling your feelings. However, that conclusion is beginning to change. New investigations demonstrate that the vast majority of our choices are done unwittingly. Presently, it is believed that just a single or two continuous choices are "restrained," and the rest happen rather unwittingly, which isn't really an awful thing. It is also conceivable to have "clashing" attitudes towards a similar thing, individual or experience. There exists a 'conscious mentality' and an alternate 'oblivious attitude' around a similar thing. This can be found in circumstances where somebody may openly seem to have a 'socially worthy' uplifting attitude towards something (the conscious level disposition) and yet their oblivious attitude makes practices that aren't consistent with their freely communicated mentality. Another vital piece of the trader's disposition is to join and adjust into both, your life and your trading. While it is vital to be an engaged trader and furthermore, one that is engaged in a quest for capability, there is a line in which the centre can turn into a fixation. Try not to cross this line! On the off chance that you discover you are getting fixated on your trading, the time has come to pull back and take some time off. Unwind consistently to abstain from getting noticeably fixated on trading. Get some activity with a specific end goal to enhance and keep up your well-being. Do exercises that you appreciate, other than trading. What's more, bear in mind to unwind. A well-adjusted trader will typically win more than a fixated gifted trader, since his or her body will be more casual, less restless and less vulnerable to negative feelings such as fear and covetousness, which cause poor trading.

Capable of Understanding Loss Aversion Better

In financial aspects and choice hypothesis, loss aversion alludes to individuals' inclination to unequivocally lean toward staying away from the loss to obtain pick-ups. A few investigations propose that loss is twice as capable, mentally, as additions. Loss aversion was first exhibited by Amos Tversky and Daniel Kahneman. For instance, they directed a test in the BBC Horizon narrative – How You Really Make Decisions. A gathering of individuals was given a choice, they could have a £5 note or flip a coin to get £20 or nothing. The greater part of them picked the hazard free offering of £5. Another gathering was given a £20 note and a choice to give £15 back and keep the £5 hazard free or flip a coin to keep the £20 or lose it all. A great many people in that gathering flipped the coin, which is fairly odd as the two were given a similar hazard free alternative of accepting £5. Researchers have led a comparable report on monkeys, acquainting them with money and giving them the alternative of buying the natural product. The monkeys in the investigation hinted at being less opposed. In trading, there might be exercises, for example, exploring information that is regularly assessed as positive in light of how it trades. In the meantime, the movement may be assessed as negative on the grounds that for some it might be exhausting to do. This will deliver clashing states of mind towards that particular action. The majority of this demonstrates there might be hidden 'states of mind,' both positive and negative, impacting your trading exercises, trading thoughts, your association with money and maybe even how you contemplate yourself. If states of mind that aren't supporting the objective of amplifying trading benefits exist, they ought to be changed.

Encouraging Private Moments and Leisure Trading

When you are building up your trading abilities and trading attitude, ensure that you're having a ton of fun in the meantime, and treat it like an amusement. Build up a calm domain where honing and learning are entertaining. This is the place where "paper trading" can help you. "Paper trading" is an incredible approach to hone you by trading in a calm domain where you can have a fabulous time while learning and moving forward. When you are prepared to trade with genuine money, trade to win! Be casual yet engaged. Try not to consider it excessively important or you will lose your edge and wind up noticeably tense and pushed. Rather, stream with the business sectors, and don't imagine it any other way, you are there to win! The US Navy has some awesome colloquialisms: "It pays to be a victor!," and "Second place is the primary washout!," and this is valid for trading too. If loss aversion is something that we have created through a huge number of years of advancement, would we be able to truly change our conduct? Most likely not, but knowing is a large portion of the fight. You can begin to examine your activities and act in a similar manner when loss repugnance kicks in. I realise that from my experience. The primary week I began trading, I saw tremendous achievement. I made a benefit of about €4000, and I was over the moon. On the 6th day, I made some goliath blunders. I had three trades on in the meantime, and every one of them was finishing out. If I had abandoned it, I would've still been in benefit over €3500. However, I chose to cover my loss and bend over every one of the trades. I did that in various circumstances and lost the majority of my benefit. After that had happened, I began to ask why I had done that. Why chance the greater part of my benefits for an additional €500? I didn't comprehend my conduct, as I've never been a card shark. I had no clue what made me act so nonsensically. In the wake of finding out about loss abhorrence, it began to bode well. When this was going on, it felt like I was on autopilot. I continuously asked myself, is this truly a smart thought? Presently, we comprehend what a mentality is and how it is framed. In the following video of the arrangement, we will find out about the mental structure of dispositions so you can comprehend the impact they have, great or terrible, on your trading exercises.

Trading Psychology Diagnosis: Identifying the Root of Trading Problems

Each trained physician realises that analysis goes before treatment. We need to comprehend what is turning out badly before we attempt any sort of arrangement. The core of most critical thinking technique is some approach to burrow to the underlying drivers. What's more, communitarian talks with all the applicable specialists are vital to that. Auto mechanics take part in a similar procedure, they tune into the motor, look in the engine and run tests before they recognise issues and start to settle them. In any case, shared trades are insufficient without great visual models. The fishbone (or Ishikawa) chart is a typical decision for that model, yet numerous others exist. Quite a bit of trading psychology, similar to a lot of generally connected psychology, is issue centred. We begin with an issue, and we hope to distinguish and evacuate or limit the reason for the issue. This is like the structure of a drug. We begin with side effects, analyse an ailment and look for a treatment that will cure the illness.

Traders constantly look for answers for their trading issues before they really comprehend the wellsprings of those issues. Similarly, tutors and mentors of traders offer their answers without really experiencing an intensive indicative process. Be that as it may, that is insufficient for critical thinking to take care of the issue. You should have the capacity to:

- develop solutions for those causes
- distinguish what choices must change to execute those cures
- have a visual of the effects of changing those choices on whatever remains of the framework or outline
- comprehend the tradeoffs that unavoidably should be made versus the client and business interests
- potentially enhance further if those trade-offs are undesirable or excessively restricting

Neglecting to do those things, before choosing a solution for an issue, will commonly cause different issues. Then again, doing all that is practically identical to rehashing the choice procedure of the earlier advancement exertion. Issue solvers are never offered time to tackle the issue equivalent to the first advancement exertion. The main great answer for this problem is the reusable learning that was created amid the earlier improvement exertion, where they ought to have effectively done a rich causal trade off examination, enabling them to settle on the first choices in view of solid information. Along these lines, when an issue happens later, it turns into an activity of distinguishing the information hole that wasn't recognised beforehand, rapidly shutting that crevice and then fusing that new learning into the current information as basic leadership apparatuses. After that, it perceives how that would change the plan choices. Along these lines of believing, it is tied down by a few critical inquiries.

Question 1: Is There Really an Issue Here?

This may appear like a bizarre inquiry. You've quite recently drawn down, and you've been baffled in your trading. Obviously, there's an issue! The issue is more unpretentious. Any fruitful trading is a probabilistic venture. Hit rates and Sharpe Ratios don't develop to the sky. Individuals are questionable, and markets install a considerable measure of instability. Therefore, losing periods are unavoidable, and dissatisfactions will be experienced. Similarly, as we anticipate that baseball hitters will strike out sometimes and football quarterbacks will toss deficient passes once in a while, we can expect losing trades. A trading approach with a 60% hit rate could be extraordinarily productive, yet it will, at present, experience strings of losing trades with consistency. The trade lop-sidedness began with OPEC and the oil value stuns in the 1970s and oil imports from that point forward. This is an enormous issue, yet the recipients of this trade irregularity battle to keep things the way they are. (Coincidentally, next time you hear somebody at FOX running down our nation's environmentally friendly power vitality endeavours, thumping the Chevy Volt or denying environmental change, consider this: Fox's second-biggest investor is an extremely rich person in Saudi oil sovereign. This means, we start the finding by looking at a significant specimen of past trading, not only the most recent couple of days or trades. A regular informal investor making many trades a day may look at the month's outcomes and results from the previous year. A more extended term trader may need to gather information over a year or more before certainly distinguishing an issue. As such, to distinguish an issue, it's important to see that current outcomes miss the mark regarding past ones and that current drawdowns are not like past ones. That requires a legitimate verifiable view. When traders expect an issue to exist without an adequate chronicled examination, they risk tinkering with strategies that work and exacerbating those techniques. This is genuine when traders start to trade frameworks.

They end up plainly debilitated when the framework has a (typical and expectable) drawdown, so they start to change the framework, front run the framework and so on, just to transform the mishaps into extended droops.

Question 2: If There Is an Issue Introduced, Is It Related to an Adjustment in the Market(S) You're Trading?

An extraordinary instance of this has been the current decrease in instability in money markets. Numerous traders who profited from force and pattern trading have endured this low unpredictability period since moves never again expand and, without a doubt, tend to switch. This prompts disappointment and debilitation. The key tells for when trading issues are identified with changes in business sectors is that individuals trading comparative methodologies are likewise encountering execution challenges. This is one reason it's vital to have a wide system of trading associates, regardless of the possibility of trading autonomously. If the greater part of traders trading comparative styles are encountering drawdowns, you can firmly expect that not every person has transformed into an enthusiastic bundle of nerves in the meantime. Uneven trade connections are currently emptying money out of our nation at an emotional rate. We are significantly more open to imports than a significant number of our 'trading accomplices' are. We purchase from them, they don't purchase from us, and we simply let this proceed for a seemingly endless amount of time. If your trading issues are broadly shared and can be connected to shifts in how your business sectors have been trading, no mental activities will take care of the issue. Nor is it an answer for put one's head in the sand and expectation that business sectors will "pivot." Or maybe, the response to the trading issues is to adjust to the new condition and look for new wellsprings of edge that can supplement one's customary trading. For instance, one may discover mean inversion or relative esteem methodologies that pleasantly supplement one's directional/slant/energy trading. The mix of trading approaches really broadens returns and delivers a smoother P/L bend.

Question 3: If There Is an Individual Issue Show Is It—or Has It Been—Exhibit in Non-Trading Parts of Your Life?

Here is an imperative issue. Numerous individual issues, such as nervousness, outrage, sadness, consideration deficiencies and impulsivity, appear in trading. However, they do not appear only inside trading. For instance, a man may experience difficulty with persistence and dissatisfaction in individual connections, and those same issues manifest in his association with business sectors. A man may have confidence issues in life that appear as negative intuition designs in times of market loss. When the enthusiastic examples, thought examples and conduct designs that meddle with trading are happening and interfering with different parts of life, it is a solid sign that just taking a shot at trading won't be adequate. It bodes well to look for proficient offer assistance. In the 70's, the trade adjusts plunged underneath zero in view of oil, and the nation reacted with preservation and looking for choices, until Reagan. To exacerbate the situation, Reagan lectured on 'organised commerce,' as being used modestly outside work to break American unions. (In any case, Reagan additionally implemented standards against "dumping" and other trade infringement.) The genuine break in our adjustment of trade obviously starts around the time that NAFTA and the World Trade Organisation became effective. After that, it went completely nuts after China was acquired. In the vicinity of 2001 and 2009, we lost 1/3 of the greater part of our assembling occupations, more than 50,000 processing plants and whole enterprises. We emptied trillions of dollars from our economy. Sadness, nervousness, consideration shortages, addictions, bipolar turmoil and relationship issues cause massive influence on a high level of individuals in the all-inclusive community. Traders are not excluded from these general issues. Expecting an intense subject matter to affect trading is essentially a trading issue, and it may keep you from getting the correct sort of assistance. No measure of writing in a trading diary will rebalance neurotransmitters in your cerebrum or understand the contentions you convey to your marriage. When you see the issues influencing your trading and also influencing different aspects of your life, it's a solid sign that a more broad way to deal with change will be required.

Question 4: If the Issue You're Confronting Happens Extraordinarily in Trading Settings, Do You Require Mental Training or Do You Require Additional Coaching of Your Trading?

Here, again, is a critical refinement. Particularly for fresher traders, disappointments and other passionate issues emerge in trading on the grounds that they are still youthful in their expectations to learn and adapt. What they require is not just passionate training, but rather directly from experienced coaches who can enable them to rectify trading blunders and reliably apply trading abilities. Indeed, even experienced traders can experience drawdowns and disappointments, since they are committing trading errors that a coach can get. I, as of late, worked with a trader who was exceptionally demoralised as a result of a drawdown that happened in light of the fact that he was not observing relationships among his positions. What he thought were a few free trades ended up being variants of a similar trade, once the national bank showed a conceivable arrangement move. He lost money, since he was excessively gathered in that one, merged trade. This is yet another motivation behind why it's exceptionally useful to be associated with systems of companion traders. Ordinarily, such connections offer shared tutoring that can address situational issues and errors in trading. Here is the trap of our uneven trade problems, these "facilitated commerce" understandings increment sends out. The reason this is a trap and an issue is because they increment imports more. In this way, from one viewpoint, the understandings make and improve intrigue bunches that push for continuation and extension of the problems. They also increment trade shortages, which deplete our economy. Drawdowns and interruptions of trading are more mental and situational. A few mental methodologies can be useful, including behavioural strategies (introduction treatment) for tension and execution weight; subjective rebuilding systems for hair-splitting, presumptuousness and negative idea examples; and arrangement centred ways to recognise and grow one's own particular accepted procedures. (Particular utilisations of these strategies can be found in *The Daily Trading Coach*. The making of best practices is a noteworthy theme inside *Trading Psychology 2.0*. A review of intellectual and behavioural methods for enhancing trading execution can be found in *Enhancing Trader Performance*)

Absence of Training

Point the finger at it on the fervour to make huge amounts of 'moolah' in trading, yet some novice traders hop the weapon and trade genuine money on a live record immediately, without rehearsing their abilities on the demo. An unpractised trader can wipe out a record speedier than you can state "edge call," which is why we encourage beginner traders to open a demo account first. Demo trading enables apprentice traders to get their feet wet without putting their well-deserved money on hold at first. This enables them to have a vibe of the market condition, to change their trade designs as they see fit and to hone legitimate hazard administration. Without legitimate instruction and preparing, you may be missing evident prompts from the market. For example, outline designs, Japanese candle arrangements or moves in showcase assessment.

Issue in Trading Technique

Behavioural strategies are aptitude building techniques that you rehearse progressively, amid issue circumstances. You actually are showing yourself new aptitudes and new propensity designs. For instance, an extremely straightforward behavioural system is enjoying a reprieve amid trading at whatever point you feel on edge, baffled, exhausted or demoralised. You rapidly perceive that you're not in the correct attitude for trading, and you enjoy a reprieve from the screens. Acknowledging the issues categorically and figuring them out are considered to be the greatest notions for the traders. Thus, they are required to assess them in every definite interval. Amid that break, you may participate in different aptitude building exercises. For example, unwinding preparing to back one off and diminish strain. Behavioural strategies are ordinarily rehearsed outside of trading hours, with the goal that the abilities wind up programmed continuously when issues manifest.

Passionate Trading

Indeed, even experienced Forex traders succumb to passionate trading every once in a while. Enthusiastic clamour may introduce itself as unchecked fear, expectation or eagerness. These feelings, thus, show themselves through hurtful trading practices. For example, overtrading, trading too extensive, cutting winning trades and letting losing trades run.

Changing Market Conditions

At times, the issue isn't with your trading psychology but with moving Forex economic situations. You might be very restrained and doing everything as indicated by design, yet in the event that your trading approach sometimes falls short for the market condition, you could, at present, wind up somewhere down in the red.

Arrangement Seeking

Arrangement centred procedures are ones that inspect what you are doing amid your best trading, both as far as trading hones/forms and mental self-administration are concerned. The objective of arrangement centred work is to "accomplish a greater amount of what works" and turn out to be more predictable with the goal that accepted procedures can transform into repeatable best procedures. *Trading Psychology 2.0* contains 57 best practices, without anyone else's input and different traders. The section on Building Strengths grasps an answer centred way to deal with distinguishing what you excel at and building your trading around it.

You have presumably experienced a couple of losing streaks all over, however, you inevitably recovered it by making the vital changes. Unless you're ready to pinpoint the foundation of the issue, you'll likely have a considerably harder time bobbing back. In the event that you are experiencing this circumstance, odds are that the weight to get back operating at a profit is making it troublesome for you to evaluate what the issue is. Keep in mind, diagnosing your concern is the initial step to curing it! The better we can decide the foundation of the issue, the better we can address it.

A Powerful Technique for Changing Your Trading Psychology

What traders regularly recognise as mental issues in trading are typically the consequence of a basic issue and not simply the issue. Effectively managing the issue implies distinguishing and tending to its motivation. The approach starts with acknowledgment. We are not going to wipe out dissatisfaction, instability or emotional episodes. Trading works in a situation of vulnerability and hazard. That will evoke undesirable musings and feelings, on occasion. It's OK to be human and to have human emotions. It will happen. When we acknowledge that these examples will manifest, we would then be able to effectively expect them. Rather than labelling them insane, we need to make them our core interest. Once we're in that condition of acknowledgment, we need to make full utilisation of a clear and capable anxiety administration schedule. We tune into serene, unwinding music, close our eyes, moderate and develop our breathing and sit still while backing off and concentrating on the music. We utilise the breathing to bring our body's level of excitement down, and we utilise the music to increase our subjective core interest.

Through this routine, we keep ourselves out of the 'flight or battle' method of stress and into a method of tranquil sharpness instead.

Enhancing Trading Leadership Quality

A typical view, held by traders and mentors of traders, is that enthusiastic variables represent the distinction between trading achievement and trading disappointment. Some hold that feelings ought to be controlled, kept under tight restraints and made optional to the discipline of tenets. Others hold that feelings ought to be acknowledged and experienced carefully and when conceivable, utilised as data. In either case, the objective is to guarantee that basic leadership is accomplished through an appropriate trading process and not driven by the enthusiastic encounters and motivations existing apart from everything else. The anxiety administration routine requires some training, so we need to rehash the activity a couple of times each day, for a few days, to end up noticeably great at achieving that 'quite ready' state. With training, we can centre ourselves and get ourselves out of the 'battle or flight' mode on request. At that point, once we've turned out to be great at the anxiety administration, we do the activity with the music and the profound breathing. However, now we include symbolism. We envision the testing market circumstances that ordinarily trigger our dissatisfaction, misshaped considering, tension and so on. At the end of the day, while we're playing the music and breathing gradually, we're distinctively strolling through circumstances where we miss a trade, lose money, go into drawdown, trade inadequately and so on. While you're envisioning those circumstances, you need to really envision and **feel** those passionate reactions that have undermined your trading in the past. You need to feel the fear or insatiability or disappointment. Be that as it may, you're presently encountering those feelings while you are in charge, engaged and loose. You continue concentrating on those circumstances and feelings until you can remain in your quiet, engaged zone. This is an activity you'll need to do each day, prior to the beginning of trading and maybe also during late morning breaks. The reiteration enables you to effectively confront passionate difficulties while remaining in charge. Through rehashed understanding, we reconstruct our negative examples of thought and feeling. Thus, we encounter them. However, they never again characterise or control us.

Overtrading Is Not Encouraged Always

The emotive perspective of trading execution is mistaken and is not, actually, conceivably stated in some other execution area. Nobody, for instance, would fight that the way to achieving grandmaster status in chess is a component of effectively managing one's sentiments. Enthusiastic restraint, while vital for model execution, is not really adequate. All the time, passionate loss of control is the aftereffect of poor execution and not its essential driver. Consider an algorithmic trading framework that has been oversized, utilising numerous indicators over a look back period to envision future value conduct. Such an over trade methodology has negative expected returns. However, barely on the grounds that passionate elements have meddled with its execution. Or maybe, it is summing up from shamefully determined guidelines, accepting that the future will inflexibly reproduce the past. This is an essential idea, and it distinguishes would-be trading mentors from real therapists. Frequently, the wannabe mentor has a most loved device or set of methods for managing trade issues. A clinician perceives that the issues individuals experience can have many causes and at first, tries to figure out where the issue originates from. We should take an average case of a trader gripping omissions in the train. The trader trades well for some time, overtrades and loses more money than is reasonable. The trader asks the mentor, "How might I tackle this issue?" It's the wrong inquiry. The correct inquiry is, "What place is this issue originating from?" It's simply in the wake of posting that inquiry that we can make sense of a conceivable arrangement. Consider the following conceivable reasons for slips in the trading discipline:

- The trader is endeavouring to concentrate on screens persistently, for an expanded time and is getting noticeably exhausted, with a subsequent loss of resolve
- The trader is diverted by issues in his/her own life, maybe stressed about contentions at home or money related issues
- The trader experiences a lack of ability to concentrate consistently, there's clutter and impulsivity
- The trader has turned out to be baffled by late trading loss, as these trigger past sentiments of being a washout
- The trader has neglected to adjust to a lower volume/bring down unpredictability showcase and is presently trading breakouts/energy that neglect to appear

Consider an algorithmic trading framework that has been overtraded, utilising numerous indicators over a look back period to envision future value conduct. Such an over trade framework has negative expected returns, yet scarcely in light of the fact that enthusiastic components have meddled with its execution. Or maybe, it is summing up from despicable determined guidelines, expecting that the future will inflexibly imitate the past. Once we've accomplished a level of acknowledgment and restraint, we add the last segment to our symbolism work: we distinctively envision the issue situations and our negative enthusiastic and intellectual responses to those, and now we additionally strikingly walk ourselves through how we might want to manage those responses. Along these lines, for instance, we may envision missing a trade and feeling disappointment and thinking how idiotic we are. Then, we imagine ourselves venturing, once again, from the screen briefly, doing some profound breathing and training ourselves in a more useful mode, revealing to ourselves that it's OK to miss something, that open doors will keep on arising, that the vital thing is to remain centred around future open door and so on. The majority of this mental practice is done while we're breathing profoundly and gradually while tuning into the unwinding music, in a still position. So, through rehashed mental practice, we're envisioning circumstances that make us resentful, and we're honing methods for considering and carrying on dealing with those circumstances helpfully gifted trader creates methods for contemplating markets that are one of a kind, particular to budgetary markets and doesn't just create general thinking aptitudes that would prompt accomplishment crosswise over fields of execution.

Discipline in Trading

The beginning stage for recognising reasons for our trading psychology challenges is making an index of occurrences when those difficulties are and aren't happening. Along these lines, for instance, we would note when we are experiencing more difficulty with discipline in trading, and we would scribble down what is happening in those circumstances. We would write about what's occurring in business sectors, what's happening in our psyches, what's going on in our own lives and so on. We would also record events when we're faring much better in our train and what is happening at those events. As we index occurrences, we start to see themes and they give incredible insights into potential wellsprings of our trading hardships. The rehashed mental practice manufactures new propensity designs for us. As we fabricate those new propensities, we would then be able to encounter baffling and debilitating circumstances in our trading, take a couple of full breaths and take part in the helpful self-talk and activities that we've been practicing. The representation practices go about as training with the goal that we are more arranged to manage control amid real trading. The most imperative refinement is between issues that happen exclusively inside the trading setting and issues that happen outside of trading, as well as those that have happened in our past. In case we're deficient with regards to train in our own lives (maybe by not paying bills on time, by being effortlessly occupied, by being candidly vexed), that is not quite the same as circumstances where discipline slips are particular to the trading setting. All the time, the association is an enthusiastic one. The disappointment that triggers the slip of discipline is a dissatisfaction that is being felt in different parts of the trader's life and it has also been felt amid the trader's past.

Rehearsing for Trade Success

A similarity would be the execution of a doctor. The gifted doctor gets on side effects, takes a decent history and physical, settles on tests to direct, gathers the discoveries into at least one conceivable conclusion, leads more tests to separate the symptomatic potential outcomes and in the end, discovers treatment choices in view of the favoured finding. All this time, the gifted doctor is keeping up a decent affinity with the patient and drawing in the patient steadily, reassuring the patient to be as expected with data as would be prudent. Regularly, as you inventory the waxing and disappearing of issue designs, you'll see that working with a devoted trading mentor is not the appropriate response. On the off chance that the issue is a contention from your past that you're rehashing in your trading, a skilful advisor or specialist can help with this. If the issue is a considerable shortfall that has been available since our childhood, this can be tended to restoratively, maybe by means of biofeedback preparing. On the off chance that the issue is adjusting to changing economic situations, maybe what is required is some coaching from an accomplished trader. Should the doctor get the determination and treatment wrong, we would not assume that enthusiastic variables impeded an effective result. Maybe, we would search for breakdowns in the doctor's thinking and basic leadership process. This procedure is area particular, in that it is not utilised by experts in other execution related fields. The thinking procedure of the chess grandmaster does not look like that of the doctor and neither take after the thinking of an effective informal investor. You may rationally practice advertising situations of clutching trades, stressing how energised, glad and productive you'll be by accomplishing this objective, while you are propelling yourself amid a strenuous treadmill work out. By setting the treadmill at a slope and a decent speed, you will be running at a lively pace and lifting your heart rate. With reiteration, you will start to relate the objective and its passionate advantages to your body's pumped up state. It will end up being an undeniably intense flag on your radio dial. At that point, before trading and during trading breaks, you should simply get back on the treadmill. Triggering your body's work day in the state will trigger the coveted move on your dial of awareness. You will get to the conduct you fancy by purposefully setting off the prompts related to the conduct.

Positive Anticipation for Trading

Rolling out improvements involves significantly more than captivating in positive considering or getting positive pictures in your mind. On the off chance that you don't change your condition of cognisance and your capacity to move your own awareness, you'll be tuning into a similar programming for a long time. Figuring out how to move out of negative states is a gigantic accomplishment. Where emotional development happens, nonetheless, is in figuring out how to make new, positive states. It is in turning into the software engineers of our own understanding. This means, when a trigger, for an example, happens, it is more critical to concentrate on ourselves than on our trading. On the off chance that one of our examples is set off, the trading we're probably going to miss is terrible trading. We can't change an example unless we are able to intrude on it first. Venturing from trading, briefly, to upset an example gives us more prominent control over how we think and how we react to business sectors. Each time we interfere with a cycle of awful trading, we fabricate our trade muscles and make it simpler to break the examples whenever. Here are four examples that surfaced amid the current workshop, so as to change the mental methodologies of the traders at an ideal level:

- We profit, turn out to be excessively energised and hopeful, add to chance at awful levels and after that, maintain weakening loss
- We lose money on a trade or experience a drawdown period, wind up plainly baffled and start setting peripheral trades to attempt to profit back
- We lose money in a drawdown, wind up plainly negative and cynical and then pass up a great opportunity for a consequent open door.

Learn from Previous Trade Ever

Perfectionist partner thinks we ought to have profited and then, add to positions at terrible levels or take poor trades to compensate for any shortfall. Notice how in every circumstance, there's an occasion, an arrangement of considerations and sentiments activated by the occasion and after that conduct driven by those contemplations and emotions. Care implies that we are vigilant for those contemplations and emotions, with the goal that we can quiet and centre ourselves before putting our next trade. When we really know our examples, we are in a vastly improved position to foresee them and take a supportive delay before re-entering the market. After some time, this finishes the counteractive action. Regardless, we encounter loss. Despite everything, we have baffling encounters, and we feel wired now and again. However, now we have an arrangement of devices for remaining quiet, remaining centred and remaining in charge by reacting to these difficulties in the ways we've drilled.

When we acknowledge that passionate and psychological eruptions will happen, it ends up less demanding to expect them and manage them successfully. When trading firms **have** indicated enthusiasm for intellectual variables while selecting traders, they frequently have searched for general capabilities as opposed to ones particular to the trading space. Therefore, for instance, they may have competitors play out a general thinking test or they may search for decent evaluations on a school transcript. When I was showing full-time at the therapeutic school in Syracuse, I was amazed by the way that evaluation in school anticipated medicinal school grades. However, it was just in the initial two years of classroom-based restorative training. School reviews and even evaluations in fundamental science courses in the underlying years of restorative school were not important indicators of clinical execution with patients. Knowing how to study for tests did not relate exceedingly with knowing how to connect with patients, exploring choice trees of analysis and treatment and actualising genuine methodology.

Trading Psychology and Trade Management

Most people who choose to trade their own particular records are exceptionally eager to open a record and take their first trade! All things considered, it should be simple, correct? Simply push a catch and the benefits ought to take after! It's not very long after that when most discover trading requires a greater extent a profound comprehension of the Market, alongside our very own comprehension of individual psychology! Have you, at any point, experienced faltering and troubles with shutting an open trade? It's a wonder that most Forex traders, even experienced ones, battle to make strides. Trading psychology is a basic component of fruitful trading. Together with overseeing hazard legitimately, they shape the foundation of long haul consistency. Your trading psychology, its best and most exceedingly terrible viewpoints, uncovers itself in the warmth of fight, when positions are on that will have any kind of effect on your benefit. In the event that you need to comprehend the outlooks of traders, watch them at two times: when markets aren't trading and when positions are on. It's when markets aren't trading that we watch hardworking attitude, profitability, innovativeness and the capacity to create thoughts. It's when positions are on and P/L is moving that we watch, centre, train and have the capacity to follow up on all plans.

Assess Trading Methodologies

Most traders just concentrate on trading systems and discovering trade sections. They are pulled in by the appeal of pips as well as benefits and trust that trading frameworks and passages are adequate to wind up productive. Sadly, I have to blast that air pocket or else the market will do it. Kindly don't misunderstand me, applying adjusted techniques and discovering quality passages is imperative to work and merits a trader's consideration, just not 100% of the consideration. There are other imperative viewpoints, like hazard administration, trade administration and trading psychology. Lamentably, numerous traders turn out to be completely diverted by just a single side of the condition -frameworks and passages. They contribute the majority of their chance and vitality in testing and upgrading procedures, as opposed to working up the experience expected to oversee open trades and to deal with the psychology behind every setup. The second trouble is that overseeing trades is intense from a trading psychology perspective. Most trading issues are assortments of performance anxiety. Performance anxiety happen when an execution that is normally programmed turns into a question of intemperate examination. This regard for the execution makes an Interference Effect, in which the execution can never again stream normally. Such performance anxiety every now and again meddles with athletic execution, open talking, trading execution, sexual execution and test taking. Fears about the result of an execution overwhelm the execution, results are adept to endure. Execution anxiety happens as much during times of market accomplishment, as during times of market loss It is not under any condition unordinary to discover traders who are great at taking (proper) loss, yet who wind up noticeably fearful when they book a pick up and take benefits rashly (i.e., before achieving their benefit targets). Impedance Effects, following series of losses, are not any more weakening than Interference Effects from the weight that traders feel when they are profiting.

Compulsiveness of Trading

Traders, for the most part, attempt to supplant negative self-chat with positive self-talk. This is an error! When traders are drenched in the market and concentrated on the screen, they ought not to be taking part in self-talk by any stretch of the imagination. Compulsiveness is the most widely recognised wellspring of performance tension among traders. Traders have a tendency to be accomplishment oriented and frequently set elevated objectives for themselves. These execution objectives add to the pressure when the objectives are not met. When all is said in done, it bodes well to supplant execution objectives with process objectives. Rather than defining an objective of making, say, £250 a day, a trader should, for instance, set an objective of following their trading procedure (trade set-up, triggers, execution and trade administration). Compulsiveness prompts overtrading. Overtrading is the most widely recognised wellspring of loss among the traders. Traders overtrade when they feel interior weights to make money and these weights daze the trader about what is occurring in the markets at the time. Trading when instability is low, trading outside one's trading plan or qualities, trading to make up a loss and trading hastily huge sizes are cases of overtrading. Expanded levels of trading size can re-ignite performance anxiety. Traders that ace execution nervousness at one level of trading size (e.g., benefit/loss swings of up to Rs. 100) will as often as possible re-experience it once they seriously increment their size (e.g., benefit/loss swings of Rs. 500). We, by and large, adjust our feelings by the dollar sums we make or lose. This makes a bigger trade considerably more hard to oversee (inwardly) than a little trade, despite the fact that the setups might be indistinguishable. Traders frequently think they have more awful mental issues than they really have. At the point when execution tension examples have meddled with trading for a timeframe, traders regularly end up convinced that they have profound situated passionate issues that need serious psychotherapy. Regularly, the conviction that one is harmed, that one is sincerely unfit, is a bigger issue than the execution uneasiness itself. This is an exceptionally resolvable issue.

Avoiding Overtrade and False Enthusiasm

In the warmth of fight, a few traders lose their concentration and take part in minimal valuable trade administration. They may end up plainly aloof and quit searching for chances to scratch a trade that turned out badly or add to a victory. They may wind up noticeably enthusiastic and wrapped up in each tick, inevitably blowing up to little moves. They may progress toward becoming danger opposed, never hoping to get greater and leaving on the main whiff of the development against them. They may turn out to be excessively forceful and overtrade, adding to positions at poor levels. It's when trades are on that our mentalities are probably going to move, our bodies are probably going to go into 'battle or flight' mode, and our trading psychology is probably going to turn out. The talented trader supports the mentality amid the trade that was critical to arranging that trade. The talented trader realises that as much P/L originates from dealing with the position as entering it. A survey of your trade administration will probably fill in as a helpful audit of your trading psychology and recognise what you do, getting it done and what you have to do to get to that next level of execution. Most traders who are persuaded that they have profoundly established mental issues or addictive trading designs are really in an endless loop of fussbudget self-requests, expanding execution weight, mounting tension upset execution and restored self-requests to adjust for their disappointments. Before long, traders who got in such a cycle start to question whether they will ever succeed. By tending to their issues at the source, the desires that create execution weight, traders can regularly turn themselves around in a shockingly brief timeframe. Certainly, there are different issues disconnected to execution fears that can meddle with trading. The one of a kind thing about performance anxiety is that it can harrow very fruitful traders just as much as new kids on the block. This is a result of the foundation of a great part of the uneasiness and hair-splitting. It has a tendency to be available in the most accomplishment situated and effective people. It is genuinely a double-edged sword.

Utilisation of Refutation and Affirmation Trading Levels

The initial step is not to feel appended to any trade setup. My trade setups are not in a "fight" with the business sectors. Or maybe, they are trying my thoughts regarding the market. The market can demonstrate my trade investigation as right or erroneous. I utilise the accompanying strides to help manage me in this procedure. I utilise refutation and affirmation levels to test whether the market concurs or can't help contradicting my examination (not me as a trader). I, additionally, watch out for the feelings of the market by breaking down examples, candles and waves. I refresh my examination every so often and frequently to check whether value activity and the market structure have remained the same or changed. Set-and-overlook traders can do well. However, I, for one, want to utilise new value data for ceaselessly refreshing the best trading choices. Obviously, I have to keep away from re-breaking down open trades each and every second of great importance. For the most part, breaking down the business sectors each couple of candles is fine (in a similar time span as the passage or higher). Know that you must be interested in getting new data on the off chance that you can deal with your trading predisposition. In the event that I was to (furtively) trust that one specific trade setup must be right in all conditions, I will never have the capacity to sincerely dissect the best administration for the trade. Why? Since, then, I would trust that the market needs to demonstrate rectifying me. In my vision, traders must evacuate this inclination. One straightforward pragmatic strategy is to "prompt" you. Give trade administration counsel around an open setup. However, trust that the trade is not yours. This should help expel a portion of the passionate connection. Keep in mind, my trade setups don't have to demonstrate anything to me. They don't speak to me or my identity as a trader. Thus, I feel completely good with dealing with the trade. To sum up, all trade setups are simply thoughts. The market can affirm or refute them. However, don't think about it literally. Be rationally prepared for all conditions, with the goal that you can modify your trading plan to the truth on the outlines. Also, the best way to be rationally prepared is to be interested in examining new data without a trading predisposition.

Concentrating on Trade Behaviours

Somewhere close to the extremes of execution weight and smug sluggishness is an upbeat medium where traders can concentrate on self-change without attacking their outcomes. Trading resembles dating. You need to keep starting desires sensible, appreciate it while it's occurring and gain from it once it's finished. Shockingly, a trader's trading psychology can hinder and attack our clearness when taking trade administration choices. Maybe you have had some of those considerations glide in your mind while overseeing open trade setups:

- This setup will most likely win.
- This setup can never lose.
- The market must rebind now.
- The market will unquestionably hit this objective.

As a rule, traders see their trades as "great" and the market as "awful." The trades are practically similar to their own particular children. Their losing trades are, as it were, their unrewarded saint. Their triumphant trades seem incredible. Their suspicious trades doubtlessly will recuperate soon. These contemplations speak to a trader's expectation and wish when trade setups are open. Be that as it may, here is the genuine mystery of the market: it doesn't tune into our expectations. The market does not think it is fairly similar to the breeze. It blows without thought. However, it does, by and large, take after a bigger example and pattern (atmosphere and climate developments). Most traders anticipate that the market will take after their investigation, their plans and their thoughts. No, it's the trader's undertaking to take after the market as could be expected under the circumstances (flawlessness is inconceivable). A trader has a few winning trades a column and, feeling sure, builds his size to exploit his hot streak. The position, at first, goes to support him. However, it rapidly turns around when the market pushes lower. Compelled to sell his position, he understands he has lost the greater part of the benefit from his past winning trades. He is headed to recapture the money and re-enters the market, just to get hammered by a momentary wave of the offering. He now feels like he has entered a cool streak and starts trading reluctantly, with decreased size. When the market closes, he is down on the day and the week. He feels like a yank for getting to be plainly pompous after his increases.

Assessing Outcomes of Trading

Most likely, you can recognise an example in each of these circumstances. The individual is in an execution circumstance where he/she encounters weight to succeed. The circumstance has gone up against outrageous significance in the individual's eyes and now, he/she is centred on the consequences of the execution, instead of executing the execution itself. This double concentration, stressing (or cantering) on the result of execution while attempting to stay inundated in the execution, is the regular component behind all performance anxiety. Such nervousness is the absolute most regular trading issue I have experienced in my meetings with traders. Traders get a kick out of the chance to set objectives for themselves, yet regularly as not, fiscal objectives wind up making pointless weights. More compelling objectives are ones that emphasise on the way toward trading. For example, constraining loss with stops or holding trades until a trailing stop is hit. A pleasant attitude is, "Whether I simply trade the correct way, the benefits will come." This takes a significant part of the weight off the execution. In accordance with this, traders are additionally prescribed to tackle hazard incrementally. Risk puts a mental amplifying glass on circumstances and significantly builds the open doors for execution weight. Traders who endeavour to drastically expand their size rapidly find that the trade that worked out with 1 contract may not work with 10, in view of weights to (as well) rapidly restrain loss or take benefits. A continuous increase of size is much more viable than an incautious jump, for which one is candidly ill-equipped.

Self-realisation on Trading Designs

Any self-talk amid times of execution nervousness really meddles with the exact preparing of market information, in light of the fact that the piece of the cerebrum in charge of seeing and following up on showcase designs is not being enacted. It is obviously better to step far from the screen and refocus on what the market is giving you, than to act aimlessly on one's feelings of trepidation and intensify an officially troublesome circumstance. Traders need to stay mental practices to unmistakable personality states by figuring out how to put oneself in a condition of surprising quiet and centre and after that, by practicing adapting methodologies for undermining circumstances. A trader can make a connection between the mental state and the adapting reaction. When there is a distressing execution circumstance, the trader should simply conjure the practice mental state, and the adopting practices that have been over-scholarly will go to the fore. For example, on the off chance that you constantly rationally practice a technique for clutching winning trades while maintaining a quiet concentration, reproducing the quiet concentration amid following the winning trade will make it less demanding to summon the self-talk and conduct related to holding the position.

In the realm of trading, it is imperative to perceive how our feelings and behavioural examples can attack trading execution, and we have to see how our enthusiastic responses to various occasions need to change.

Mind Shift: A Different View of Trading Psychology

Acing the craft of trading can take years of experience and a prepared personality. In the present unstable markets, mental flexibility is the way to keeping up and enhance trading execution. To a trader, books on trading psychology are either amazing or repetitive. They can be amazing in light of the fact that you may very well locate the one idea that transforms you into a gainful trade. The one idea that grows your trading profession. It may not be the first occasion when you read about the idea. However, it is the first occasion when it breaks through to you. They can be accessed on the grounds that for traders who, as of now, comprehend the correct approach to think as a trader, books on trading psychology appear like tedious sound judgment. Trading psychology is a profoundly individual issue. So, I'll leave you to choose which book addresses you. While you can't change your psychology overnight, these 18 trading psychology books are valuable for drawing nearer to the correct trading outlook. One that goes up against trading psychology says that we should control our enthusiastic experience with the goal that we adhere to our procedures and our discipline. Another thought on trading psychology says that we ought to end up noticeably better at tuning into the sentiments that speak to the instinct and gut feel for business sectors. This current book recommends an alternate approach by and large. We wind up ready to see and trade advertisers better when we can make mind moves that enable us to encounter showcases in an unexpected way. Like an auto, we can make a mind change by evolving gears, enabling us to approach the world with more torque, more noteworthy force. Like an auto, we can accomplish a mind move by switching to another lane, opening another way. The reality about reliably beneficial trading is not some dim science any longer.

Psychological Clarity Is Recommended for Trading

Dynamic traders of prospects and alternatives settle on visiting fast choices, requiring a high level of mental clearness. Auditing their losing trades, they regularly find that they have veered off from their set up procedures and plans, talking themselves into choices that they could never make in paper trading practices. It is intensely disappointing to replay the day's session and see the "self-evident" signs missed and the incautious choices made. "What was I considering?" is the normal regret. Now and again, it appears as if we are not in our correct personalities. As indicated by psychological advisors, that is precisely what happens. In the warmth of trading, we move our mind states, enacting programmed thought designs that can disrupt the best-laid trading plans. The objective of subjective treatment is to recognise these reasoning examples, block them and supplant them with more helpful choices. Intellectual treatment starts with the thought that individuals have an essential need to comprehend their reality. Our need to clarify life occasions is strong to the point that occasionally, we will incline toward superstitious and mysterious clarifications to none by any means. A great case originates from individuals who experience the ill effects of an issue known as frenzy issue. Amidst totally non-undermining circumstances, such people can all of a sudden issue overpowering trepidation. Since the response truly appears suddenly, patients with freeze issue imagine their own particular clarifications for their assaults. On the off chance that their frenzy happened in a shopping centre or in an auto, they will accept that shopping centres and autos are the issue and maintain a strategic distance from these settings. In the end, the rundown of culpable circumstances duplicates to the point where panicky patients decline to leave their homes. Enthusiastic and physical imagination is a way to accomplish crisp, innovative trading thoughts. This opens the way to new systems for self-dominance in trading. We see marketing better when we move from detached data handling to dynamic handling, really playing and exploring different avenues regarding the data. We see marketing better when we move from dynamic preparing to intelligent handling, experiencing data from numerous points of view. You won't be distant from everyone else with your trading. Trading can be a desolate business, particularly for individuals who are normally more open to being with and working with other individuals. Having a mentor on your group will give the positive feeling that you have somebody you can swing to and trust to give genuine help.

It Is Your Plan That Matters

Regardless of how much your family and companions might need to energise you in the event that you share your trading with them, they are not totally autonomous. They are probably going to be too candidly connected to you to have the capacity to give the autonomous guidance you truly require the most. The truth of the matter is, they will be working from their motivation as opposed to yours. A trusted mentor is centred just on what you require and what will enable you in accomplishing what you need.

Instructing Demonstration to Expand Execution and Results

As indicated by a recent report, 1-on-1 instructing can enhance your selection and accomplishment with aptitudes preparing by up to 88%. Truth be told, this examination demonstrated that subsequent to finishing just aptitudes preparing, for example, going to a class to take in another framework, you can expect just a 22.4% change in your capacity to perform with that framework. In any case, the examination demonstrated that with the expansion of only two months of 1-on-1 instructing, this figure soared to 88%; a gigantic 65.6% increment in profitability. Presently, envision making an interpretation of that into trading and how noteworthy that could be for expanding benefits. This exploration demonstrates 1-on-1 training is the most capable approach to pick up drastically expanded execution in just fourteen days. This is on the grounds that any change to your practices, for example, utilising another trading framework or changing a current one, requires a mental change. An ideal approach to make that change rapidly and make it last is to work with an accomplished mentor so you can abstain from returning to your past frequent practices. I'm speculating that most traders know where it counts inside that their absence of achievement is because of their present outlook, but on the other hand, I'm speculating there are great reasons why they haven't made a move yet.

Training Is a Transient Speculation of Trading Opportunity

Since the capable techniques utilised as a part of 1-on-1 training are demonstrated to build up your trading psychology, you can be sure that applying the subsequent positive, benefit amicable, changes in accordance with your practices will bring about perpetual upgrades, so you can convey more predictable and gainful outcomes route into your future.

Mind Shift Is Fundamental for Execution Improvement
All games individuals have a mentor because they realise that without their mentor, they would not accomplish the outcomes they do, in light of execution. Simply take a gander at golf, games, football, b-ball and any other game and you will see the player's mentor close by.

Self-protection for Trade
Your brain's prime mandate is self-protection – keeping you alive. It will successfully finish this mission, even if it requires misleading and beguiling itself. It was worked to control both condition and result. What's more, there was a period, quite recently, when this was a noteworthy issue. The world in which our human precursors lived was perilous, so self-protection was a genuine undertaking. By looking for control over the result in the short term, the mind of our progenitors adjusted to the deadly risks that prowled in their condition. By solidly getting by, for the time being, our precursors created helping snappy passionate reactions to risks in their condition that preceded thinking, since speculative reactions to dangers are too moderate for survival concerns. As a trader, you encounter this issue each day, when feelings keep running over consistent intuition in the warmth of a trade. Amid the advancement of our feelings (recollect those natural activity possibilities that planned activity between the creature and the earth), here and now survival was more profoundly esteemed than long haul benefits. This advancement ended up noticeably wired into the enthusiastic brain as an example, so when prompts from the earth exhibited risk to life, the mind started up the feeling as an antecedent to making a move instinctually. Everything came incredibly, until the reasoning brain started to rise up out of

the enthusiastic mind. All these survival impulses were, at that point, wired for self-safeguarding, before our precursors begun considering. So, it was normal for the survival impulses that had been so effective in our more primitive past to be chosen as we developed into the present day man. The glitch is that your mind can't differentiate between an organic danger to survival from long prior and the mental uneasiness you encounter when you experience instability in your trading. (Nobody enlightened the enthusiastic mind concerning it!) And it keeps on going about as though any risk to your influence (your money) is a danger to your extremely presence. The mental self-portrait around your feeling of influence to survive and the image of money ended up connected. Furthermore, this is the place where the brain and trading wound up plainly poor associates.

Correcting the Problem of Survival Instinct

Unless you won the hereditary qualities lottery, the cerebrum/mind you use to trade is essentially not prepared to deliver achievement in trading. It was not worked to manage instability. Rather, it was worked to manage the assurance of survival for the time being. For most traders, with a run of the mill passionate engineering, this new adjustment must be taught. Generally, in trading, nonstop presentation to vulnerability and hazard has been the technique used to drive the mind to re-adjust its built up designing (this is known as introduction treatment in psychology). As rational as this strategy seems to be, it has not ended up being a viable method for driving the cerebrum to change survival systems that have, for some time, been converted into attributes all through history. As a matter of fact, introduction based arrangements re-damage the trader, so he or she turns out to be considerably more sincerely receptive to instability and the absence of control over the result that is a given in chance administration. In trading, to be viable, you need to cool the responsive primal enthusiastic hardware with the goal that you can think in the long haul about probabilities. This is not what the mind advanced to do. Be that as it may, in the event that you require your cerebrum to move from the survival nature of here and now self-protection (survival achievement) to likelihood administration for accomplishment in the long haul, you should bridle the mind's neuroplasticity and intentionally adjust it to the new standard. Much like there are treatments for stroke recovery in light of the neuroplasticity of the mind (where they re-prepare and re-course elements of the cerebrum to oblige harmed zones), so also can the cerebrum be retrained to encounter vulnerability and fear of the obscure, uniquely in contrast to the primitive hardware of the battle/flight reaction of the enthusiastic mind. To do this, you should prepare your cerebrum's reaction to instability. To the passionate cerebrum, instability is an awful thing with regards to dangers. (What's more, as long as you hazard capital, your cerebrum will see instability as an unsafe event in your condition.) Currently, your mind is sorted out to see vulnerability along these lines.

Taking Action Against Instability – Vulnerability – Threat – Fear/Anger

This is the survival sense reaction that traders encounter each day. Notice that psychology does not kick in until the feeling is coursing through your body and mind. Legitimate believing is captured before it even begins. The minute instability raises its head when capital is put in danger, it is wired to decipher that experience as a risk to self-conservation (weakness). The felt understanding of defencelessness triggers your feeling of frailty, so it is translated as a danger to natural life, as opposed to simply mental distress. From here, the reasonable cerebrum/mind is naturally commandeered, and the mind pushes you into battle/flight with its objective of here and now survival. This where you encounter fear of loss, fear of section, fear of pulling the trigger, self-attack, vindicate trading, over-trading, and so on. Psychology appeared late for the diversion and was overpowered by the primitive passionate reaction to see danger in instability.

Outfitting Neuroplasticity for Probability Management

It is a particular circuit that must be reconstructed to begin the change procedure. When sensorial information goes to the enthusiastic mind, it is first assessed by the hippocampus. In view of the memory put away there, a choice is made to send the data to the reasoning cerebrum, with the goal that rationale and reason can be connected to overseeing vulnerability and hazard (wanted result). This is known as the more responsible option. It requires greater investment for this circuit course to reach conclusions that can be followed up on. However, this is the place likelihood administration (and not life and passing choices) happens. In any case, if the hippocampus chooses that the issue is excessively undermining, making it impossible to lounge around sitting tight for a contemplated reaction, a choice is to be made (truly in the squint of a minute) and the sensorial data is steered to the amygdala, where battle/flight reactions administer passionate and behavioural reactions toward nature (the way you respond to the reckoning of trades conflicting with you or the truth of a trade conflicting with you). Here, the amygdale commandeers the reasoning cerebrum, and the trading mind is toast. The required key expertise here is to manage the enthusiastic affectability with the goal that the hippocampus doesn't go overboard and seize the sound personality from being a piece of basic leadership. Utilising diaphragmatic breathing and muscle unwinding to interfere with the Genesis example of a feeling is an exceedingly powerful strategy for passionate state administration. Since feelings are natural, they have a mark that incorporates breathing style and solid pressure. These parts of the feeling are important for the feeling to develop to the point of overpowering the normal personality. When the feeling is gone up against by an adjustment in breathing style and muscle strain, the feelings of fear and outrage can't look after themselves. You are truly removing their fuel.

The key thing is that instructing is demonstrated to upgrade execution in all fields, and the same is valid in trading. We see marketing better when we move from intelligent handling to multi-dynamic preparing- preparing numerous viewpoints through different modalities. On the off chance that we generally remained in one path, in one rigging, we'd be very wasteful in our ventures. Trading psychology ought not to be tied in with hosting your emotions or reversing them. The mind that can move is one more prone to adequately achieve its goal.

Psychometrics and Trading Psychology

From the initial phase of the Trader Training program, learners embrace a progression of mental assessments and appraisals that assist to decide identity sort, the intellectual quotient (IQ), design acknowledgment abilities, risk profile, here and now and long haul memory limits. The after effects of these tests give the assessors a premise whereupon to fabricate a more inside and out assessment of the trader, which helps with having the capacity to choose the most fitting measurements to utilise. The outcomes shape every student's individual advancement program as they advance through the preparation. The instability of the trading condition is profoundly testing. To be productive requires knowing, with certainty, how to reliably get it done. Despite the fact that most traders recognise what to do with a specific end goal to limit their loss and take out those victory trades, measurements demonstrate that they think that it's difficult to do what they know. In this book, knowledge will be given on why traders find it so difficult and what you can do to distinguish it, kill your self-undermining behavioural examples and transform your loss into benefits. Trading achievement is not just about trading frameworks and programming bundles. Through building mindfulness, you can take your execution from "losing" to "winning" whenever.

Routine for Trade

An awesome case of this happened in my current trading. I cut and diced my current P/L trade in terms of professional career and discovered one factor that dependably anticipated my everyday benefit: the season of the passage of my first trade. On the off chance that I traded at an early hour in the morning session for my first trade, I will probably be unrewarding on the day than if my first trade happened later. For sure, by checking on my outcomes, I could verify that passages inside the initial ten minutes of trading definitely diminished my day by day P/L execution. At The Trader Training Company, we utilise deductively through strategies to evaluate our learner's real-time trading conduct. The program uses Trader Psychometrics, a logical way to deal with surveying trading conduct, created by one of our Directors, David James Norman. It is the investigation and at last, the evaluation of electronic trader conduct where we have a one of a kind window into the execution of the trade. Using restrictive calculations, proportions and conditions, the electronic trader's review trail is caught and evaluated in real-time, empowering us to contemplate, hazard oversee and enhance the student's trading conduct as they are trading reproduced and live markets. This open door is totally novel to the Trader Training Company and puts our alliances in front of the business. The psychobiology of trading and contributing, procedures for settling on better choices under anxiety and weight, building flexibility and reinforcing your sensory system, including the utilisation of biofeedback preparing reasonable techniques for creating solid concentration, diminishing distractibility and fortifying self-control and poise. Creating attention to your trading and contributing convictions and recognitions, figuring out how to 'think in an unexpected way' and procedures for making a triumphant traders/finance directors outlook. The most recent neuroscience research and how to apply it to your trading and contributing to upgrading your basic leadership, including how to build up your bodies sixth sense (capture attempt), defeat loss abhorrence and lament aversion, manage trouble and tackle feelings, for example, fear and fervour.

Never Carry Burden of Employment

Here is the place psychometrics uncover psychology. The early sections mirrored an absence of tolerance on my part. I wound up plainly married to a specific market scenario, and I feared passing up a great opportunity for that move. Rather than sitting tight for advertising activity to affirm my scenario, I endeavoured to front-run the pattern. As a therapist, I know very well indeed that in any hit the dance floor with the market, you need the market to lead. My employment is to take after-market heading, not to satisfy my inner self by anticipating market activity. In any case, once my sense of self-ended up appended to the expected move, all my favour instruction and preparing went out the window. Trader Psychometrics could be depicted as another field of the behavioral fund and also a subset of psychology. It is the investigation of how traders settle on choices to trade and as we probably are aware, the term 'trader conduct' envelops a huge number of components including identity, level of hazard resilience, basic leadership competency, data absorption capacity, spatial mindfulness, design acknowledgment, IQ, enthusiastic knowledge, intellectual execution, manual and mental smoothness, even silliness and melodic capacity. Using psychometrics, I've been helping speculative stock investment administrators, exclusive traders, venture counsellors and self-coordinated financial specialists effectively explore the business sectors. A straightforward "energy to trade" won't keep going long in the business sectors. Like an expert competitor, you have to prepare and know yourself well to get it going. The individuals who arm themselves with information about their identity and their own trading style increment the chances of turning into a more engaged, taught and effective market member.

Anatomy of Losing Trade

So as to discover an answer, we should first precisely see how particularly losing trades are being made. So, how does psychometrics offer assistance? When I understood that my initial trading was harming me, I made a rigid decide that I couldn't enter the market inside the initial 10–15 minutes of trading. I made a mental exercise for myself in which I could basically quiet by myself before the market opens and envision myself trading with extraordinary persistence. Amid those activities, I advised myself that my chance was not restricted to the opening snapshots of the day and that I was working in a scenario of bounty, not shortage. This is critical in light of the fact that the issue with a loss is not simply the loss. It is the endless loop that unknowingly gets under way on the back of it. For the most part, a losing streak begins with an impeccably worthy loss and winds up in a series of loss and victory trades, like in the accompanying scenarios:

Scenario 1: Your trading day begins well, you take after your guidelines, and you concentrate on the way toward executing your trades, as per your trading technique. You, as of now, have a couple of vectors, your record is developing, and you are resting easy. At that point, the market moves out of the blue, and you end up in a loss. You finish off the trade according to your leave methodology, it is no major ordeal, despite the fact that you don't care for it. It's alright, you know you are well ahead, and you can recuperate effortlessly. The following trade doesn't work out, it is possible that you begin feeling marginally irritated as you see your well-deserved benefits dissolving without end, and your self-talk begins whispering in the back of your mind now. "Gee golly, I worked so difficult to make those benefits… I trust I won't stuff it up again like last time." But you are ready to assume the loss as indicated by your hazard necessities. What occurs next is, your concentration moves from being in the present to slipping once again into the past. You strikingly recall the last time you had an awful loss, and now you begin fearing the future, trusting you won't rehash exploding your trading account. The endless loop has begun. You think that it's elusive your musicality, regardless of what you do, you appear to be on the wrong side of the trade. Value climbs, you go long. However, value drops down very quickly, and you wind up in another loss. You go short to get back with the pattern, yet now value hops up once more. You begin what I call 'project trading,' and your trading account experiences a series of loss. You have begun entering and leaving your trades incautiously, capitulating to your desires, since it gives you transitory alleviation from the passionate power of the inclination. In the event that you don't figure out how to prevent yourself from project trading, the point will come where you surrender candidly and let your loss keep running until your record explodes.

Scenario 2: You have been doing truly well. You figured out how to make a decent benefit, and you can't quit taking a gander at the quantity of your trading account with satisfaction. As the trading day approaches the end, you need to simply make another Rs. 10 to round up the record. Be that as it may, rather than making another Rs. 10, you now end up with a Rs. 20 loss. These are the hardest for traders to leave, they would prefer not to annihilate their attractive trading record, they would prefer not to give the benefits back, and these are the circumstances that are most inclined to wind up as a victory trade. You lose everything, feeling crushed and vanquished.

Scenario 3: You have quite recently made an Rs. 800 loss. Neglecting your trading methodology, you are holding your trades too long on the grounds that you need to make the entire loss in one trade. As opposed to taking your benefit, you wind up with another loss. The cerebrum is intended to think in settings and contrast what is presented and what has quite recently been. Thus, on the off chance that you simply made a Rs. 1000 in the past trade, and now you are in an Rs. 800 benefit, regardless of the possibility that your system gives a left flag, you most likely don't take your benefit. You disregard it, since that little voice in the back of your head is disclosing to you that if you simply hold the trade for 5 more focuses, you would have recouped the loss and perhaps made back considerably more. You need that extra Rs. 200 to get square.

Inclination of Profits

On the off chance that your past loss was Rs. 600, then you most likely are glad about the Rs. 800 in light of the fact that now you are Rs. 200 in a net benefit. What do the above scenarios all have in like manner? You didn't take after your strategy, you comprehend what to do, yet you didn't do what they know or maybe you offered into your inclinations as well as allurements and hopped into trades for all the wrong reasons. Your trading process now about recouping the loss, as opposed to making benefits. You quit thoroughly considering your entrances and bounce into trades, you think excessively whether to escape a trade or not, until the point when the loss has turned out to be great to the point that you are seeking after a retracement, so you can get out at a lesser loss. This kind of believing is counterproductive. Much the same as the renowned coin hurl illustration; the present trade has nothing to do with the past trade. Each trade ought to be dealt with, overseen and assessed as a solitary, individual trade. In any case, what am I saying is, you realise that obviously, you have heard and perused all the immense tips on what to do and what not to do. However, here and there, it appears that you are not responsible for your conduct. A large number of you will feel like I precisely depicted your trading knowledge here, and if you can see yourself in the above scenarios, don't give up. You are not the only one, and all the more vitally, it can be settled. The motivation behind why it is so trying for traders to defeat their self-disrupting behavioral examples is that they are searching for the arrangement inside the set of trading.

I frequently hear traders say, 'I simply must be more trained, tolerant and so forth.' It never works on the grounds that the issue itself is never the issue, an absence of discipline or patients is only a manifestation of a more profound main driver, and once you reveal what the underlying driver of the issue is, the self-attacking conduct has a tendency to just disperse without you expecting to apply any resolve or force. That is the reason why, as I would see it, composing a trading diary is not extremely helpful, as most traders remain in the limited states of their reasoning. Despite everything, it doesn't give them knowledge or understanding about why they do what they do and how to make strides.

What Is the Arrangement?

Each individual has an oblivious programmed behavioural methodology on the best way to react to specific circumstances. That is the reason we continue encountering similar difficulties again and again, until we end up mindful of these methodologies and can deliberately transform them. An awesome beginning stage for revealing those behavioural examples are behavioural profiles. Not all, but rather, many solutions to your life's difficulties can be found in seeing how you unknowingly act in specific circumstances and what the outcomes are. Research demonstrates that the best traders share a typical characteristic, they comprehend why they do what they do. They have an abnormal state of mindfulness. They perceive their qualities and their impediments and built up an approach to work with it. A device that I find valuable is the Disk behavioural profile. The Disk profile gives me an incredible understanding of the common qualities and shortcomings of a trader with regards to their trading and what we have to chip away at. The individuals who comprehend their regular behavioural inclinations can assume responsibility. On one hand, they can characterise a trading methodology that complements their identity and then again, they can supplant behavioural propensities that are inconvenient to their trading achievement and are consequently significantly more inclined to seek winning trades, in the correct route, at the ideal time and get the outcomes they want.

Consistent Behavioural Examples

A trader whose behavioural example is inside the compliance, vitality is precise, calculative and thoughtful. They are consistent and logical, which makes them extraordinary experts but lesser traders. They need to be correct, driven by sureness. They are exceptionally organised and rigid, as they would prefer not to be right, which makes them most appropriate for a more extended term slant trading technique. They need to be exact, as their greatest fear is failing to understand the scenario, which may make them pass up a major opportunity for incredible trading open doors as they very much want to sit on the sidelines than being in a trade that they question. Their basic leadership system will be founded on various pointers in their methodology. The main marker lets them know there is a setup, the second gives them the confirmation and the third level of pointers give them the assurance to take that trade or not.

Examine your system on how you make a loss. You will understand that you rehash a similar couple of slip-ups again and again. At that point experiences the behavioural examples as portrayed in the Disk profiles and relate back your qualities and shortcomings. Utilise your normal behavioural examples to outline a trading philosophy that is suited to your necessities and inclinations. You have built up the mindfulness for your shortcomings, and the following stage is to either transform them into qualities by modifying your approach in a similar manner and furthermore, to receive new and more valuable behavioural examples to end up noticeably a more able trader.

Five Guiding Principles of Trading Psychology

When you initially began trading, you discovered that outside diversions cost you money in your trades, and you discovered sound judgment approaches to manage them. As you advance in your trading, you will discover inward diversions, things that originate from inside yourself will cost you money in your trades. In the gathering, George's notice titled *Principals and Psychology of Day Trading* will be talked about. The remainder is a gathering of stories about trading principals and basic false impressions that George frequently sees in himself and in others, amid here and now day trading, both in the pits and as an off floor trader. He has seen numerous traders' trade into demolishing in light of the fact that they were adamant in clutching regular false impressions, until it was past the point of no return. He feels perceiving and understanding the issues are basic to discovering achievement in trading. Among the things George will discuss are: "never add to a losing position," "it is the market's response to news that matters," "when everybody is in, the time has come to get out," "size kills," "it is constantly simpler to enter a losing trade," "when you awaken, your senses aren't right." Good trading discipline requires that you pick a stop and benefit objective before entering a trade. However, picking the correct point for a stop is frequently troublesome. Trading is not a simple calling to ace, and similarly, as it is vital in focused games or execution expressions, brain science is the way to progress. Trading analyst, Brett Steenbarger, records five vital principles that will lead you to the correct way. Here are five vital principles that relate particularly to accomplishing an effective trading brain science.

Principle 1: Trading Is an Execution Action

Trading doesn't, for instance, require a high IQ. There is no trading quality that fruitful traders have and unsuccessful traders don't have. There is, additionally, no individual that is best to trade. Trading is tied in with building up your insight, aptitudes and capacities. The exploration proposes that expert traders represent well more than seventy-five percent of all offer and fates contract volume. It is difficult to maintain accomplishment against these experts without sharpening one's execution and by ensuring that you don't lose your capital in the learning procedure. Trust in one's trading originates from the authority presented by one's learning and advancement, not from mental activities or experiences.

Principle 2: Success in Trading Is a Component of Gifts and Abilities

Numerous traders imagine that it's their brain research that keeps them from progress, since they are on edge or frightful. While exorbitant nervousness ought to be tended to, usually it's not brain research but the absence of aptitude that torpedoes traders. Brain research bolsters your trading and can help you to enhance your execution of what you definitely know. It can't make you into a talented trader if you haven't built up those abilities. For traders, this implies finding a prevalent fit between your capacities and the particular markets and systems you will be trading. Numerous execution issues are the aftereffect of an imperfect fit between what the trader is great at and how the trader is trading. The 80% and higher win loss proportions promoted are not a down to earth trading strategy or an expert trader. I saw the subtle elements of one trading framework that bragged an 85% prevail upon loss proportion ten years. When I saw the points of interest, I understood it just traded twice every year and left by the end of the second day! An "expert trader" is not going to sit before a screen all year to just be in the market for four trading days! An expert trader needs to discover trading techniques that offer steady benefits a seemingly endless amount of time. He takes a benefit at a point where he has actually demonstrated he has a decent likelihood of progress with sensible stops. There are a few straightforward approaches to set benefit goals before entering a trade. One is to look at past highs and lows that can be considered past help or resistance. Leave your trade just before the market starts a trial of that level. You can utilise Gann levels or Fibonacci retracements as your benefit objective. If I get a turn close to the high, I will more often than not exit just before the market gets to a mostly back.

Principle 3: The Centre Ability to Trade Is Design Acknowledgment

Actually, it would corrupt your execution. Endeavouring to control compelling feelings like fear, eagerness and expectation draws your consideration far from the market. You can't deal with a trade when your emphasis is on your interior state. The absolute best traders figure out how to live with and utilise their feelings. You are human. It's difficult to be a robot. Suppose you are trading on a basic specialised flag, like a Doji star on a five moment Bond outline. A Doji star is a five-moment bar where, after a market move, the open and close of the five-minute bar are a similar cost. You may have a channel that characterises a "market move" as having the Stochastic on the five-minute outline to have moved from over sold (under twenty) to over purchased (more than 80). You may offer instantly on the Doji, with your stop one tick over the high of the Doji. With this flag, you can backpedal and contemplate advertise history to decide the circulation of the greatest productivity before the market in the long run switched and would have hypothetically ceased you out. You can make a conveyance of the quantity of five moment periods that go until you were ceased out.

Principle 4: Much Example Acknowledgment Depends on Certain Learning

Your psychological distraction is vital when the business sectors are shut. In a few regards, it's significantly more essential than when the business sectors are open. If you can't concentrate on your outlines, rehearsing your specialty through re-enactment trading and building up a blueprint for your next trading session, it would be hard for you to centre when it truly checks, i.e., when you are trading and money is hanging in the balance. There are times when a market is out of season or simply floating unobtrusively. In many circumstances over my trading training, I have taken the lead. "Never offer a dull market." The reason is that the vast majority are NATURAL BUYERS. Has a stock agent, at any point, called you done when anything exceptional was going ahead to simply offer? No, individuals need to "purchase" things with their money. So, when the market is in a get-away mindset. Not doing anything unique, the more serious hazard is being on the short side. On the off chance that a specialist needs to make a commission, he knows it is less demanding to bring a "purchase side" thought to a customer. If he brought an "offer side" thought to a customer and the market was acting dull, the customer couldn't envision that a sharp auction is not too far off, "not in a market that is this very."

Principle 5: Emotional, Psychological, and Physical Variables Upset Access to Designs We Have Obtained Verifiable

Traders and financial specialists gather money before they start to trade and just when they have sufficient capital, they start to trade. So their basic perspective is, "I now have some money, I need to purchase something." People, by and large, search for something to purchase. So, a market that is going up is for the most part, pulling in an ever increasing number of purchasers. Market tops are, by and large, portrayed by rising open premium and rising day by day volume. In a down market the general population that already purchased is attempting to get out. Traders that search for circumstances on the short side of the market is, for the most part, more advanced in their trading approach. They have traded for some time and can see the benefit potential in taking an interest in a down market. In all likelihood, they began their trading profession like the larger part of traders, as purchasers. So, in an up showcase, the number of inhabitants in individuals in the market continues expanding directly into the best. In a down market, those that were long are attempting to get out. At the point when the market begins down, short traders are pushing, yet the down pattern doesn't generally set in unless the aches are selling. Market bottoms are, for the most part, described by declining open premium and declining volume. At the base, nobody thinks about a market, and by and large, hardly any individuals are trading the market.

Trading requires split second judgment, both when you're in the pit or sitting at a screen. A basic transient dithering can be the distinction between a decent trade and an awful trade. Ordinarily, traders need to go through to the specialist for a sore throat and request a fix of anti-toxin to thump it out of them, just to have the specialist instruct them to take a solution of another pill shape anti-toxin. They would disclose to me that these are not sluggish, they will have no symptoms. Principles of trading psychology are no robot science in terms of their implementation ability. In line with it, the discussed principles are not very complex as well, in terms of critical understanding. Thus, they may play pivotal roles in ensuring trading benefits. The most critical inquiry I can ask a yearning trader is: Are you occupied with an organised preparing process? Just perusing articles in magazines, sites, web journals and books, is imperative, yet it is not preparing. Preparing is simply the methodical work to manufacture abilities and sharpen execution. It requires consistent criticism about your execution on what is working and what is not, and it requires a relentless procedure of penetrating abilities, until the point when they wind up noticeably programmed.

Managing Trading Psychological Risks

The most troublesome issues we confront as traders are the ones that we don't know exist. Certain human inclinations influence our trading, yet we are regularly totally uninformed about how they are influencing us and our main concern. While there are numerous human propensities, we will take a gander at three that, if not overseen, can hinder the street toward accomplishing our money related objectives. The monetary risks of trading are genuinely notable. If we measure positions too vast or bring about an excessive number of keeps running of losing trades, our capital will end up noticeably exhausted. Lose a large portion of your money and all of a sudden you need to twofold your staying capital, just to come back to break even. On the off chance that you trade each day and normal 55% winning trades, you'll bring about keeps running of four back to back losing trades generally consistently. Measure those trades too extensively and you'll be searching for another occupation or diversion. When managing to trade a specialised way, we can see where we blundered and endeavour to settle it for next time. In the event that we leave a trade too soon in a move, we can modify our leave criteria by taking a gander at a more drawn out time allotment or by utilising an alternate pointer. When we have a strong trading plan and still lose money, we have to look at ourselves and our own particular brain science for an answer. When we manage our own personalities, our objectivity is skewed. Therefore, we can't appropriately settle the issue. The genuine issue is blurred by inclinations and shallow technicalities. A case of this is the trader who does not adhere to a trading plan and neglects to understand that "not adhering to it" is the issue, so he consistently changes techniques, trusting that is the place the blame rests.

Sorts of Trading Risks

The risk of boredom: Many traders are pulled in to trading in view of the likelihood of extended P/L moves in a generally brief timeframe. Our sound trading technique offers a minimal of such fervour. In fact, there are long stretches of moderately level execution. In the event that the trader is trading for needs other than productivity (fervour, snappy wealth), he or she is able to surrender the technique following quite a while of treading water.

The risk of drawdown: Many traders liken a trading edge to a smooth value bend. Not really! As we specified in the before the chapter, even a technique with a 60/40 win/loss proportion will encounter a progression of four losing trades 2–3 times, all things considered, per 100 trades. On account of our arbitrary request of wins and loss, we ended up with long stretches of drawdown, though unobtrusive. The trader who likens drawdown with disappointment will desert even a decent technique.

The risk of drawup: We made up that term, if you pondered, but you get the point. If drawdown is the sum, your portfolio loses an incentive in a timeframe. Drawup is the sum your portfolio raises. In a generally brief period, we had a progression of victors ahead of schedule in the year, putting the portfolio up 20%. A technique with 60% champs has around a 13% shot of giving you dashes of four sequential wins. Why would that be a hazard? After a major drawup, numerous traders wind up plainly pompous and change their position estimating and trading recurrence, refuting their edge. Their desires raised, they think that it's harder to get past the unavoidable times of level execution.

The risk of sequencing: Quite just, even with an exhibited edge and reasonable loss limits, we can't know ahead of time the sequencing of our champs and failures. The record is up liberally for the year. However, invested the same amount of energy treading water as rising a great part of the technique's increases was gotten in a moderately brief timeframe. However, we can't realise what that exact time will be. That implies we need to continue down successions and level ones with a specific end goal to get to the triumphant periods. The risk of sequencing is a psychological hazard, regardless of the possibility that you have an edge, and it is a hazard whether you trade in a mechanical framework or in an absolutely optional way. Simply, on the off chance that you have X% chances of winning, you can decide the likelihood of experiencing dashes of wins and loses. If you see those streaks as strange occasions when they're measurably expectable, you will react to them anomalous with tension, self-question and likely miss the open door. When we have a series of wins, we think we have a hot hand. We think we've made sense of the market. We feel presumptuous, and we act as needs be. On the other hand, when we have a series of loss, we believe we're on an icy streak. We think we've lost our edge. We lose certainty, and we act as needs be. We believe we're squandering our opportunity, going no place. We feel exhausted, and we act as needs be. The best mental treatment adjusts mental hazard, the hazard we see with a genuine market chance. We finish that by knowing it as definitely as conceivable, the verifiable execution of our trading techniques. That is moderately simple when we're trading mechanical frameworks. Numerous product projects will furnish us with itemised reports of framework execution, including drawdowns, the most extreme number of progressive champs, washouts and P/L bends. What numerous traders don't know is that they can acquire comparable reports for their discretionary trading. Projects, for example, Trader DNA and stages, for example, Neoticker and Ninja Trader gather trading comes about for traders and ascertain execution measurements, like those used to assess trading frameworks. These insights can be gathered to be mimicked, and in addition to live trading, it empowering traders to decide their edges before putting money at risk.

Assessing Money Related Risks

When you are figuring out how to trade, money related risks transform into mental ones rapidly. We may have a 55% win proportion, yet we don't know how that 55% will be dispersed after some time. Consider Henry's P/L forecaster delineated previously. We have a little trader, with a Rs. 33,000 account, who has a normal win equivalent to their normal loss (Rs. 1000 every week after commissions) and a 55% winning rate. The above outline indicates one conceivable way for their two-year (100 weeks) P/L. By and large, the trader is very fruitful. The two-year return on capital is sufficiently 33% to help a vocation in the portfolio administration world. Yet, take note of that the initial 15 weeks that are spent in the red. In addition, there is a drawdown late in the period in which about 33% of benefits are lost. These unfavourable occasions are completely expectable and having nothing to do with modified or poor trading. They make up a large number of the mental risks of trading. The analyst, Donald Meichenbaum, presented a strategy for push administration that he called stretch vaccination. He found that presenting individuals to low levels of an expected stressor helped them adapt to genuine anxieties when they happened. Assessing your execution, knowing your reasonable drawdowns, drawups and level exhibitions ahead of time is a sort of a stress vaccination, setting you up for the results you're probably going to confront when you trade well. We are very much familiar with how feelings can upset trading. Less refreshing is the manner by which trading can play with our heads! As in prescription, a little immunisation can go far in anticipating significant ills.

Mindfulness Is Power

While there is no enchantment projectile for conquering the majority of our issues or trading battles, getting to be mindful of some conceivable base issues enables us to start to screen our considerations and activities, so that after some time, we can change our propensities. The consciousness of potential mental traps can enable us to change our propensities, ideally making more benefits. How about we take look at three basic mental eccentricities that can regularly cause such issues?

Sensory Derived Bias

We pull data from around us to shape a conclusion or predisposition, and this enables us to work and learn, as a rule. Nevertheless, we should understand that while we may trust we are shaping an assessment in light of genuine confirmation, frequently we are definitely not. On the off chance that a trader watches the business news every day and structures an assessment that the market is going higher, in light of all the accessible data, he may feel he arrived at this conclusion by stripping the media work force's suppositions and just tuning into the certainties. This trader may still confront an issue: When the wellspring of our data is one-sided, our own particular inclination will be influenced by that. Indeed, even realities can be introduced to offer belief to the predisposition or assessment, yet we should recall there is constantly another side to the story. Moreover, steady introduction to a solitary assessment or perspective will persuade that it is the main viable position regarding the matter. Since they are denied counter proof, their supposition will be one-sided, based on the accessible data.

Staying Away from Vague

Otherwise called fear of the obscure, staying away from what may happen or what is not absolutely clear to us, it keeps us from doing numerous things and can keep us secured an unrewarding state. While it might sound absurd to a few, traders may really fear to profit. They may not know about it deliberately, but traders regularly stress over extending their customary range of familiarity or just fear that their benefits will be taken away through expenses. This may definitely prompt self-harm. Another wellspring of predisposition may originate from trading just in the business with which one is most well-known, regardless of the possibility that that industry has been, and is anticipated to keep, declining. The trader is staying away from a result in light of the instability related to the venture. Another normal inclination identifies with clutching the washouts for too long, while offering the champs too rapidly. At the point when costs vacillate, we should factor in the extent of the development, to decide whether the change is because of commotion or is the aftereffect of an essential impact. Hauling out of trades too immediately frequently comes about because of disregarding the pattern of the security, as speculators receive a hazard opposed attitude. Then again, when financial specialists encounter a loss, they regularly move toward becoming danger searchers, bringing about an over-held losing position. These deviations from sane conduct prompt silly activities, making speculators pass up a major opportunity for potential increases because of mental inclinations.

Tangibility of Trading Anticipation

Anticipation is an intense feeling. The form of anticipation is frequently connected with an "I need" or "I require" sort of mindset. What we envision coming is eventually, however, the sentiment foresight is here now, and it can be a charming feeling. It can be so agreeable, truth be told, that we make feeling reckon our concentration, rather than accomplishing what it is we are suspecting in any case. Realising that a million rupees will appear on your doorstep tomorrow would make an incredible sentiment fervour and reckoning. It is conceivable to wind up "dependent" on this inclination and along these lines, put off taking instalment. While income sans work taken to the entryway is more than liable to be snatched by the energetic mortgage holder, when things are not exactly as simple to drop by, we can fall into utilising the sentiment suspicion as an incidental award. Watching billions of rupees change hands every day, except not having the certainty to take after an arrangement and take a lump of the money, can mean we intuitively chose that, imagining the benefits is adequate. We need to be beneficial, yet "needing" has turned into our objective, not gainfulness.

Managing Risk Trading

When we know that we might be influenced by our own psychology, we understand it might influence our trading on an intuitive level. Mindfulness is frequently enough to rouse change in the event that we work to enhance our trading. There are a few things we can do to defeat our mental barricades, starting with expelling inputs that are clearly one-sided. Diagrams don't lie. However, our impression of them may. We stand the most obvious opportunity with regards to progress if we stay on goal and concentrate on basic methodologies that concentrate benefits from value developments. Numerous awesome traders evade the sentiments of others, with regards to the business sectors and acknowledge when a feeling might be influencing their trading. Knowing how the business sectors work and move will enable us to conquer our fear or voracity, while in trades. When we believe we have entered an obscure area where we don't have the foggiest idea about the result, we commit errors. If we have a firm understanding, at any rate probabilistically, of how the business sectors move, we can construct our activities in light of target basic leadership. At long last, we have to lay out what we truly need, why we need it and how we will arrive. Tune in on the musings that go through your mind right when you commit an error and consider the conviction behind it. At that point, work to change that confidence in your regular day to day existence.

Enthusiasm to Combat Trading Risks

Numerous traders thus trust that they have enthusiastic or trading psychology related difficulties with their trading when, as a general rule, they simply don't have legitimate hazard and money administration procedures set up that are suited to their trading style and size of the trading bank. This is the thing that I call the 'fitness hole.' This can be accomplished just by playing Judas on the procedures and quantities of your hazard and money administration systems. To give you an illustration, the traders of my elite gathering need to fill in a business trading plan. Without coming up short, every trader, so far, has utilised a 1 – 2% hazard run the show. However, when I survey their trading execution throughout the end of the week, the starting 98% of traders let their loss keep running past the 2%, except for a couple. Think about what, they are the ones who are reliably gainful. Our inclinations can influence our trading, notwithstanding when we don't think we are trading on the one-sided data. Likewise, when a result seems unclear, we fail in our judgment, despite the fact that we have an origination of how the market should move. Our reckonings can likewise be obstructions from accomplishing what it is we think we need. To help us in these potential issues, we can evacuate one-sided inputs, acquire comprehension of market probabilities and characterise what it is we truly need from our trading.

Price Action Trading Psychology for Consistent Result and Profit

Price based trading is the way in which experts on the floor trade today, without the utilisation of pointers or other specialised instruments. Numerous online traders have become acclimated to depending on markers, as opposed to concentrating on price alone. Very frequently, these pointers require steady advancement to guarantee importance for the market being traded. Furthermore, pointers fall behind price. Value activity is the most genuine association that a trader can have to the market and subsequently, ought to be the sole factor in deciding how to day trade. In a meaning of Price Action trading (PA) technique, it is a demonstration of reacting to the way that price acts or carrying on amid a timeframe. With PA, you will trade what you see and not depend on any intricate marker that you didn't know how it's been figured. You act in view of some set principles that respect value conduct. Truly, as people want to control things, circumstances and even other individuals some of the time. Along these lines, when that natural craving meets the wild market, there will undoubtedly be a few, should we say, subjective disharmony included. At the point when circumstances don't unfurl how we need or anticipate that they will, it makes us disappointed, irate or pitiful. With regards to trading, this is precisely why you can't expect a specific result on a specific trade, in light of the fact that on the off chance that you do, you will kick off an enthusiastic tempest of negative sentiments that reason with you to submit account decimating trading botches if the result you expected on a trade isn't the result you got. To abstain from committing these errors, it's important that you comprehend the brain science of benefit targets.

It Is Timeless

Once a trader is outfitted with the learning to go up against the business sectors, he or she can, in a flash, perceive setups that will prompt reliable benefits. Unfavourably, markers may have a timeframe of realistic usability, a period when the pointer was best, may have passed. Value trading is constantly significant, as it trades on the general conduct of price, not a solitary procedure utilised by oscillators, Bollinger Bands or other profoundly mechanical methodologies. Basically, trading amid the main hour gives the liquidity you have to get in and out of the market. By and large, the market just patterns throughout the day, under 20% of the time. Most new informal investors imagine that the market is recently this perpetual machine that climbs as the day progressed. As a general rule, the market is truly exhausting. The one time of day which reliably conveys on sharp moves with volume is the morning. Expecting you are doing this professionally, you will require some genuine money. Day trading isn't something you ought to attempt with your lunch money. In the event that you were trading with Rs. 100,000 per trade, what amount of volume do you think your stock needs? In the event that you are truly perusing this book, the main reaction from you ought to have been about what the price of the stock is. Accepting you were imagining that, you require countless offers trading hands at regular intervals. Reason being, you require enough volume to enter the trade, yet in addition, enough that you can conceivably pivot in a matter of minutes and close out a similar trade you simply put on, despite the fact that value activity is best prescribed for any individual who's quite recently starting in the money related market. I could review my first experience with FX showcase. I was so overpowered with a ton of various trading techniques. They all seem extraordinary in principle, yet appalling by and by. I've figured out how to settle down for value activity procedure, and the reward was colossal. Also, value activity works for a wide range of market sorts. The technique has been known to be a compelling day trading procedure for almost all fates, monetary standards, lists, Forex and even stocks.

It Is Adaptable

Discovery methodologies, pointers and nitty-gritty specialised investigation all have one lethal defect, these methodologies are awfully particular to take a shot at on an everyday basis. Markets are inalienably unusual. A more noteworthy dependence on a scientific recipe likens it to a stricter approach. Strict methodologies may create not very many trades consistently. Some days may have zero trades. At the point when a trader can't make the benefit on an everyday premise, he or she is probably going to switch markets. Such excessively intense methodologies require the reconfiguration of pointers or the whole strategy. For instance, if a trader's marker can't recognise any productive setups, the trader is probably going to move to another market. For instance, the Euro. This trader may not know that the pointer is not intended to work for the Euro or on the off chance that he or she is if the marker expects to streamline to work for this new market. Discovery techniques are a bother and may have calamitous outcomes if the trader chooses to analyse. As Mark Douglas examines in his book *Trading in the Zone*, each trade you take is absolutely detached and free of the last trade you took or the following one you will take. This fact is the establishment of understanding benefit targets and why they give traders so much inconvenience. The reason it's the establishment is that the vast majority will accept emphatically that if the last trade they took had a specific result and their present trade setup appeared to be identical (as that last one) upon passage, the same or fundamentally the same result should occur. Be that as it may, this reasoning is precisely where the inconvenience begins, as Mr. Douglas brings up again and again in his book, each trade's result is questionable and is basically an arbitrary occasion. Unlike pointers, value activity trading unadulterated market perception and connection. Utilising goal and high contrast manages, a trader may put trades by understanding the market. Since such systems depend on a hidden comprehension of how markets function, value traders are more qualified for envisioning future market movement. Market Traders Institute is committed to helping its customers see how markets function and its preparation projects and programming are intended to enable traders to be in the best position for future market movement.

It Simplifies Trades

Traders who depend on programming to manage the course of price regularly share a "more is better" attitude. Traders who utilise markers once in a while share this misguided judgment by filling diagrams with pointers and jumbling up value show. Most markers don't work concordantly with each other. More than likely, they will deliver clashing signs, in this way, confounding the trader. This is the reason programming ought to be joined with preparing and it's why Market Traders Institute's Ultimate Charting Software accompanies a 21-day web based preparing system to keep a jumbled value show. No procedure is safeguarded and value activity comprehensive. No procedure or framework will, without any help, give you predictable outcome or benefit. Each time we talk about consistency in Forex trading, much to our dismay that it cut over the way we decipher the market, the way we adhere to a methodology over some undefined time frame, the way we keep to a use estimate and the time we open and close the trading terminal consistently. It can be hard to see how you could profit in the market if each trade has a basically irregular result, since that reality is, by all accounts, in a struggle with the way that traders do profit reliably after some time, and it is conceivable. The trouble lies in the way that you have to hold two distinct understandings of trading in your brain at the same time that appear to be in strife with each other. The principal understanding is that you can profit reliably on the off chance that you execute your trading technique reliably after some time. The second conviction is that you can't control the market and each trade has an arbitrary and autonomous result of some other trade you take.

Desire Is the Enemy of Trading Achievement

Presently, we should delve into the brain science behind why individuals battle with benefit targets and with trade exists when all is said in done, benefits or loss. As I suggested in the opening, desires give individuals inconvenience in the business sectors. A trader who doesn't accept or possibly doesn't know that each trade has an irregular result that is autonomous of whatever other trade won't be rationally arranged to manage a trade result that doesn't line up with his or her desires. This is the reason the establishment of fruitful trading is based on a comprehension of the arbitrariness of each trade. When you genuinely comprehend and acknowledge that each trade has an irregular result, paying little heed to what occurred on your last trade, you shouldn't be frustrated or even amped up for the consequence of your present trade, since you ought to have no desires. When trading, perceiving the season of the day and how the cost is moving is exceedingly essential. The open objection session frequently characterises the general pattern for the day, as major money related establishments push and draw the market amid these hours. Considering this conduct permits value traders to show signs of improvement thought of how the cost will plot amid whatever is left of the day. Figuring out how to trade the market with value activity techniques enables traders to put trades in view of their own insight and comprehension, as opposed to depending on an outsider to give orders. Certainty is a vital piece of a trader's brain science, as an excess of it can cause overspending and too little can make traders pass up a major opportunity for benefits. Value activity trading demystifies the business sectors, demonstrating that gut impulses don't work. Trading on what is seen, instead of what a source is exhorting is invigorating and regularly, exceptionally productive. The main desire you ought to have is that if you take your trading technique/trading edge over a sufficiently substantial specimen estimate, you should turn out productive towards the end of that example measure, expecting you are utilising a successful trading procedure, obviously.

Way to Approach Profit Targets and Trade Exit

You may have perused my article on set and overlook trading and moderate trading, at that point the present lesson about the brain science behind leaving a trade will enable you to comprehend why I take that set and overlook/moderate way to deal with my trading and why I educate different traders to do likewise. Because of the absence of control we have over the market, the main 'trade administration' method that genuinely gives your trading edge/technique the most obvious opportunity to play out and work to support you over a progression of trades, is basically giving the market a chance to play out without your obstruction. After we enter a specific trade, we can't know how far it will move for or against us, so we should know about this reality and oversee trades appropriately. Investigate the accompanying chart for a visual portrayal of arbitrary outcomes utilising a similar edge (for this situation, offering a key resistance level) can create two altogether different/irregular results. The trader doesn't know how far the market will move far from the level or whether it will pivot (invert) or begin to incline from that point. All he knows is that blurring key outline levels is his edge, and he should execute it, again and again, to see a benefit after some time. This trader is going out on a limb. However, he or she is accepting an open door to profit. This is precisely how a clubhouse or "the house" works. An expert trader thinks like the house in a gambling club or even like a bookmaker, as far as chances/probabilities are concerned. Gambling a little sum on a trade can yield immense prizes. On the other hand, when these colossal prizes happen is an irregular desire. There is an irregular desire on any given trade, which implies there's an arbitrary circulation of champs and failures for any given trading edge. You can't know whether THIS trade will be productive or not. All you know is that IF you take after your trading system, you ought to be gainful over a progression of trades. You need to rationally acknowledge that regardless of the possibility that you go for 200 pips on a trade, it might just go 175 pips. That is something you need to manage, and it's where the ability of a trader comes in. A talented trader will utilise their gut trading feel now and again to leave a trade, and there's nothing amiss with doing so. However, it takes preparing, time and experience to create. On the off chance that you look at my article available wizards and regardless of the possibility that you read the Market Wizards books, you will acknowledge that the greater part of those renowned traders were not utilising mechanical passage/leave rules, they utilised watchfulness and gut feel regularly.

Value Profitable Trading Frameworks

Trading is not tied in with 'taking care of business' constantly. As Mark Douglas accentuated, it's about probabilities, particularly, figuring out how to think in probabilities. When you join a high-likelihood trading edge, like my value activity trading methodologies, with a comprehension and acknowledgment of the arbitrary result of each trade you take, you set yourself in a place to benefit reliably in the event that you trade with discipline over a sufficiently vast specimen estimate. You may ask why I see our mind as an apparatus. As far as the money related market is concerned, our brain is the best instrument ever. The sort of thought, outlook and question you solicit specifically demonstrate the kind of progress you'll have. It will intrigue you to realise that our brain experiences real examination through inquiries and answers. Anyway, why wouldn't we be able to discover the correct things to ask, particularly while breaking down value graph? Note that value activity levels work best in business sectors with high liquidity. This is the reason it works so well in the Forex showcase. In view of its high liquidity (most noteworthy on the planet actually), the Forex advertise delivers a portion of the best value activity levels of any money related market.

A major misstep numerous traders make is that they treat value activity like a plan or format trading strategy and simply chase for candles that fit their reading material criteria. In trading, everything is relative, and you have to put value data in connection to what has occurred sometime recently.

Healthy Psychological Profile for Successful Trading

For most traders, trading is about markers, stock screeners and monetary reports among other things. Sometimes, traders do understand that there are a ton of things in play with regards to deciding a triumphant and a losing trade. Gratefully, however, by and large, the human personality makes a stunning showing in that it is frequently unnoticed, unless you give careful consideration. You will rapidly find how your mind begins to process the data and subsequently, in the process, having a sound perspective and an inspirational disposition can impact the basic leadership process. Paul Farrell watches that 95% of traders don't make it. 80% of the informal investors lose money. One examination discovered that dynamic financial specialists turn over their portfolios too much (258% every year) and made 12% of their money. Inactive purchase and hold financial specialists with just 2% portfolio turnover had better returns. What's more, most informal investors experience the ill effects of their hyper dynamic market moves. Numerous psychological well-being experts characterise a "dubious" condition as being upsetting. Vulnerability happens as a result of an excessive amount of data or due to too little limit. The very fact that we can't manage accessible data is upsetting.

Considerable Variables for Trading

Accessible trading data far surpasses one's ability for settling on fundamental trading choices, so one can just take care of some of this information. The restricted limit is the main consideration in trading achievement and in understanding anxiety.

Three variables are basic to effective trading:
1. a sound psychological profile
2. the capacity to settle on precise choices from a lot of data
3. money management and trading discipline

A shortcoming in any of these zones diminishes one's ability for preparing data, bringing about anxiety, poor trading choices and loss. Loss, thus, can deliver push, bringing about more loss. Pursuers who have taken the Investment Psychology Inventory Profile may review that their test outcomes were part of these three noteworthy ranges. Pretty much every basic part of trading can be viewed because of psychology. Traders who can stay persistent at trading and sit tight for the correct open door are the only ones who have figured out how to take control of the mental parts of trading, when contrasted with another trader who is yet to discover an adjust in sitting tight for the correct set ups to happen. A straightforward undertaking, for example, purchasing and offering a security requires the psyche to factor in the data that you have inquired about, the intimations from the specialised markers or in the event that you utilise any or the signs from the value activity itself and also doing speedy computations with respect to how much finances to assign or hazard to a trade, where to set your benefit and stop loss levels et cetera. These assignments, and some more, are done intuitively, and in a matter of not as much as a millisecond. When you begin glancing around, you will, at some point or another, understand that having sound psychological well-being is fundamental with regards to your long haul trading achievement. This is valid for informal investors or financial specialists as well as in pretty much any field.

A Healthy Psychological Profile

A solid mental profile may effectively envelop all parts of trading. In any case, certain mental attributes seem unmistakable from basic leadership and money administration. Everybody has an alternate arrangement of past encounters. Because of those encounters, one builds up specific states of mind toward life. These states of mind might be open or prohibitive. Open dispositions create development, include change promptly, arrange individuals toward self-change and deliver joy and achievement. The fruitful trader, for instance, may depict himself with such statements:

> *"I appreciate life without limitations. I am continually investigating new thoughts, going to new places, encountering change and having some good times. I endeavour to get all that I can out of life, and I energetically anticipate every day."*

> *"I am in the best of well-being since I eat appropriate sustenance, get a lot of activities and rest soundly. I am never excessively focused on anything in light of the fact that I don't feel weight—just test."*

In spite of the fact that an open state of mind is not fundamental to trading achievement, best traders are very open. An open state of mind will help a trader in the market since it upgrades data preparing limit. Despite the fact that the fruitful trader still has a constrained limit, his dispositions toward life keep his ability at the most elevated conceivable level. The losing trader, by differentiating, regularly has a shut state of mind toward life. Some portion of this shut demeanour incorporates various guard instruments against winning. For example, the fear of achievement or the fear of disappointment. Any type of protectiveness brings about detachment, building defensive dividers and opposing change. Consider the accompanying proclamations that a losing trader may use to depict himself:

> *"I am truly unfortunate. Each time I attempt to trade, something turns out badly. I wind up losing. Other individuals make it unimaginable for little folks like me to be a champ. Maybe that is the reason I am so discouraged constantly. Money, beyond any doubt, has been my ruin."*

> *"Trading is extremely distressing to me, maybe on the grounds that I stress over what will happen constantly. Be that as it may, I likewise stress over what will happen on the off chance that I escape the business sectors. I'll likely never have the capacity to excel in life."*

The losing trader has shut himself off from the world. Some data may still overcome him. However, it is all dimly shaded by his prohibitive mentality. His shut personality seriously limits his ability to manage data, and he feels 'pushed.' Take investigate sports, which is regularly observed as one of the nearest handles that can be contrasted with day trading. Competitors don't simply invest energy in sharpening their aptitudes, they commit a decent measure of time in forming and preparing their psychological well-being or psychology too. It may sound unoriginal to state this. However, fights are first won in the brain. Additionally, a competitor has effectively won or lost a race in their psyche, and it's similar for a trader too. In the event that you had an awful day and you chose to trade, odds are that your diverted personality will, in the long run, misdirect you into taking the trade that could bring about a loss, unless you got very fortunate in picking the correct security to trade.

Consideration of Trendy Market for Success

Trading psychology is not something new, and there have been unlimited measures of materials and research done on how to prepare one's psyche to be effective in trading. Trading psychology is an essential part of trading on account of the market, all things considered, shows an aggregate psychology of alternate financial specialists. Consider the case of a positively trending market, where the business sectors are rising. Financial specialists are becoming tied up with the rally since they are aggregately bullish on the business sectors, maybe for reasons known or principally straightforward avarice in light of associated weight. Similarly, there are many occurrences when even uplifting news in the business sectors ends up being motivation to offer. Such minutes flag a critical viewpoint from financial specialists and regardless, the business sectors simply appear to take a gander at everything as half vacant. Accordingly, when managing the business sectors that show the aggregate psychology, as a trader, it is imperative to comprehend this conduct as well as prepare one's mind with the end goal that the trader is in better control. Psychology in trading has two critical capacities. Right off the bat, the market itself is an impression of the more extensive financial specialist psychology and basically mirrors the state of mind of the speculator. Furthermore, the trader's own particular psychology assumes a greater part with regards to deciding the achievement of the market. Stock costs don't move in light of the fact that a fleeting moving normal crossed over a long haul moving normal or on the grounds that there was some other specialised trigger. Stock prices move as a result of human feelings. Despite the fact that high recurrence trading or algorithmic trading has expanded over the previous decade, an ever increasing number of traders are presently controlled by rationale and conditions. People still remain the significant market members in the share trading system. Subsequently, it is worthless to forget about psychology in trading.

The Psychology of Fear and Greed

When discussing psychology, there are two words that are frequently tossed out in the open. Fear and Greed! Fear in the securities trades is when financial specialists avoid the hazard and look for well-being in resources that don't yield exceptional yields (or yield any profits now and again) as an insurance of one's capital. The general deduction here is that the speculator is excessively apprehensive, making it impossible to contribute their money due to expecting that they would wind up losing their capital, as opposed to making any benefits. Voracity in the securities trades, then again, is when financial specialists look for higher returns, therefore going for broke. Here, the general origination is that financial specialists are idealistic about the economy or the general securities trade and consequently, are willing to go out on a limb. These same feelings additionally assume a huge part with regards to an individual trader also. For instance, would you be going out on a limb by adding to your positions when you are frightful? Then again, have you at any point thought about how a triumphant streak normally begins one winning trade after another and you begin expanding your position sizes? This is only fear and ravenousness in play on an individual level, while the more extensive securities trade cycles are an impression of the more extensive contributing group. Money markets crash in history are only these mental cycles in play, activated by speculators because of some awful news. By and large, amid the pinnacle of the share trading system crashes, you will regularly discover national banks and even governments turning out in help. For the most part, the account of the time being that national banks debilitate to cut financing costs or direct money into the economy. These words, as a rule, have demonstrated to mitigate financial specialist supposition, subsequently gradually lifting the secured trades back on track without really implementing any of the focuses that were discussed.

How Trading Psychology Makes a Difference

By creating order and keeping feelings good and gone, informal investors can utilise trading brain science, further bolstering their good fortune to make benefits as well as to limit chance, particularly when things turn sour. A typical way traders lose money is the point at which they begin adding to a losing position. Depicting these minutes may appear to be straightforward on paper, unless one has truly encountered this. The conviction that one's investigation is correct and that the market will switch bearing in the following couple of pips is one reason why traders think that it's hard to cut their losing positions. In the meantime, it is trading psychology or the absence of it that frequently puts a trader in fear with the end goal, and they wind up rashly stopping a triumphant trade. While a touch of market information is fundamental, the feelings frequently prompt such juvenile choices by traders that they end up being exorbitant encounters as a rule.

Keeping up Healthy Psychology

For informal investors who are accustomed to trading and out for quite a while, it can begin to wind up plainly dull, if not tedious with regards to day trading. This can be much more emphasised on the off chance that you are practicing on only one specific market. For instance, it is basic to discover many effective fates informal investors concentrate on simply trading the E-smaller than usual S&P500 prospects contract. While one can, without much of a stretch, reject the dullness and continue grinding away, over some stretch of time, the informal investor can fall into an inclination in the business sectors, which can lead them to settle on wrong trading choices. Another factor is the point at which a trader assumes a loss. Now and again, contingent upon one's conviction on a trade, this can be much more noteworthy as the trader's mentality would be stuck in a predisposition and would prompt rehashed examination that somehow conveys a similar inclination. To keep up a sound attitude, the initial step is to enjoy a reprieve from the business sectors. This implies not looking at the diagrams for some time, keeping in mind the end goal to clear up any assumptions one has about the business sectors. Alluded to as looking with a new arrangement of eyes, taking regular breaks can help traders break the dullness of trading as well as distinguish new trading openings or even dangers that they neglected to see already. It's a given that to keep a sound mentality, traders need to concentrate on reflecting or seeking a diversion that they like, something which is totally inconsequential to trading or the money related markets. A few traders get a kick out of the chance to feel like they are taking a break, when in reality they either wind up perusing a book that relates to the business sectors or viewing a narrative about the money related markets. Seeking after interests, particularly one where physical action is required, can be an awesome approach to practice oneself physically and rationally. Traders ought to concentrate on different angles. For example, on their environment. Managing a miserable circumstance with somebody at home or managing a genuine loss can affect the human personality. Along these lines, it is frequently said that traders (particularly on the off chance that you trade as a profession) should know either how to manage their feelings or remain off the business sectors, until they manage the mental obstructions.

Trade with Top Grade

Trading may appear to be simple, particularly when the money begins to stream in. In any case, a trader is regularly tried when their trades turn sour or when they take a major hit to their value. Frequently, just the ones who lift themselves up and keep on moving on, while gaining from their errors, are the ones who figure out how to make it till the end, with some of these even managings to make a good benefit. In the event that you haven't yet contemplated the significance of trading brain science, take some time out and glance back at your trading comes about. As a rule, the response to why you cut off a triumphant trade or added to a losing trade or even made a major benefit lies in your reasoning by then.

3 Keys to Mastering your Trading Psychology

Mastering your trading psychology is the initial step in your approach to effective trading. Regardless of whether you're trading money, shares or outcomes, trading psychology is a basic stride to be noticeably predictable in the monetary markets. I think this is not quite the same as what the greater part of you might be expecting. However, these three keys will help you with your trading psychology. Did you realise that, by far, most of the traders at last FAIL, in light of the fact that they concentrate all their consideration on a certain something…having an awesome trading strategy. While this is obviously of incredible significance, it is just a single little piece of the master plan. Actually, there are 3 key components that you should ace, keeping in mind the end goal, to wind up plainly an effective trader. In this book, I'll be explaining each one of them, one by one. For a considerable length of time, I examined the graphs, searching for some kind of framework that gave me an edge over the market. The favourable position that would enable me to be reliable week in and week out, a trading framework that was reliably gainful with no draw down! Holy Grail! I contemplated trading psychology! I thought taking misfortunes was being an all-around trained trader! The harder I worked at concentrate the outlines, the more time I spent on the diagrams, the more awful my P/L and trading execution appeared to be! Despite everything, I thought it was my entrances and leaves that made a difference the most. I was taught and thought that trade psychology was simply being strong to take the misfortunes and seek after more victories! Psychology has significantly more to do with accomplishment in the business sectors than most traders will give credit. Appropriate trading psychology can be separated into 3 key zones which traders may concentrate their endeavours on changing.

Key 1: Focus on One Method

You can concentrate on any technique that you pick. In any case, concentrating on one technique, particularly for new traders, is vital to set yourself up for progress. This doesn't imply that you are constrained to trade one procedure for whatever remains of your life. Or maybe, the fact of the matter is to ace one technique first, before adding more to your trading plan. Essentials and assessment are the primary drivers behind most of the value developments in the Forex showcase. In Forex, a trader will give himself the most obvious opportunity with regards to progress on the off chance that he executes a trading strategy in view of the basics and conclusion. In accordance with this, traders are constantly prescribed to deal with making their vision. Who would you like to end up and where would you like to go? How solid is your vision? This is a lot more intense and vital than why you are trading. I don't trust that a "why" is sufficient or simply needing to "profit" is sufficient to keep you concentrating day by day, to remain driven and trained over the long haul and to stay with your trading plan. On the off chance that you make a dream of which you need to wind up and work towards it every day and persistently enhance it, I trust you can end up noticeably relentless! A decent vision will keep you doing the things every day and that will pull you in a positive manner.

Your trading strategy is fundamentally how you trade. What must occur with the end goal for you to pull the trade trigger? Most trading techniques depend on markers. For example, RSI or MACD or a mix of a couple of various pointers. By and by, I favour not to trade in light of pointers. Having the capacity to just read the Price Action off the outlines will give you a significantly more grounded base in deciding your trades. Whatever your decision is, having a decent trading procedure is imperative when attempting to end up a productive Forex trader. The inquiry, obviously, is the thing that does 'great'? What constitutes a "decent" trading methodology? Most traders characterise a "decent" trading system as one that has a high rate of achievement. In all actuality, you have to ask, how has this 'achievement rate' been set up? Over what number of trades would it say it was resolved? 10 trades? Or 100 trades? What's more, shouldn't something be said about posting the inquiry, whether all trades made after the exact strides of the trading methodology? It is not as simple as finding a trading procedure, for those cases to have a 70% achievement rate and then simply running with it. Odds are, whether you've been in the trading diversion for quite a while or not, you will realise that it is never that clear.

The specialised examination is an extremely fledgling and retail approach to trade the Forex markets. In the event that you ask huge money traders at banks and subsidies what kind of specialised examination they use to enable them to settle on trading choices, you will probably get an exceptionally confounded look on the traders' front. No trade with billions of rupees to contribute takes a gander at an outline secured with moving midpoints and markers to make trade calls. Or maybe they tune in to what the national banks are letting them know. The specialised investigation has been made, to a great degree, prominent, on the grounds that it talks in absolutes on the off chance that this example appears then this is the outcome if the moving normal crosses this then that will happen, and so forth through essentials are interested in translation. Retail traders truly like "without a doubt" results. However, what they ordinarily discover (or possibly they stick to the dream for ever) is that nothing in trading is as straightforward as purchasing a pattern and profit. It is not necessarily the case that specialised examination is totally pointless, a remarkable inverse really. The key is to utilise specialised examination as a planning device to enter and leave trades line with the general basic and sentimental picture. A blend of 80% essentials and notion consolidated with 20% specialised investigation is an entirely decent place to begin. With essentials, the significance of any financial markers lies in what the Central Bank is concentrating on. Every Central Bank will just concentrate on maybe a couple things at any given time. In the event that, for instance, the Central Bank is concentrating on swelling and development, then creation numbers will have little effect on the development of the money. However, GDP and CPI will have an incredible effect. Forex production line has an extraordinary financial timetable that is free and gives you a decent summary on what each monetary marker implies.

You should not be a specialist on the intricate details of each and every pointer, all you have to know is that the primary markers are what the Central Bank is centred around to settle on choice on what apparatuses they will use to authorise money related strategy. What is the Central Bank stressed over or concentrating on? All traders ought to take after the Central Banks lead. Never battle them on the grounds that the trader will dependably lose!

Key 2: Have a Trading Plan

Having a trading plan is a fundamental key to turning into an effective Forex trader. Without a trading plan, the trader is flying visually impaired and may succumb to taking irregular trades. In the event that a trader does not set aside the opportunity to figure a thoroughly considered trading plan, it is practically sure that they will fizzle at the trading and contribute amusement. Your trading plan is your target way to deal with entering, overseeing and leaving your trades. The arrangement's sole target ought to be to take out the feelings from your trading choices. Utilise your arrangement and stay with it until the point that it gives you input that something should be balanced. Your trading plan must have basic components. For example, the strategy you trade, your trading edge, trade administration, objectives, comes about following and how you will gain from your trades request to take your trading to the following level of progress. You ought to characterise what achievement is for you. For the vast majority, achievement is the capacity to make their living 100% from the business sectors. That is a truly decent objective and a totally achievable one.

We are, on the whole, unique. A few of us have £5,000 put aside that we can put into trading. Some have just £500 and for some, those sorts of figures are only in their dreams. We are, on the whole, extraordinary. We, as a whole, have distinctive funds, diverse points/objectives and distinctive purposes behind trading the Forex Market. Money Management or Risk Management is that vital piece of trading that decides how much money you will hazard on a solitary trade. This sum will be controlled by what your individual objectives are and furthermore, how much money you need to really put resources into the market. When in doubt of thumb, when you are prepared to begin trading, genuinely it is best to hold your hazard down to 1% and base your Money Management around that. Sadly, there are a lot of 'Forex Gurus' out there on the Internet who don't specify the significance of managing your hazard (stay far from these sorts of individuals) or say that it's alright to change more; say 3% or even 5% (inconceivable!).

Your arrangement ought to give a target gauge with the goal that you can deal with your trading business impartially and roll out improvements to constantly enhance your outcomes. Trading designs don't need to be unpredictable, yet they ought to be sufficiently adaptable to change after you pick up information from the extensive pool of trading comes about. Keep in mind that a major piece of accomplishment in any walk in life is to accomplish something reliably finished in a drawn out stretch of time. This can be measured by following a trading plan over countless. The truth of the matter is, it doesn't make a difference how incredible a trader you believe you are. It is basically numerically demonstrated that amid your trading exercises, you will have misfortunes and not only one overall, but many misfortunes. The inquiry you truly need to ask yourself is, do I make due amid this episode of misfortunes? Or will it wipe my record out?

Key 3: Build a Winning Psychology

There is a typical misinterpretation encompassing traders who have turned out to be effective. Many individuals imagine that these effective traders have something unique about them that they themselves don't. While this can be valid at times, 99% of whatever remains of the time, it's completely false and misdirecting. Winning traders have figured out how to take after a trained arrangement that has given them the conviction to stick to it, regardless of what the business sectors or any other person say or does. So as to build up a triumphant psychology, you should first comprehend the overall population's psychology in the business sectors. Dread (offering) and ravenousness (purchasing) are what chiefly command the business sectors with pit stops loaded with inner conflict (cost going sideways).

There is one key segment that influences each and every trade you take…you. Your trading psychology all the time is the contrast between an effective trade and an unsuccessful one. You can be the most grounded person on the planet, yet you are human and as a human, you have feelings. Trading is an exceedingly charged passionate amusement, particularly when you are trading a lot of money. Normally, your feelings can surpass and impact your reasoning/conduct as a trader. Once in a while, you will subliminally take a trade in view of your feelings, regardless of whether you are 'Requital Trading' or simply being plain eager, it is all down to how solid your trading psychology is. You could have the best trading strategy in the world, yet in the event that you have a frail trading psychology, it means nothing. We should investigate a portion of the courses in which your feelings could have an effect on your trading choices.

Concentrate on what you CAN control versus what you CAN'T control. Withdrawing yourself from results and figuring out how to concentrate on the procedure, process and the procedure of immaculate execution of your day by day standard and chip away at your vision. This will make executing your trading plan and hazard administration simple. In the event that you are concentrating on money, you are overlooking the main issue. Money is the final product of perfectly executing your "edge" or trading technique after some time. Eagerness is the thing that a trader will enter a long position after the market is now up to the path, past its normal day by day go. Dread is the reason individuals clutch losing positions too long, way past the amount they were eager to lose on the trade. Like the group, all appear to offer, at the very least, conceivable time just before the offering has wrapped up. Try not to take after the crowd to the butcher. Figure out how to gain by the crowd's mix-ups. Dread can immobilise numerous traders. At the point when their trade begins to conflict with them, they begin to freeze and for some individuals, freeze transforms into inaction. What ought to be done is, the trade ought to be left without feeling according to your pre-trade design. You don't need to like taking a lost, yet while you are in the warmth of fight, all that you do must be chilly and ascertained. On the off chance that you escape a trade for a 2% misfortune and it keeps on moving against that position another 10%, you would be glad to assume the

2% misfortune over the 10% hit. Remember that the vast majority need to be correct. The vast majority can't concede when they are incorrect, until the point when the agony turns out to be unbearable and there is positively no decision to leave the position. For the most part, it's the trader constraining the positions shut, in light of the fact that there are no more edges to support the misfortunes.

Keep in mind that nobody wins 100% of the time. This implies you should figure out how to acknowledge misfortunes as being a piece of the trading amusement. These misfortunes will dependably come as a thoroughly considered stop misfortune strategy that was resolved before you put the trade. On the contrary, if you are holding overnight positions, there is dependably the likelihood that the market may move or hole against your position and cause bigger misfortunes than you may have expected. Do you have a fiasco design? If not, consider making one on the grounds that there is nothing more awful than losing more money than you proposed and not knowing how to deal with this bigger misfortune. Work on these three segments of your trading psychology. On the off chance that you do this, where will you be in 2 years? 5 years? 10 years? Will the exertion be justified, despite all the trouble? Totally! You can just lose if you don't take after your trading psychology guide or in the event that you quit!

Developing Your Mind for Trading: Building the Inner Team for Consistent Profitability

Sustainable development is among the greatest difficulties any business pioneer faces. However, it isn't another issue. It is evident that all dealers need to endeavour to accomplish it. The main issue with this oft cited comment is the thing that you see is affected by what you are feeling, no special cases. In the event that no one but dealers could see the actualities plainly without feeling, they would be liberated from the oppression of passionate thinking. At that point, exchanging would be simple. Yet, nothing could be further from reality. Despite the fact that conditions are altogether different for present day business people, the basics of feasible development continue as before. Most traders can't create and keep up the soundness of brain, which makes their conduct conflicting. Also, there's a basic explanation behind that Trading is so nonsensical. It pushes around the greater part of our intrinsic inclinations, and it makes being steady an extremely troublesome accomplishment to accomplish.

Never Stick to Singular Decision

The trader's weaknesses in the execution appear as faltering, self-questioning, anxiety, over-trading or drive trading. These are side effects of the issue that the trader endeavours to cover without getting deeply involved in the issue. This is the place most traders remain stuck until the point when they figure out how to look at the self-constraining convictions to which their exhibitions are established. Up until the point of that snapshot of retribution, most trying traders truly don't have any acquaintance with themselves. As one trader taking my gathering course put it, "I didn't comprehend what I didn't know when I began this course. Presently I recognise what I know." According to Jon Kabat-Zinn, a well-known care master, care implies focusing especially; intentionally, right now and nonjudgmentally. This vital concentration on the breath enables us to take advantage of that regular capacity of our own to be completely present and mindful of where we are and what we're doing, while not being excessively responsive or overpowered by what's happening around us. Some of our soonest composed records of the act of care reflection recommend that it began in India, two or three years ago, and it was performed basically in religious settings. These days, with science backing its advantages, care contemplation has advanced past its religious setting and is honed by individuals all around the globe, paying little mind to statement of faith and aphorism. Deals and showcasing specialists frequently discuss "one of a kind offering recommendations," or "USP" which Entrepreneur characterises as the "factor or thought exhibited by a trader as the reason that one item or administration is not quite the same as and superior to that of the opposition." An organisation's real reason offers to ascend to its USP. At the point when a business has a reasonable vision, it's less demanding to make items and administrations of significant worth. Revlon organiser, Charles Revson, for example, constantly used to state that he sold expectation, not cosmetics.

Trading Mind Bring Self-development

How about we gain from this current trader's adventure into understanding the self by tailing him as he awakens and understands that he needs to construct the brain with which he trades. What he finds is that he truly needs to build up the mind that he conveyed to trading into a mind that can deliver accomplishment in trading. It was not that he had a "terrible" personality. It was quite recently that a promise to self-advancement is required to move past wilful barricades and into a steady benefit. In the same way as other individuals preparing to end up traders, he had been effective in a profession before trading. He clarifies, "I put in 25 years in the Air Force as a flight build for an extensive freight fly. It is an immense plane with many confounded frameworks that you need to remain over or you will experience difficulty. I was a piece of an unbelievably all around prepared group that flew that plane. We, as a group, were set up for anything. As a group, we were profoundly taught and positive about our ability to keep our plane flying. On the off chance that one individual was having an awful execution or day, there was another person in the team to help them and get them once again into the attitude expected to fly that plane. Naturally, I thought to teach and certainty that served me as well as a group part flying the plane would likewise serve me in trading. It didn't. My learning and certainty, created as a major aspect of a compelling group, disintegrated as I traded. The issue is that I held a conviction that I could not be right, and I could "right" any circumstance - this is not the way it works in trading. Additionally what I found is that, as a flight design, I was a piece of an outside group. Everyone built up specific decides that gelled into a superior group. The issue, as I inspected the circumstance through this course, is there is no outside group in trading. The group that must be created is inside. This is a totally unexpected creature in comparison to an outside group. When I came to trading, I was not set up for that, and my trading account demonstrated it."

Building up the Inner Team

"What I have found, however, is that inside each of us are the credits required to assemble a superior group. Be that as it may, you need to create it. You're not going to just luck out and fall into it. In the Air Force, groups are working with extraordinary purposefulness. Every individual contributes his aptitudes to the general accomplishment of the group. In trading, you need to build up these parts of the self. There is nobody there to do it for you. As I have built up these parts of myself, my trading has taken off. I now recognise what to search for and how to bring these inward assets into my working mindfulness. I call this my trading team. It has a significant effect."

If you need to make an adaptable business, you need to see that it is so urgent to construct mark value and passionate associations with clients. It's those connections that connect clients to your items and will keep them coming back to you. Building a brand is tied in with creating and supporting those connections after some time. Here are some fundamental tenets to interface, shape, impact and lead with your items and brands.

- **Pick your intended interest group:** The surest street to item disappointment is to attempt to be everything to all individuals.
- **Associate with general society:** Make your group of onlookers feel a passionate connection to your image that is grounded in trust in your items.
- **Attract your clients:** A basic, moving message is significantly more compelling than one that tries to feature excessively numerous item components, capacities or thoughts.

No advertising arrangement can safeguard a brand personality that isn't full grown. Try not to have a much-showcasing spending plan to talk about. Make convincing substance for the distributor and online networking locales to begin producing mindfulness among target client bases and develop. Luckily, inside every one of us (as this trader portrays) are capable, indwelling assets that can be produced from an elite perspective. In any case, how would you approach building up the mind that trades?

Opportune Understanding of Mind

To begin with, the sincerely savvy trader finds that his brain is more nuanced and muddled than he thought. What he finds is that the brain is not only a place where "his considerations" happen. Or maybe it is better comprehended as a panel or a board room that is populated by different contending powers. Each of these board individuals from the advisory group goes to the meeting with a plan and course where they need to take the "corporate self." In the undeveloped personality of a trader, attempting to end up plainly reliably productive, the prevailing "board individuals" are damaging in nature, while different less-predominant "board individuals" are frightful that change will bring about losing what they have. On the off chance that you have ever experienced self-question while endeavouring to pull the trigger or have gone ahead of schedule from a trade expecting that you would lose money, you have encountered these individuals from the self as they control the board of trustees of the self, otherwise called an undisciplined personality. Doing everything yourself can be enticing before all else when reserves are few and desire, high. While there's nothing amiss with a hands-on approach, going up against more than you can deal with, particularly in territories where you need understanding, can be harmful. In the time of the worldwide independent economy, it isn't hard to discover capable aptitude, yet you need to know where to discover it. There are currently many sites and online commercial centres that give specific assets from outline, advancement and deals to back lawful administrations and keeping the money. Best of all, you can attempt little undertakings at low ventures. The trap knows precisely what you need to be done and putting assets toward finishing substantial objectives. By creating enthusiastic control abilities to quiet the body and psyche, care would then be able to be utilised to open the entryway of the brain and look at both your ideal life and the convictions that drive your trading. What's more, what you find is that you don't have considerations and convictions. They have you. Furthermore, in your blindness to their impact, they have been running your trading mind and your trading account into the ground by figuring out how to observe these diverse components of the self through care, an awesome open door for the re-creation of the self winds up noticeably conceivable.

Assuming responsibility of the Mind

Care contemplation is simply cerebrum work out. That is all it is. What's more, there's developing examination demonstrating that when you prepare your cerebrum to be careful, you are really redesigning its physical structure through a procedure called neuroplasticity. As Emmet and Mark Murphy write in their book *Leading on the Edge of Chaos*, getting new clients can cost an association around five times more than holding current ones. Actually, a 2% expansion in client maintenance can have an indistinguishable impact from diminishing an organisation's expenses by 10%. To put it another way, decreasing client deserting rates by only 5% could build gainfulness by 25% to 130%, contingent upon the business. Effective maintenance begins with the underlying contact a business makes with a client and proceeds all through the lifetime of the relationship. Bain Capital has even evaluated that for specific ventures, a 10% expansion in client maintenance is generally proportional to a 30% increment in an organisation's esteem.

Be Calculative on Monetary Decisions

Managing the Mind That Trades: Micro Management of a Trader's Psychology

A basic segment of effective trading is brain research. By the term brain research, we allude to the perspective a trader ought to have while trading. All the more particularly, trader brain science manages controlling trader's dread, trader's ravenousness and trader's train. Trading is a very energising movement. The inconvenience is that it is not really conceivable to feel energised and profit in the meantime! Think about a club where beginners celebrate over free beverages, while proficient card counters coldly play many games, collapsing more often than not and squeezing their leverage when the card tally gives them a slight edge over the house. There is a huge amount of guidance on trading setups out there in the blogosphere. Some of it is great, the majority of it is awful, yet none of it impacts your trading as much as your own trading brain research. The "psychological distraction" is normally the missing connection that shields a trader from trading gainfully. Why is trading brain research so essential? It is on account of individuals who are not wired to trade. Our brains are built to propagate survival, not profit. That is the reason such a variety of traders know precisely what to do to profit, yet at the same time, do the correct inverse.

Trading Procedures are Recommended

As much as traders find out about how vital passionate and mental disposition is in the execution of trading, not very many traders really deal with the mind that trades as they travel through the procedure of a trade. This turns into the establishment from which the trader figures out how to deal with the psyche while he is trading. Managing loss is sincerely the hardest thing a trader must manage. Loss affects our feelings. When we assume a major loss, amidst a ten trade drawdown or get halted out of a stock that promptly turns around and winds up hitting our arranged target. The loss trigger prompts vindicate trading, micromanaging, poor basic leadership and various other trading brain research traps. Fix the loss trigger by grasping little loss. Keep in mind that little loss means you are accomplishing something right. You are adhering to appropriate hazard administration. You realise that this loss amounts to nothing on the off chance that they are sandwiched by some greater wins. Sadly, a trader's trading brain research can block and damage our lucidity when taking trade administration choices.

Understanding Trading Psyche

Maybe you have had some of those contemplations schemes in your mind while overseeing open trade setups:
- This setup will without a doubt win.
- This setup can never lose.
- The market must rebind now.
- The market will clearly hit this objective.

As a rule, traders see their trades as "great" and the market as "terrible." The trades are practically similar to their own children.

Their losing trades are, as it were, their unrewarded legend. Their triumphant trades seem unsurpassable. Their far-fetched trades most likely will recuperate soon. With a specific end goal to accomplish a business, restrained fair personality from which to trade (the Traders State of Mind), a trader must be careful. This part of the administration of the psyche is centred on getting the cerebrum and the mind prepared to trade. Normally, arrangement for the trading day starts the prior night. Also, setting up the mind proceeds when the trader awakens and before he gets up. At that point, a timeframe is given to mental planning and practice that incorporates a supplication/contemplation/focusing period where the trader tunes his brain into the pinnacle execution association of self that is appropriate for trading. It is here that the trader can volitionally build a psyche established in quiet, taught, unprejudiced nature. With his mind now quiet and prepared for trading, the trader begins his day. The prior readiness prepares the trader for the trading day with the goal that he/she is fit to trade from a perspective grounded in quiet, restrained specialist. Be that as it may, this is insufficient. This quiet, trained expert must be kept up through the cycle of a trade.

Psychology and Process Conjoin

All that arrangement is washed away inside a brief time frame if the brain is not prepared for the procedure of the trade. What I have found is that the early arrangement phase of mental status is useful for around 30 seconds to 30 minutes. This is the place a specific brain science of execution should be coordinated into your genuine trade design. Your trade design and your mental arrangement are not independent. Your brain is a basic piece of the trading framework. It is the thing that drives your stage and procedure. So this driver must be prepared to drive his framework in a capable manner. The typical explanation behind this is, the trader fears disappointment and feels that he can't assume another loss. The trader's sense of self is in question, diminishing tension by shutting a position dread of position inversion and subsequently, feeling let down requirement for moment delight.

Looking for Set-ups

Numerous traders turn out to be quickly blinded by a tricky predisposition while in this stage. With a direness to act, they approach their outlines looking for set-ups. This very criticalness to act sullies the mind that should be quietly sitting tight for set-ups. Rather, trusting that they must be "accomplishing something" to be trading, the expertise of persistence (important to sit tight for trades to come to them) is vaporised from the attitude in a glimmer and supplanted with a criticalness to trade. Abruptly, they are pursuing trades that are questionable choices, best case scenario. This predisposition gets them into inconvenience, since it sets them up to take trades, not in their trade designs or has a higher hazard to compensate parameters than their trade design manages. Numerous traders have made a decent showing with regards to setting up the brain for the trading day, just to disrupt them toward the start of the trading cycle because of this inclination. Along these lines, this point is basic to dealing with the brain science of the trading mind. Your occupation is to calmly sit tight for set-ups to come to you. Your occupation is not to get things going. Numerous traders live beyond words for their next trade. While we investigate each trade, our general directing concentration ought not to be additions and loss at the time but rather, after some time. Try not to stress over that one loss. This prompts urgency inclination that will smell destruction with your brain. Keep in mind, in the fantastic plan of your trading, that one loss is good for nothing. Rather, consider, not fixate on, the following 100 trades. This will keep you concentrated on the procedure and not here and now comes about.

A Trade Warms Up

Have you, at any point, seen what occurs in your mind when you begin seeing all the affirmation coming in as you watch a conceivable trade set up? The hotter the trade gets, the more an untrained execution brain science is tried or tempted. This is a minute to take the delay and direct your brain research so that, in your energy, you don't get in ahead of schedule. On the other hand, maybe, in your reckoning (untrained execution mind) you continue looking for more affirmation, until the point when the trade possibility is finished. Is the mind that watches the set up quiet, persistent and trained? If not, you have to prepare yourself to be. As you go to pull the trigger, what is your mental creation? It is safe to say that you are pulling at the bit to bounce in (elation) or is your trigger finger incapacitated and unequipped for tapping the mouse (delay)? This is a minute for which you should get ready. It is not a minute that is pushed aside until the point that it can't be disregarded. All the "man-up" risking you can summon now is a risky pointless activity on the off chance that you have not built up the mind that is set up for this minute.

Request Confirmation

When they hear that "cha-ching" of a request being filled, something emotional occurs in the brain of numerous a traders. They are currently dedicated to the trade, and there is no chance to get out of it, though the hazard is genuine now, and you could lose your money. This is the place numerous traders begin a descending winding in their capacity to deal with a trade adequately. Their psyche has not been sorted out to unite the best possible components for trade administration. Traders need to take a delay here and remember themselves. They have now moved from searching for chances to misuse (hostile facilitator) to shielding turf (protective organiser). It is right now that it is basic for the trader to reassert his execution brain science or it will be a long ride down.

In the Red

There is nothing more terrifying for the advancing trader than to watch a trade flux. The trade is ricocheting around and investing a decent piece of energy in the red. You can see the red pointer light and can feel the dread and energy. The mind begins truly de-compensating and the take steps to adherence to the trading plan are getting destroyed. Planning for this circumstance ought to be a piece of each trader's training. The trader must figure out how to control it or the trader's execution mind moves from concentrating on execution to being focused on losing capital. The trader's employment is to keep up the mind that is centred on the execution of execution. However, an enthusiastic seizing is in progress. This is the reason this minute in trading should be expected and prepared for. Else, it shields you from turning into the trader you could be.

Stuck by Marginal Profits

This is one of the greatest minutes that isolate a scratch trader from a reliably productive trader. In the event that the trader has not dealt with the mind that deals with the trade before this minute, there is a capable desperation for him to take the benefit right on the time from the trade, while the trade is still beneficial. At that point when he gets the money for out and feels the transitory passionate help, he watches the trades move to his objectives, simply like his trade design lay out. The issue is that the trader's passionate state has not been overseen in some place along the movement from trade section to being in the red while in the flux, to the snapshot of benefit. The key accentuation here is on preparing. The trader is taking the mind he arranged before trading started and reasserting it, reckoning these minutes with the goal that he set up for the unpleasant states of trade administration.

Leaving a Trade – Taking a Loss

Amid the procedure that is being laid over here, the accentuation is on the administration of the mind that executes the trade and not on whether you are winning or losing. On the off chance that you deal with the mind that trades, you execute your trade design from a pinnacle execution perspective. Your procedure will deal with the champs and washouts. Your employment is to deal with the mind that trades. Putting on a trade can be alarming. Your well-deserved money is hanging in the balance, and you would prefer not to lose it. Anyone who has traded a paper account with progress and made the move to genuine money knows the effect fear has on your trading. Dread shows itself in trading by making it hard to pull the trigger on a trade, leaving before hitting targets, hauling out of trades before the stop is hit and other smaller scale overseeing issues. On the off chance that dread is appearing in your trading, diminish your hazard. The little the potential loss, the less frightened you are of the trade.

Leaving a Trade – Winning

A standout amongst the riskiest things that a trader can do is to get energised by a win while he is still trading (after your trade day is over, is an ideal opportunity to commend the win). While trading, the reasoning personality is extraordinarily impacted by the enthusiastic express that you convey to the demonstration of trading, especially to the assessment of set ups. When you can rest easy, you are bringing a mind bolstered by elation into the assessment of set ups. What's more, elation will make you accept with the assurance that the great circumstances will roll and afterward, you never again can assess your trading hazard successfully. When you win in trading, the quiet, trained, unprejudiced nature you attempted to accomplish before you began trading is kept up by directing your feelings and psyche. Until the quiet, taught, unprejudiced nature is re-built up, you are not fit to trade with a mind intended for trading achievement.

Investigating Your Trades

Specific accentuation and consideration should be set in the brain with which you survey your trade day. Is it accurate to say that you are whipping yourself for the slip-ups you made or the last open doors you now find in your graphs and execution? Then again, would you say you are going about as a kind, savvy instructor to yourself? The latter makes a passionate space for figuring out how to happen, while the former makes an enthusiastic vortex that keeps passionate reactivity at the cutting edge and bargains the limit with regards to learning.

Toward a Peak Performance State of Mind

This is the work of the inward round of trading. When you set up a procedure that presents into your working personality a pinnacle execution state for trading, you can start to rehearse it in these particular minutes in the trading cycle.

A Psychology Checklist for Trader

Every fruitful dealer will state it is essential to have a framework set up that empowers us to computerise and sort out our activities all through the trading day. This trading framework ought to be a well-equipped machine that should work in view of a couple of basic parts: sound trading propensities energised by legitimate attitude (trading psychology), cash administration (your capacity to overcome risks) and strategy (for executing trading systems). Actualising sound trading propensities and routine will help with every one of the segments above. Fruitful trading is regarding key standards to limit stretch. Sound trading propensities result in brilliant outcomes. The reasons fluctuate and incorporate stresses over income or the economy, yet many feel that the market is set out in a fall. These bearish proclamations appear to be the same old thing. It can be hard to keep up long positions in stocks when everybody appears to differ with you, yet the best brokers disregard the features and take after their principles.

Trading Success is Dependent on Individual Psychology
At any given time, a ton of the general population requiring a top are presumably looking for features, as opposed to benefits.

There is no capability test required to wind up noticeably a market analyst or a blogger, and anybody with an email delivery can utilise WordPress to offer market conclusions. A portion of the locales looks refined. One well-known site plays out an apparently ceaseless cluster of straight relapses and declares that nothing ever attempts to be agreeable to them. The Ideal Trading State will fluctuate from individual to individual and will normally be discovered just through experimentation. In any case, for myself, and I speculate for most others, it's a quiet and centred condition with no diversion. It's regularly expressed that we have to trade without feeling. That is junk. You're human. You can't trade without feeling. Your point ought to be to guarantee that you take after the procedure, regardless of the nearness of feeling which may whether or not with your procedure. Actually, regression analysis is a procedure that has some constrained applications in the business sectors and ought to dependably be joined by a few tests for trading importance. The best trial of whether something works in the business sectors is just its gainfulness. Ideas like r-squared and correlation coefficients can't pay a trader's home loan. However, they can make membership income for bloggers.

Experience Develops Trading Psychology

Brokers need to disregard the features and feelings of others and concentrate on what the business sectors are really doing. Many will observe this to be among the greatest difficulties they confront in trading. It is normal to take the market feelings of regarded investigators. In any case, there is never an assurance that anybody will be appropriate in the business sectors. Bloomberg, as of late, met 88-year old Joe Granville, who estimates a 4,000 point drop in the Dow Jones Industrial Average amid 2012. More youthful merchants have most likely never known about Granville, who once moved markets in a more straightforward time. The vast majority of

what individuals whine about when they say they're experiencing trading psychology issues are not psych issues, by any stretch of the imagination. Regularly, it's something more fundamental. For example:
1. An insufficient methodology unequipped for giving an edge
2. Absence of faith in their system because of deficient testing and advancement work
3. Endeavouring to work in a time allotment or market 'specialty' which does not suit their way of life or hazard resistance
4. Powerlessness to adjust strategies to suit changing economic situations
5. Improper administration of hazard

Positive Trading Approach is Key to Trading Success

Keeping up a positive trading disposition will enhance your cash administration and risk management skills. A negative trading attitude will modify your reasoning and mentality. Your disposition will decide if you are gainful with your trading. Your state of mind is more imperative than your market information and even your level of understanding. It is critical how you respond to the market and not what the market will do to you. Continuously break down every single trade, victories and failures. Having a trading diary will enable you to distinguish what works for you and so on. It will channel you the correct way. It is, by a long shot, the most supportive technique for individual trading reflection. Controlling feelings is likewise required in such a manner. Passionate swings and enthusiastic anxieties affect your mental perspective and will influence your trading choices. When you trade with feelings, you don't trade obviously and normally. A few books discuss isolating your feelings from trading. Trading includes the most passionate product on the planet, which is cash. Cash outlives loathe, love, insatiability and whatever else you can ever envision. The best way to control your feelings as a dealer is to have a strong trading plan. Yes, brain science identifies with the psyche. In any case, the brain does not work in confinement. It's a piece of an entire personality body framework. Furthermore, it gets its fuel from the body.

Discipline in Trade Enhances Psychological Advancements

The concentration is entering in trading. Ensure you don't have any diversions around, no web perusing, no telephone replying and no children playing. It ought to be simply you and the graphs. Give the graphs a chance to address you, and they will guide you. Trading and the entire psychology is sufficiently hard, worrying around a temperamental trading stage, poor graphing and design, terrible web association can take a hard toll on your trading and the future achievement of your business. The train is interpreted in the capacity to take after your trading plan. The train is the quintessence of the greater part of the mental issues. Set aside the opportunity to assess your arrangement before speculation to put a trade, break down economic situations before pulling the trigger. Discipline is one of the key qualities you need so as to have the capacity to manage diverse circumstances in trading from the point you choose to enter your trade, to how you deal with your trade, to setting and sitting tight for your objectives. Notwithstanding what instrument you are trading, whether it is stocks, fates or forex, it is imperative to create sound trading propensities appropriate from the earliest starting point, this will quickly track your trading to progress and benefit.

Mastering Fear and Impulse

Following various years of securing the information of how to trade, most traders discover their trading minds are still traded off by fear, seemingly out of the blue. All of a sudden, all that learning is trapped by fear, exactly when they require that information exhibit as a primary concern to settle on strong trading choices. Conflicting outcomes take after paying little mind to how much their trading framework is changed or changed to make the outer train. At long last, the trader goes to the awkward acknowledgment that the issue is not with their procedure, their framework or the business sectors (regardless of these all functioning admirably in reproduction), the issue is the six crawls between their ears and especially with the way they bargain or don't bargain with their feelings of trepidation. Traders read about master traders who appear to be conceived with the correct traits for trading. These master traders trade impartially with an intense train that enables them to stop their feelings at the entryway. What's more, understudies of trading, who read about these attributes of effective traders, frequently attempt to imitate the passionate control and perspective they read about. They, as Dorothy in *The Wizard of Oz*, click their shoes and mysteriously envision themselves having the "right" passionate and mental attributes.

They may even watch a trader brain research DVD, tune into a guided reflection, mess around with their mind waves or take in some Neuro-Linguistic Programming (NLP) traps with expectations of a simple fix. Attempt, however as they may, the passionate exciting ride of their trading holds on. The missteps understudies of trading make are that they contrast themselves and these uncommon individuals who are conceived with a hereditary inclination and enthusiastic demeanour that is appropriate for trading. In spite of the fact that they are uncommon, many yearning traders set these off-the-rack outstanding traders up as the mental model for their trading.

Being Able to Achieve Determined Characteristics

People may come furnished with a specific hereditary legacy under the correct conditions, are communicated such that it gives a man favourable position in specific spaces. Taken to an outrageous, you additionally observe this hereditary building in reproducing mutts for specific attributes. This sort of hereditary designing is basically unrealistic in people. This does not imply that characteristic determination is not used to upgrade execution. In spite of the fact that people are significantly more unpredictable, the Russian and Chinese have utilised quality articulation to guide youngsters with an athletic guarantee to an incredibly preferred standpoint. Also, a few traders win the hereditary attribute lottery for trading. By far, most don't. They need to figure out how to build up a brain science worked for trading. Else, they keep on choking in the grip – when the money numbers. Traders are constantly prescribed to imagine earlier thought on what is feeling. It is essentially the Body/Brain/Mind activating to any disturbance to recognisable status. In particular, the segments of a feeling (e.g. fear) are:

- Excitement – the body turning up
- Feeling – subjective experience of the feeling. Considering is traded off

- Inspiration – what the feeling is instructing you to do (evade, assault, approach)
- Meaning – the presumption that ends up plainly wired into your mind)
- Disposition – hereditary qualities

Fear is a biological issue that traders need to get. Regardless of the amount they read about what the brain should look like to trade well, little is talked about how the trader approaches building the extremely enthusiastic and mental aptitudes and dispositions important for effective trading. Just because nature did not furnish you with the "right stuff" for your trading mind, it does not imply that you can't support your brain research. So you assemble the perspective expected to effectively execute your philosophy and turn into a reliably productive trader. Similar to other best entertainers in different areas, what isolates them from the pack is no more ability (everyone has ability at the best), worse learning of their art, but it is the enthusiastic administration (or passionate insight) to utilise that ability and information in the grip to deliver crest exhibitions. They need to lead their feelings of fear head on, instead of denying them. The same is valid for traders, significantly more so.

Building Trading Attitude

Sustain is of significantly more essential value in building up an attitude than nature. Nature may give potential. However, the individual must build up that potential with the goal for it to end up noticeably able. This implies, regardless of the possibility that you didn't win the quality pool lottery, you can prepare your enthusiastic and mental inclination, further bolstering your good fortune in trading. Dangerous passionate inclinations about money, worth, hazard and vulnerability are hereditarily passed on starting with one era, then onto the next. They are not deterministic qualities. They have learned examples that wind up plainly wired into your cerebrum/mind as propensities. It's not hereditary qualities, but it is an adjustment to the condition. This is the way the money account to which you adjusted appears in your trading. It is transmitted through the eras and your mind's adjustment to the condition. Furthermore, fear-based propensities and convictions can be de-built and re-sorted out into a significantly more trader neighbourly perceptual guide. It is constantly prescribed to the traders to deconstruct the combination of vulnerability and stress. The majority of us experienced childhood in conditions that applied weight on our creating mind that composed us to "not commit errors" and to concentrate on sureness, as opposed to the administration of uncertainty. It is from this always adjusting cerebrum that our "brain" develops the way we decipher reality. For most of the traders, when that cerebrum has moved toward development, it is one-sided to look for conviction and maintain a strategic distance from vulnerability. This is just an organic inclination of the human mind that has been opened up by what we are instructed about hazard and instability. This is an association of the mind that is not going to function admirably in trading. That specific adjustment can function admirably in different areas, yet not in trading, where the accentuation is on grasping the administration of vulnerability and hazard. You conveyed a mind adjusted to look for surity and keep away from assurance in the profession of trading. The fear based personality that rises up out of these versatile strengths trades with an inclination to not lose on the grounds that it fears loss. Presently, science and brain science have planned against the sort of mind that a trader needs to convey to trading – a mind that is OK with vulnerability.

Instability and Fear into Probability

Most traders (who come to perceive that, by far, most of the trading is an internal diversion) come to understand that their recorded story, now implanted in their neuro-hardware of conviction, is the thing that must be changed. There are no traps or enchantment projectiles. Most traders wade through years of desensitisation (of their feelings of trepidation and self-constraining convictions) before finding steady achievement in trading. This procedure rewires convictions about self and vulnerability that in the long run open the likelihood of trading on another level. Luckily, this re-association of the trader's psyche can turn out to be more streamlined when we start to see how significance is sorted out in the cerebrum/mind. There is no single association of the self. There is no last "me." "Me" is just the present association of self-convictions that you hold as genuine. We don't see reality, we see shadows cast and there is dependably an eyewitness deciphering what it is encountering. Traders come to hold certain suspicions about the market. Some of these suppositions have been worked out and have turned into a viable method for hitting the dance floor with the market. However, the market does not mind what presumptions you endeavour to put on it, nor does it have consciousness of the "facts" put upon it by people. Before traders perceive that they are the issue (and the potential arrangement) to trading issues, they, for the most part, have traded for various years and are fruitful in re-enacted trading. They know how to trade a system that functions in a classroom. It is the point at which the danger of capital is placed in play that their "certainties" about the market are tested. It is now that the trader is not isolating vulnerability from stress or fear. This circumstance is very trainable. The suppositions of self that have moved toward becoming hard-wired as self-constraining convictions (their unexamined certainties) are not fizzling in light of the fact that they don't know how to trade, but since they are not prepared to work in a domain of vulnerability. What's more, the default versatile program is to respond from fear when perplexity emerges from snapshots of vulnerability (an ordinary event in the execution of trading).

Relying on Rational Thinking

On a very basic level, traders need to take in an arrangement of aptitudes and instruments by which they do mind surgery on their passionate conviction framework. This is a long way from applying rationale to enthusiastic thinking. Trading turns into an extraordinary place to see, "in advance and close," the trader's convictions about the self in real life. There is no avoiding "reality" as it has been sorted out inside the self. Your trading account turns into the gauge of the adequacy of the convictions from which you trade. Most traders find that their "realities" are just unexamined presumptions about the world that drive their observation. It is, as of now, the presumptions behind the self-constraining convictions can be watched and recreated. Yet, the convictions should be found with regards to feeling established in neurobiology and lumping convictions into the reasoning personality. Building your convictions into overseeing hazard, as opposed to staying away from chance is then conceivable. Nervousness now can be controlled and tuned in to, not from an avoidant spectator but from a restrained and fair onlooker, with altogether different results. "Reality" they see enables them to be available in their trading in an unexpected way. The hole between re-enacted trading and live trading limits, as they prepare their perspective to grasp instability from a point of view of teaching, persistence, boldness and unprejudiced nature. Long ways from the restless perspective that made them either or trading rashly as fear cleared their reasoning limit away. The significant move is that the trader is never again trading to win or lose, which he can't control with assurance. The trader is currently dealing with the mind that creates the execution of his execution of the trade, which can be made do with a high level of assurance. The result is still vulnerability along these lines of trading. However, the trader has now given his technique and trading framework the benefit of the likelihood of an effective trade. He is responsible for the mind that oversees instability. This is trading the zone or being in a trader's perspective.

Self-constraining Trading Convictions

Applying care as a device to your trading enables you to bring the self-constraining convictions that harm your trading into your mindfulness, where they can be worked with. Rather than floating on the streams of inconspicuous self-constraining convictions that breaking point the way you oversee instability and hazard, you turn into the designer of the story you convey to trading. Instability moves toward becoming decoupled from stress and fear. Also, you create internal assets that enable you to deliver into your mindfulness, persistence, strength and unprejudiced nature that live as potential outcomes in the totality of your being. Even with instability, you never again must be constrained by your apprehensions to deliver conflicting outcomes. Rather, you convey a perspective to the vulnerability that makes the likelihood of fruitful trading. Trading is a trip into the likelihood of who you can be. The "you" that you conveyed to trading is once in a while the "you" that will get you achievement trading. Fear direction and care are simply the foundations of re-sorting out trades. It is your obsession that gives you the inspiration to learn and utilise these apparatuses to wind up who you should be for reliably fruitful trading. Trading turns into the trip into self-authority. These days, it has a tendency to be Forex. In any case, it used to be supplied in the 80s, when I was in my high scholars, proceeding onward to penny shares (those under one GBP), in view of the extensive ascents and then choices trading on the grounds that again of substantial potential picks up and afterward onto fates, at that point spread wagering for comfort. Today, it is Forex and records as a result of use (value for the money) and furthermore, simplicity of trading and long trading hours and liquidity, making my trading methodologies simpler to send.

Out of Theory and into the Trading Room

What does this hypothesis look like in trading? How about we investigate? Jim is a trader who is actually a scientific genius. He has profound working information of PC frameworks, aviation and mechanical designing. Now he is a lawyer who rehearses licensed innovation law. In the recreation, his trading mirrors the unmistakable considering and fair-minded perspective that you would expect out of a man with this sort of preparing and experience. In any case, when he trades and hazard enters the photo, he doesn't "see" the majority of the alternatives and examples that are reflected in his diagrams and pointers. His preparation is exceptionally one-sided towards assurance (recall individuals' lives and costly gear were in question in light of his estimations), instead of the administration of hazard and instability. He was prepared that losing was impossible. Consider all that accentuation on "not committing errors" and making decent evaluations, as opposed to learning as we grow up. At that point, as a specialist, you are prepared to "over architect" with the goal that the structure won't come up short. You see the concealed predisposition here? This preparation ended up noticeably routine and went away from the plain sight of his mindfulness. Presently, it is an unexamined inclination that hues the perceptual world he sees.

Vulnerability Means Fear of Being Off-Base

This presumption that instability must be disposed of, now a conviction inserted in the neuro-hardware of his cerebrum, turned into the unexamined conviction (or recorded story) that he carried with him into trading. This conviction was profoundly viable for him, both as a scientific genius and as a patent lawyer, where a high esteem was set on assurance. Be that as it may, this same considering, so effective in one space, was delivering close frenzy for him while he was in a trade. Thus, he escaped trades too early, and he took his benefits too rapidly, some time before he achieved his objective (he could not be right and lose the benefit he had in his grasp). Once in a trade, nothing was sure. Dealing with the trade was an activity in the administration of instability, as opposed to assurance. Instability, still intertwined with fear, activated and his sound and clear intuitive mind was defiled by fear. From this fear based perspective, alternatives that would have appeared to him while in an unprejudiced perspective were cleared away and supplanted by the negative expectation of stress.

The Brain's Role in Trading Performance

Money related choices are among essential life-molding choices that individuals make. We audit realities about budgetary choices and what intellectual and neural procedures impact them. In view of subjective imperatives and a low normal level of monetary proficiency, numerous family unit choices disregard sound money related standards. Family units commonly have under-expanded stock possessions and low retirement reserve funds rates. Financial specialists over-extrapolate from past returns and trade again and again. Indeed, even the best corporate directors, who are normally exceptionally instructed, settle on choices that are influenced by pomposity and individual history. A large portion of these practices can be clarified by surely understood standards from psychological science. A blast in amazing aggregated evidence, especially how down to earth, minimal effort "prods" can enhance monetary decisions, is effectively giving clear direction for adjusted government control. In 2004, Brian Knutson, a partner educator of brain research and neuroscience at Stanford University, found that trading stocks changed a similar piece of the human cerebrum that was related to sexual desire and medication mishandling. This neural system, for the most part, called the "joy focus," starts up in the reckoning of prizes and can dull or even abrogate the frontal flap, where psychologists trust a large portion of our thinking is completed. Does this mean stock traders will begin showing up in "most needed" publications and be decreased to pushing tech stocks in dull rear ways? Not likely, but it highlights some intriguing mental issues that putting trades brings out in generally rational individuals. Numerous monetary choices impact individuals' lives, and these choices are made at many levels in the economy. For instance, what contract a family unit picks influences its funds considerably. The specifics of what contracts are accessible and how they can be portrayed are regularly compelled by government arrangement.

Let the Brain Play Inquisitive Games

The mind's frontal projections are included in motivation control, judgment, arranging, planning and executing of behavioural plans. Among frontal projection, the issue is schizophrenia, dementia and consideration shortfall issue. At the point when people neglect to satisfy their New Year's resolutions and different expectations, we usually credit their inability to an absence of inspiration research. Notwithstanding, it finds that the capacity to catch up on such plans is essentially identified with frontal projection execution on neuropsychological tests. It might well be that traders who have issues with following trading rules have considerably more extensive neuropsychological shortfalls, not simply impermanent slips in inspiration or train. How well these money related biological community works is touchy to insight at all levels, extending from mortgage holder perplexity or guilelessness to open feeling that impacts arrangement, to whether vast banks accurately comprehend (and 'value') the systemic hazard characteristic in our entangled present day monetary system. The monetary emergency of 2008, trailed by the Great Recession, is a case of how botches and unreasonable impetuses in this framework can snowball to the debacle. As of not long ago, there has been restricted intellectual and neurological proof with respect to the instruments that underlie money related choices. In the eighteenth century, English savant Jeremy Bentham expressed that man is administered by two inspirations: the quest for joy and the evasion of torment. Knutson's tests have demonstrated that financial specialists are liable to comparative thought processes. As per Knutson's analyses, financial specialists tend to act sanely until the point that an occasion causes them delight (better than expected pick up) or torment (a loss). He asked members in his examination to browse three ventures - a generally safe security and two supplies of variable hazard and reward - to "contribute" in a set market. The bond paid out an insured Rs. 1. One of the stocks had a half shot of paying out Rs. 10 per trading round and a 25% possibility of losing Rs. 10. Alternate stocks had a half shot of losing Rs. 10 and a 25% shot of picking up Rs. 10. The members knew the stocks would have fluctuating payouts. However, they didn't know which stock was which. Essentially, they needed to judge the stocks by the outcomes in each round of trading and on the general history, as the test proceeded, much like trading a developing business sector for which little data is accessible.

Removing and Controlling Hazards

Most traders begin making normal trades. The balanced, delight and agony focuses of the cerebrum were most dynamic, yet the sound focus was prevailing. After a surprising addition or loss, be that as it may, the joy and agony focus turned out to be more predominant and expanded the likelihood of the subject settling on an unreasonable choice. A loss incited chance unwilling conduct and a pick up provoked hazard looking for conduct, both of which expanded the odds of loss, either through excessively preservationist choices (bonds the distance) or excessively rash ones (consistently wagering on the high-chance stocks). These two unique parts of the cerebrum were basically overwhelming the seat of soundness, bringing about a pull of-war between the two extremes (hazard avoidance and hazard taking). These discoveries help clarify a portion of the behavioural contributing issues that financial specialists have perceived throughout the years. Cerebrum science is mostly to a fault when we pursue a year ago increases too long and miss offering at a benefit, appreciate loss and over-sell a portfolio, rather than esteem averaging or make any of the other expensive choices that turn out to be not really discerning financial specialists. Discernment, it turns out, is the standard, yet times of madness can create as abruptly as a hurricane. Consider the accompanying practices for careful trade:

- Arranging, defining objectives and starting activity
- Checking results and adjusting to mistakes
- Mental exertion in seeking after troublesome objectives
- Inspiration, readiness to participate in real life
- Managing enthusiastic driving forces
- Dynamic considering
- Maintained consideration even with diversion
- Basic leadership, trading consideration and changing methodologies
- Arranging and sequencing activities
- Settling rivalry between plans

These sound like a veritable who of sound trading practices. Indeed, in any case, they have been taken from a rundown of basic elements of the cerebrum's prefrontal cortex given by Elkhonon Goldberg and Dmitri Bougakov in their section "Objectives, Executive Control, and Action," which is a piece of an incredible review message on the mind called *Cognition, Brain, and Consciousness and altered* by Bernard J. Baars and Nicole M. Enclosure.

Extensive Approach towards Neuropsychological Shortfalls

Dr. Goldberg, the co-creator of the previously mentioned part, proposes that participating in errands that require the utilisation of the frontal flaps may, in reality, increase the quality of their capacity. This has significant ramifications for the treatment of dementia and consideration shortages and may likewise assume an essential part in enhancing execution at such intellectual undertakings as trading. Strikingly, the exploration referred to in Dr. Goldberg's part demonstrates that the prefrontal cortex is most required in undertakings that include oddity. Well-known errands that are standard don't require a similar sort of consideration, focus, arranging and judgment. It might well be that handling new difficulties is most animating to mental health, while routine (consider the ways of life of many resigned individuals) is to the least extent liable to improve subjective working. The primary issue raised by Knutson's discoveries is the addictive idea of trading as an action, isolate from the acknowledgment of loss or additions. It has, for quite some time, been suspected that individuals look for money as a way to different things - speedier autos, greater houses, full wardrobes. The consequences of the examination propose that money itself or rather, the demonstration of gathering money might be the reward. Knutson found that fast trading itself - the storm of data requiring speedy choices - can really drive a man's psyche into a state in which he or she will normally commit more errors (In Knutson's examination, the members were not permitted to settle on just a solitary choice and sit out whatever remains of the investigation as an esteem speculator would).

Resistance from Hazards

For a considerable length of time, behavioural specialists have known that individuals' basic leadership is incredibly influenced by how decisions are encircled. For example, the same fiscal wager encircled as a decision between a specific versus hazardous pickup and a specific versus dangerous loss inspires altogether different decisions. (We tend to take certain additions; however, will look for hazardous loss to dodge certain loss). Studies utilising utilitarian attractive reverberation imaging find that we exhaust less psychological exertion in taking a beyond any doubt pick up than in picking dangerous increases, beyond any doubt loss or hazard loss. It might well be that traders don't give their benefits a chance to run just in light of the fact that they take the path of least resistance psychologically. On the other hand, traders might be hesitant to set and take after stops due to the more noteworthy psychological exertion required. Incidentally turns out, in any case, that this taking the path of least resistance and keeping away from troublesome choices may not be an element of sluggishness. An exceptionally intriguing examination leaving the Institute of Neurology at University College London finds that the encircling impact on basic leadership is intervened by a passionate focus on the mind: the amygdala. This is a similar mind focus that intellectual neuroscientist Joseph LeDoux has connected to our reaction to stress and injury. In another investigation about financial specialist conduct, it was discovered that oversights do really torment the youthful and unpractised. In a 2004 MIT investigation of trader execution (Fear and Greed in Financial Markets: A Clinical Study of Day Traders), the analysts found that unpractised traders were significantly more inclined to passionate slip-ups than experienced traders were. This proposes traders have a decent shot of making sound (and ideally gainful) trades on the off chance that they're willing to invest the energy expected to dull the mental highs and lows that accompany trading. Similarly, as specialists move toward becoming desensitised to blood and race auto drivers' progress toward becoming desensitised to speed, traders can conquer the enthusiastic elements associated with profiting that would somehow dull their edge.

Considering Financial Aspects in Trading

A concise history of money related financial matters will set the stage. In the mid-1950s, Modern Portfolio Theory (MPT) started to formalise thoughts of how a sound financial specialist would put resources into an arrangement of advantages by tolerating the hazard to acquire higher "returns" (which are rate changes in resource costs). This hypothesis framed the establishment of monetary financial aspects for a very long while and made many astonishing and sharp expectations. For instance, about how speculators pick which stocks to hold and what advertiser costs would come about because of these choices. By the mid-1980s, a few scientists started to reveal realities about the total securities trade that was hard to clarify with this completely sound perspective of the world. For instance, an exemplary paper that is regularly referred to as the start of behavioural back exhibited that stock costs vacillate excessively to be defended by a discerning hypothesis of stock valuation. This arrangement of irregular certainties just became more grounded. More money related financial experts, at that point, started to make new scientific models where speculator conduct was represented by progressively reasonable mental powers. The suggestions are noteworthy. At the point when blood stream is coordinated far from the mind's official focus, the frontal cortex and the amygdala and related passionate focuses are initiated, we are probably going to underutilise those official capacities - thinking, judgment, arranging - and react to our (enthusiastic) encircling of decisions with an absence of exertion. Running with our emotions may very well be the reason we don't thoroughly consider our decisions. It is additionally likely that we outline our decisions contrastingly amid times of centre/fixation versus passionate excitement. Upsetting scenes in the market, enacting the amygdala, are probably going to evoke a confining that is not the same as the cautious trade arranging we lead when we are cool and quiet. Research, for example, finds that fear and outrage shade our basic leadership about getting ready for psychological warfare related dangers. Passionate elements have likewise been found to shade basic leadership about monetary decisions. Trading can be a game for the individuals who have the stomach for it, yet easy-going financial specialists shouldn't hop into day trading with their retirement reserve funds. You wouldn't endeavour heart surgery on a companion or drive 160 mph without preparing, and you ought to keep away from day trading unless you're in it for the whole deal and willing to sit through the expectation to learn and adapt.

Anticipating Risk Reward and Psychological Contribution

Regularising speculations in light of a risk–reward trade-off anticipates that people will contribute a constructive division of their riches in money markets and will hold a substantial, expanded arrangement of stocks. In any case, a vast assemblage of observational confirmation demonstrates that financial specialist conduct regularly veers off from this regularising benchmark. These deviations are precise and offer ascent to an arrangement of adapted actualities that describe the trading examples of individual financial specialists. For instance, one powerful and surely understood trading design among singular speculators is the attitude affect – the more prominent inclination to offer stocks that have gone up in cost after they were purchased ('victors') contrasted and stocks that have gone down ('failures'). The main impact is apparent in singular trading records from retail financiers, proficient money administrators' trades and research facilities that precisely control the measurable procedure of value developments. While the manner of impact is currently a strong observational actuality, its motivation is still wrangled about.

Regardless of the possibility that you're not inspired by day trading, Knutson's investigation holds significance. Any stock contributing, even esteem contributing, is trading. It's quite recently spread over a more extended period. By taking as much time as necessary on money related choices and giving your reasonable personality time to reassert it, you stand a decent possibility of diminishing the behavioural mistakes that will hurt your portfolio. Some of the time, thinking back on our trading choices, we think about whether we were in our correct personalities. How precise worries end up being! A portion of the best trading brain research intercessions are the ones that keep us in our correct personalities as we settle on choices under states of hazard and vulnerability.

The Psychology of Taking Losses

When working in monetary administrations, you end up used to examining the impact of loss aversion on client conduct. In any case, loss aversion is an imperative factor in a larger number of choices than we most likely figure out. It is absolutely significant over all parts and channels. Loss aversion is a trademark that depicts how individuals are characteristically perplexed of loss. At the point when looked at against each other individuals loathe losing more than they like winning. Hence, loss increasingly poses a threat than increases, despite the fact that the incentive in money related terms might be indistinguishable. We over esteem the things we have, overcompensate when we can't have something any longer and oppose change. We despise loss. But since the loss is incessant and inescapable, our scorn of it ensures that we endure. Policymakers regularly need to settle on giving constructive and antagonistic motivating forces to urge individuals to pick specific alternatives and how much accentuation to put on these two angles. For instance, in the current national choice in Scotland, the U.K. government utilised the two endorses and guarantees to advance the separatist motivation. However, which of these two perspectives convey more weight on individuals' choices? In mental science, there is an unmistakable response to this inquiry, instantiated by Daniel Kahneman and Amos Tversky's "loss aversion" rule. This standard affirms that the subjective weight of punishments is bigger than that of potential prizes. Subsequently, for instance, individuals ought to maintain a strategic distance from lotteries which give a 50–50 chance for level with estimated increases and loss on the grounds that the negative repercussions weigh heavier than the positive ones. We should investigate the mental components that make us act along these lines.

The Endowment Effect

Assume that Nathan and Mae are two understudies at a similar school. It is arbitrarily confirmed that Mae will be given a school mug, which she gets the opportunity to keep. Mae, at that point, records the slightest amount she would need to be paid to offer the mug. Nathan, similarly, records the most he'd pay to purchase the mug. What do you anticipate will happen? You'd think if the human mind were balanced, that the simple demonstration of having quite recently gotten a mug would not instantly make us esteem the mug substantially more exceptionally. However, when this examination is directed, the understudy given the mug (Mae) should be paid significantly more to part with it, all things considered, than the understudy not given the mug (Nathan) would spend to get one. This Endowment Effect, as it's called, implies that we tend to esteem things all the more exceedingly just by owning them. You realise that the minor canine statue you procured some place (maybe you don't much recollect where)? You may not part with it, despite the fact that you could never get it now if given the open door. We would rather not lose what we have.

Risk to Way of life

On the off chance that a potential loss could be ruinous or would undermine their way of life, individuals will ordinarily reject the choice totally. This is one motivation behind why spread wagering organisations have a pre-concurred stop loss on the vast majority of their records. This shields client from their awful wagers by restricting potential loss. In the event that there was no program stop loss set up, most clients could never consider this kind of betting.

Victors and Losers

Where individuals are given a circumstance where both a pickup and a loss are conceivable, individuals tend to settle on outrageous hazard loath decisions. For instance, a man is given the decision between little-ensured increases for more than 5 years (e.g. a store based record) and a securities trade connected item that conveys a generally safe of a huge loss. Individuals tend to concentrate on the huge potential loss and regularly select the previous, less hazardous alternative. This is the reason counsellors will concentrate on the substantial upside capability of a securities trade connected speculation and endeavour to play down any potential for extensive loss.

The Familiarity Effect

We tend to like things more as we become more acquainted with them. This applies to sustenance (a considerable lot of which we appreciate progressively the more we eat them), rooms (we begin to wind up plainly more OK with spaces that we are used to) and individuals (after some time, we quit calling individuals as "outsiders," regardless of the possibility that our communications have dependably been shallow). It even applies to objects (my office seat is easily well-known to me). Maybe this mental propensity is established in the transformative should be protected: things we know about are more averse to contain concealed peril. On the off chance that you've been around that person commonly, and he's never attempted to kill you, he's presumably not going to attempt today. This Familiarity Effect, where we lean toward that which is well-known to us, makes the loss more troublesome. We may experience considerable difficulties with individuals in our lives, especially when we don't care for them much or they don't treat us well. So, we keep investing energy with companions we don't care for, as opposed to searching for obscure outsiders (who might obviously, in the end, progress toward becoming companions). Furthermore, on the off chance that we lose what we're as of now comfortable with, we need to experience the obnoxious procedure of getting to know new things.

Awful Decisions

Where the decision is between a specific loss and a bigger loss that is only likelihood (i.e. there is a shot of no loss), decreasing affectability can bring about inordinate hazard taking. This clarifies why individuals will keep on gambling in the wake of racking up the considerable loss. Their mentality is centred on the potential for their next wager to win the big stake and wipe out their loss. Individuals can turn out to be so sincerely included in such circumstances that they neglect to see that they are simply adding to their loss. Feelings and venture choices are exceptionally poor associates. Tragically, the dominant part of financial specialists settles on enthusiastic choices on the grounds that, truly, not very many really have a well-thoroughly considered speculation design, including the guides they work with. Retail financial specialists, for the most part, purchase an off-the-rack portfolio assignment demonstrate that is intensely weighted in values under the fantasy that over a sufficiently long time frame, they will, by one means or another, profit. Sadly, history has been a merciless instructor about the estimation of hazard administration.

Awful Association

At the point when two things are matched over and over, the passionate response we need to one begins to seep into the enthusiastic response for the other. This happens through a procedure known as Classical

Conditioning. That is to say, in any case, that we start to esteem the insignificant characteristics of things that are significant, even when those qualities have nothing to do with the esteem itself. For example, we have extremely constructive emotions towards our sentimental accomplice who has certain identity idiosyncrasies (or physical qualities), so we grow exceptionally positive emotions towards those eccentricities, coming to trust we would experience serious difficulties with somebody who doesn't have them. Or, then again, it could imply that we begin to lean toward items made by a specific brand since we have a positive relationship with the brand itself. Actually, many brands besiege us with promotions, endeavouring to inspire us to connect positive things (e.g. engaging quality, riches and an alluring way of life, quieting scenes of nature) with their logo. They apply Classical Conditioning to us like Pavlov did to his pooches. Simply take a gander at filtered water advertisements, which connect a specific brand with a specific way of life. This implies we'll exaggerate what we have, to some degree, since we connect an incentive with unessential components that don't create esteem themselves. We are opposed to discarding our shirt with the in vogue mark, since that logo brings out esteem, even if that shirt looks terrible on us. Furthermore, bear in mind how dismal it is that you'll never again locate a sentimental cooperation with idiosyncratic characteristics X, Y, and Z, that you now find so lovable and charming after your last accomplice had them.

Energy of Proprietorship

When a man purchases a thing with the goal of expending or utilising it, the base value that they are set up to offer the thing for is frequently higher than the most extreme value they would be set up to pay themselves. This is known as the blessing impact. The responsibility seems to expand the apparent estimation of a thing, especially for merchandise that is not traded much. This is the consequence of our hesitance to surrender a thing that we officially possess. Such conduct can be found in the lodging market, where vendors regularly need to bring down their underlying asking cost as purchases, often times, are not set up to pay the value traders to esteem their homes. The gift impact is most unmistakable for new products. For example, autos, where proprietors esteem their merchandise considerably nearer to the first price tag than potential purchasers do.

Grouping Effect and Loss Aversion

These two practices tend to work together, intensifying the issues of speculator botches after some time. As business sectors are rising, people are persuading that the present value pattern will keep on lasting for an uncertain period. The more drawn out the rising pattern lasts, the more imbued the conviction moves toward becoming, until the remainder of "holdouts" at long last "purchases in" as the money related markets develop into a "euphoric state." As the business sectors decay, there is a moderate acknowledgment that "this decrease" is something more than a "purchase the plunge" opportunity. As losses mount, the tension of loss starts to mount until the point that people try to "deflect promote loss" by offering. As appeared in the diagram underneath, this behavioural pattern runs outlandish to the "purchase low/offer high" venture run the show.

Status Quo Bias

Loss aversion is an intense force in avoiding change. Individuals have a general inclination towards the present situation (e.g. their current provider) over changing to a superior option. This is frequently ascribed to a mix of loss abhorrence and the enrichment impact. In any case, the dread of disappointment in settling on a wrong choice may have an influence on inactivity. This clarifies why it is frequently hard to urge clients to switch providers, even when you may have an unrivalled offer. This recommends it is vital to consider both loss aversion and passionate components while focusing on your rivals' clients. Unconditional promises and free trials are extraordinary methods for diminishing the danger of loss or lament that many individuals feel while considering changing from what they know.

Trading Desires

If you somehow happened to win Rs. 100 at a gambling club and five minutes after that, you make a shocking wager and lose that money, odds are, you wouldn't feel as awful as would if you were to have Rs. 100 stolen out of your pocket. Why? It's because in the primary case, you didn't have sufficient energy to acclimate to the world where you had an additional Rs. 100. So, your mind is probably going to encounter the main situation as generally earning back the original investment (however likely with a few, however not all that much, lament). You got a big chance and after that, got unfortunate, which took you back to where you began. So, on the whole, you neither picked up nor lost. Then again, in the second situation, it feels like an immaculate loss (your Rs. 100 in the opening, contrasted with what you're used to). To put it another way: Taking Rs. 100 out of your ledger and placing it in your pocket doesn't make your cerebrum feel like you've picked up Rs. 100, since you've just gotten used to the world where that money is yours. Though winning Rs. 100 arbitrarily at a clubhouse feels like a reward, that is over what we, as of now, have, so losing that money (before you've gotten used to having it) practically takes you back to where you began.

Assurance Impact

The assurance impact prompts occasions that are in all likelihood being given less weight than their likelihood legitimises. Because of loss aversion, it is human instinct to need to take out hazard, as opposed to diminish it. For instance, as opposed to offering 4 at the cost of 3, individuals react better to 1 free with each 3 bought. The last is all the more convincing on the grounds that the zero cost has more assurance. For sites, it likewise implies that if guests are marginally uncertain about how veritable or secure a site, is they will tend to amplify the hazard. This can prompt guests relinquishing a trade. It likewise clarifies why guarantees are such capable limited time apparatuses. An assurance takes out any instability about a circumstance, regardless of whether it's around an application being acknowledged or getting the promoted offer/rate. Individuals are frequently uncertain on the off chance that they will meet all requirements for offers, so an assurance expels this worry. An investigation did by Kahneman and Tversky for their prospect hypothesis showed that far-fetched occasions (1% to 2% likelihood) are overweighed by a factor of 4. Be that as it may, for a practically certain occasion, the distinction is significantly bigger. In tests, a 2% possibility of not winning was given a weighting of 13% (or an 87.1% shot of winning).

Danger of an Uncommon Occasion

Where the chances of an occasion are little (e.g. around 0.001% or less), individuals turn out to be totally apathetic regarding varieties in levels of hazard. Or maybe passionate factors and how a hazard is surrounded are the key drivers of how individuals respond to these levels of hazard. This clarifies why individuals are frequently excessively eager, making it impossible to wager on extraordinary occurrence or why they purchase different lottery tickets when there is an expansive big stake. Research has additionally discovered proof that rich and striking depictions of a result help to decrease the effect of probabilities. Specifically, individuals are all the more intensely impacted (as far as the weighting of probabilities) if an occasion is depicted by utilising frequencies than by utilising standard pointers of likelihood or hazard. This is the reason gaming locales have a tendency to advance the number of champs, as opposed to the shot of winning. From a changed viewpoint, it recommends utilising rich media to breathe life into occasions and abstain from utilising theoretical ideas of the likelihood that individuals battle to get it.

In spite of the greater part of the arm waving and beating on the table by counsellors touting long haul normal returns, time-in-the-advertise and so on, the mental effect of the loss is very genuine. These mental instruments set us up to feel that loss is much more regrettable than it truly is. We are frightened to lose what we have, exaggerate to loss when they do happen and harp on the loss that has happened before. However, much of the time, we recoup from a loss speedier than we would anticipate. Months after the fact, our everyday presence is generally less modified by the loss than we would expect. For the time being, we blow up more to lose than we recognise. In the long haul, we're less hurt by loss than we foresee.

Why Stock Traders Fail (And Others Succeed)

In the most recent decade, a considerable measure of examples of overcoming adversity to originate from securities trade trading have amazed, so has the measure of fizzled financial specialists. Consistently, a great many unsuccessful dealers rush to abandon the share trading system and their mission for riches. However, trading has never been more realistic and there are hundreds, if not a great many more newcomers on the trading floor every day. Trading stocks as a profession are a standout amongst the most charming employments a man can have. Hell, you don't require garments. You can resemble me and take off of quaint little inn down to the PC in your clothing. A lot of traders (or speculators) approach this business with the possibility that maybe a couple "enormous" moves will change their lives or then again, that after a string of little loss, one final blow will get them "back to even" or compensate for the droop. And keeping in mind that this is unquestionably conceivable, it is not likely. In addition, for each example of overcoming adversity, you can discover in which a tremendous bet is paid off, you will discover incalculable stories of burden.

Scarcity of Precise Market Conception for Diving into Trade

Having a poor outlook is the most exceedingly awful issue for newcomers entering money markets, since they have a tendency to trust they'll make it "enormous" and turn out to be overnight moguls. Be that as it may, the probability of that incident is exceptionally thin, just on the grounds that it requires genuine investment and push to contribute accurately and see any positive outcomes. Additionally, traders think since they haven't seen an arrival on their ventures inside an initial couple of days, it implies they've fizzled and should leave the trading floor. By having this poor mood, it prompts disappointment. A standout amongst fascinating points in trading and truly all through numerous territories of life is the thing that could be called for irregular support. Arbitrary support, as it identifies with destructive trading hones, happens when a broker ascribes an irregular result to ability or absence of expertise. The market, once in a while, compensates unfortunate propensities and rebuffs great propensities in light of the fact that the market is so unique. It is particularly negative if another trader, who wins a couple of trades, with definitely no arrangement at all, credits this accomplishment to 'instinct.' Arbitrary fortification can likewise hurt experienced traders who encounter a series of loss and trust they never again have the expertise. Irregular support can make long haul negative behaviour patterns which are greatly difficult to break. It is equal to a betting fanatic as they continue playing, since they win sufficiently enough to keep them there, obviously, they are losing their money as time goes on. A fruitful card player may likewise encounter a critical draw down, surrender his demonstrated methodology and in doing so, gives his edge back to the house.

Over Expectation is Discouraged in Trade

You make a trade and score a major victory. Now, you feel large and in charge and like you have this trading thing in order. This is absolutely justifiable, given that is a characteristic human feeling. How about we take a gander at trading Forex? What do you have to do to wind up noticeably a trader? Everybody supposes they'll be making a reliable 6 figure pay in a couple of months or even years. Disregard the way that the business is brimming with some extremely canny individuals, who have invested years figuring out how to be a predictable dealer. Disregard the way that you're going up against associations that have a great many rupees to toss behind their dealers as help. For example, examination and framework testing. Disregard the way that these same associations are playing on an unexpected field in comparison to you. All you require is a couple of pointers, a handle that doesn't screw you excessively, some money management, and in a year or two, you'll be carrying on with the high-life. To put this obtusely, anybody with a couple of rupees extra can agree to accept an online investment fund, and unexpectedly, 'wave enchanted wand,' they are a 'stock trader. Do you think it is insightful to permit a handyman, attorney, specialist or teacher to begin a profession in one of those fields with no sort of instruction or preparing? So, why on the planet do individuals think they can simply open a web based trading account and have predictable accomplishment with no preparation or training?

Never Downgrade Morale in Cases of Loss in Trade

Traders invest gigantic measures of energy making strong systems for money markets. However, disregard their capital. Speculators don't consider the measure of capital they have and will chance on one stock. Truthfully, many don't consider setting well-being net or have a money management design, and it winds up costing them everything. Having no restrictions and no ransom choice is terrible in light of the fact that it regularly sets the tone for disappointment. By having the farthest point of, say 2% of your general capital, it can be a sensible approach to diminish loss and keep you from taking a chance with the greater part of your capital as well. Securities trade trading plans are something which have turned into an esteemed device to most speculators; a great many new brokers don't devise a trading plan. As interesting as it sounds, having no arrangement, not even an essential trading plan, could spell fiasco, since they don't have any kind of plan or manual for taking after. It additionally implies they don't know how or when to stop. The significant reasons, in such manner, incorporate contributing excessively capital without a moment's delay, contributing excessively on one hazardous stock and making the wrong move when the market shifts. Subsequent to busting a couple of trading accounts, you will understand that trading is no simple deed, and you require more learning than basically knowing when to purchase/offer. So, you began perusing books, peruse through discussions and agree to accept trading courses to gain more information.

Trading Plans and Regularity Prevents Frequent Losses

When do we understand that irregularity can make series of loss in extraordinary trading plans and furthermore, series of benefits in poor trading plans (and furthermore situations which fall in the middle of these cases)? How would we change in accordance with trade gainfully finished in the long haul? While each trading arrangement is distinctive, every trader must have a recorded trading plan which traces how they will trade. This arrangement ought to be all around inquired about and lay out sections, ways out and money management rules. Along these lines, the dealer will know, as time goes on, if their arrangement is defective or effective. It is likewise critical to hazard a little rate of capital on each trade. Chance levels of each trade ought to be shrouded in the trading plan under the money management area. This offers breathing space to the broker as they will have the capacity to withstand a series of loss and be less inclined to roll out an untimely improvement in their trading plan when it is not required. There are continually going to be requesting difficulties to overcome, with a specific end goal to prevail in stock trading. The three focuses are only a couple of the hindrances that have made a huge number of individuals neglect to prevail with securities trade trading. They are, for the most part, exceptionally straightforward errors to make, yet they can be effective reasons why more fizzle every day. You find out about pointers that disclose to you when the cost is overbought. Fibonacci numbers that task cost into what's to come. Candle designs that flag inversions in the market. Before long, you experience investigation loss of motion. A condition of over breaking down a circumstance so a choice is never taken.

Dynamic Decision-making for Trade Success

The business sectors are, to a great degree, dynamic and in steady flux. This gets a component of haphazardness that can make benefits for untalented dealers and loss for gifted brokers, and it happens constantly. A trader should likewise decide when a specific series of loss or benefits can be credited their aptitude and when it is irregular. The best way to do this while you are learning is to approach the business sectors with a trading plan and hazard a little rate of capital on each trade. It is additionally critical to recall that even the best traders and trading techniques encounter series of loss, and this is not a motivation to desert the procedure. A trading plan is to control your trading towards the correct heading. It covers everything from the passage, leaves, hazard management, markets traded, time span and position estimates. It is your plan for progress. There can be many reasons why you are not gainful. It could be trained issues, mental components harming your trading or just having no edge in the business sectors. Without a trading plan, you will never realise what the reason is. Be that as it may, when you set aside the opportunity to comprehend what major reasons make generally fall flat. See all the more how you can dodge them and ideally, you can wind up noticeably effective in the stock trade trading world.

Which Trading Personality Are You: Warrior, Nomad or Settler?

Do you think you are a Warrior? Or are you a Settler? Or may be a Nomad? Recognising your prevalent identity sort changes the way you approach life. In the event that you know yourself and on the off chance that you comprehend other individuals, you can unhesitatingly handle your profession and your own connections, knowing precisely where you are originating from and what every other person is looking for. Warriors, Settlers and Nomads give a progressive system which fathom your own needs and the necessities of others. In light of the idea of developmental brain science, it uncovers the determinants at the centre of our characters. In light of the known development of human cognisance, there's a hypothesis that expresses that there are three identity sorts we have acquired from our progenitors: the Warrior is compelling, undaunted and authoritative, the Settler is friendly, instinctive and versatile, and the Nomad is anxious, magnetic and creative. Our identity and how we have been raised are key to the choices we make in life. In the event that you need to be a fruitful trader on Wall Street, you better be exceedingly insightful and have a motivating hardworking attitude. You likewise need a specific identity – solid, valiant and modest. Here are the six characteristics you'll require in the event that you need to make it. Terrance Watts concocted his hypothesis of Warriors, Settlers and Nomads (WSN) in view of transformative brain science. It is a technique that numerous advisors and experts utilise today. I have, indeed, utilised it when running instructional classes in relational abilities inside organisations.

Characteristics of Trading Personalities

There are diverse sorts of traders. However, a typical normal for the majority of them is a collected mind that knows not to experience passionate feelings for a market, see when the tape keeps running against you. Adamant traders frequently end up searching for work. This is especially valid for the individuals who take directional wagers, either on level cost or spread positions. They should have the trust in their capacity to find, in the future, what others in the market don't and survey whether occasions undermine or strengthen that view. Basically, the thought behind WSN (Warrior, Settler and Nomad) is that we, as a whole, have a blend of the three identity sorts inside us, yet generally, one is more prominent than the others. Once in a while, contingent upon our folks/family condition, we figure out how to "shroud" certain components of our identity with training, we can likewise upgrade those different parts of our identities that are less prevailing. There is no "best" identity sort, as each has constructive and contrary qualities, much the same as every single individual ever conceived. It is practically difficult to do what a decent trader expels. However, as much feeling from the procedure as could reasonably be expected. How did they really feel when the market drops 1000 focuses in a day? It is truly horrible for anybody with a position in the market. However, great traders need to see the circumstance impartially, as a purchasing opportunity. At the point when fiasco strikes, they have to take a gander at it as just information. There are diverse sorts of traders, yet a typical normal for the vast majority of them is a collected mind that knows not to go gaga for a market see when the tape keeps running against you. Hard-headed traders regularly wind up searching for work. This is especially valid for the individuals who take directional wagers, either on level cost or spread positions. They should have the trust in their capacity to find in future what others in the market don't and survey whether occasions undermine or fortify that view.

Warriors in Trading

Warriors get a kick out of the chance to be in charge, they get a kick out of the chance to be correct. They are confident, definitive, prevailing, stubborn, immediate and candid. They are high achievers, set elevated standards, go up against the test and can think and react quickly. Warriors experience difficulty accepting they are to blame. They can be savage and now and then, manipulative. They can be effectively perceived by lethargic non-verbal communication, watchful eye and carefulness when discussing them. They can be exceptionally private people. They complete things are excruciating of errors and aversion failure to decide. The most recent research recommends people are not warriors in their qualities, subsequent to surveying the contemporary nomad seeker gatherer populaces. Present day warriors have an immediate, direct way to deal with life. They are great at completing things, yet are narrowly minded of the individuals who are less definitive than them. They are systematic, sensible and can think and react quickly. Be that as it may, warriors additionally experience difficulty conceding shortcoming and can be manipulative and savage in their assurance to take care of number one. They are effortlessly perceived by their lethargic non-verbal communication, a watchful eye and careful reaction to questions. They are not excited about discussing themselves. 'Most legislators are warriors,' said Watts. 'Yet, despite the fact that Tony Blair tries hard to be one, he simply isn't sufficiently heartless.' Camilla Parker Bowles, Steve Redgrave and David Coulthard are great illustrations.

Settlers in Trading

Settlers are 'individual' in nature. They jump at the chance to share, to please and be thoughtful. They can be meek and think that it's difficult to state 'no' when made a request to get things done. So, they may everlastingly be heaped on at work. They are idealistic, lively, kind and delicate. They need to care for you and need to be preferred and cherished. This favours them. Pioneers have superb relational abilities, and they are regularly upbeat to discuss themselves, yet will dependably inquire about you. They can settle on choices effectively, yet will, for the most part, be impacted by others' sentiments. The present day settler is a social butterfly. Pioneers get a kick out of the chance to share and being preferred is crucially imperative to them. They are bright, open, kind and touchy and abrogating hopeful on their way to deal with life. The non-verbal communication of pioneers is graciously responsive, and they speak effortlessly about themselves. 'Ruler Charles is the outright exemplification of the current settler,' said Watts. He additionally incorporates Frank Bruno, Carol Smillie and Fern Britton, moderator of Ready Steady Cook.

Nomads in Trading

Nomads, as the name proposes, are life's vagabonds. They like experience, they despise schedule. They need consideration. Travelers look for fervour and change. They have vitality, responsibility issues and are fantastically cordial and sensational. They can be flighty. Wanderers need consideration, so they may tell more lies or over overstate. They will talk uproariously and regularly be more disgusting than others. The nomads throughout your life will dependably perk you up with some fun. However, they will definitely, consistently be late. The present nomads continually look for change, energy and new things. They are active, emotional and can frequently be found in employments which require an outgoing person. For example, acting. They have an irresistible energy and will regularly be an extraordinary wellspring of motivation for others. Nomads likewise have leanings towards flightiness. They have a couple of hindrances and can be embarrassingly loud and blunt, now and again, in a puerile way likened to touchiness. Average nomads incorporate Richard Branson, Elizabeth Hurley, Posh Spice and Jamie Oliver. Social orders are, in reality, much more battle ready than roaming ones. Nomads are the strays. They cherish change, shading, sentiments and should be the focal point of consideration. They loathe being controlled by individuals, circumstances, calendars or occasions. They are "individuals" regularly with an enthusiasm for expressions of the human experience or execution.

Impacts of Trading Personalities

Trading as a profession is an intriguing vacation decision since it is a gigantic adjustment of hazard and reward. Many individuals see it as their method for getting rich speedily, yet numerous traders scour for a living for a considerable length of time and never 'make it' as a fruitful trader. So why might you turn into an expert trader or fiddle with it low maintenance around different employments and obligations? Money is presumably the essential driver. Be that as it may, why money? Would you like to be rich? Do you view money as a marker of progress? Would you like to demonstrate individuals wrong or satisfy desires of other relatives or companions? No scholarly capabilities are required. You needn't bother with a degree. You needn't bother with an immense measure of start-up capital. Anybody can trade, yet not everybody can trade well. Flexibility is a basic segment. In the greater part of the cases, we would all adoration to act naturally utilised or have the sort of work life adjust where you can work the hours you need, require some serious energy off when you need and be liable just to yourself. This in itself can be an issue. Society directs that being fruitful is having money and having made it yourself. Acquiring many thousands or millions absolutely in light of your basic leadership capacities appears to make you significantly better than the rest with scholarly perfection. Obviously, we are every one of the mixes of these identity sorts. However, envision for a minute what may happen if two warrior sorts experience passionate feelings for and frame a long haul relationship. You can expect firecrackers! On the off chance that a Nomad and a Warrior get together, the floating methods of the Nomad may madden the Warrior, while the controlling inclinations of the Warrior may make the Nomad need to flee. Obviously, these are gigantic speculations, but I have found the theory an exceptionally helpful one to utilise in restorative work. It is critical to recollect that practically no one will be an unadulterated sort and most display attributes from each sort.

Attributes of Each Trade Personality in Present Financial Situation

Money: Warriors are destined to be keen on profiting. This is a technique for self-satisfaction and a marker for progress. Nomads may progress toward becoming traders, since they have something to demonstrate. Pioneers are destined to trade, since they consider it to be an approach to give a decent pay and may even be trading in light of the fact that their family needs them to.

Positive Trading: Settlers won't feel like they are treading on anybody's toes as they are constantly reproachful of themselves. Nomads adore this since they aren't splendid at staying at things, thus something that includes no capabilities and they can learn as and when they need is great. Warriors are aggressive, so they will search for reasons why they are superior to different traders.

Opportunity: Nomads appreciate having the capacity to trade at whatever point they need and the flexibility to go for broke as they need. Warriors will appreciate the opportunity on the grounds that there is no discriminatory constraint, no limit to what they can accomplish.

The settlers are the identity to be awkward with the not knowing component of whether they will profit or not.

Trading Loss Dealing: The Nomads will acknowledge that loss happens when trading yet won't be considering loss when taking a trade, just the benefits that could be made. Travelers acquire a loss. They will probably accuse anything and anybody aside from themselves. The Settler will point the finger at them, the Warrior will endeavour to gain from it and proceed onward. The Warrior won't just hope to recover what they lost, they additionally make more benefit to finishing everything, though the Settler will be satisfied to profit back and afterward refocus on another trade.

Evaluating Possible Problems: Settlers may get exceptionally harmed unwillingly and quit trading when they have accomplished their day by day objective. Warriors will wind up assessing why they made a loss to gain from them and will audit their objectives and techniques to continually figure out how to be better. However, at that point, stiff necked attitude may likewise lead the Warrior to trust their procedure is constantly right, even when it's definitely not. The Nomad will be the person who figures out how to do things one way and sticks with it since it works, and they can be very apathetic now and again. Something they could do with gaining from a Settler – persistence and steadiness.

However, recognising which sorts of each character we contain is quite recently the starting: Watts is worried that present day society is hot-lodging an abundance of warriors. As society progresses, we will undoubtedly observe more warriors, since they're the ones that survive. Be that as it may, society is making an excessive number of warriors. Everybody is so driven these days and urged to the slight specialist, we are winding up noticeably unnecessarily confident at a youthful age, prompting overabundances of brutality.

Why Is Trading Failure In Our DNA and How to Fix It?

There are a few reasons why analysis of a specimen may not be effective, and it is not a well-established actuality as to why it is harder to break down a few examples over others. Each trader knows this situation: you found an incredible setup and entered a trade, at that point, the cost conflicts with you and you purchase more, since you trust that cost will, in any case, go up. Furthermore, as cost goes down further, you continue purchasing until the point when you are left with a colossal loss and need to close your position since it harms excessively. Been there, done that. How would we know this? Since 90% of all traders lose. On the off chance that you are one of the 90% of traders that lose, at that point you realise that 100% of what you have perused, listened or found out about trading isn't right. It's not your blame. Not very many expert traders will share what they know with pariahs. We will do only that. The dread of coming up short is a widespread feeling that nearly everybody has or will involvement. It is the main calculation that stands our method for accomplishing something that we need or potentially coming to our goal(s). As a kid, maybe it was a dream of being the last individual in a group.

This same dread is something that specifically influences us as grown-up minds, the conditions are typically somewhat extraordinary. As a starting trader and even an accomplished trader, we confront challenges day by day, and the stakes are somewhat higher than being decided for a group. Suffice to state, it is great practice to make every effort to move past this dread into acknowledgment and gain from our mix-ups.

Study the Pulse of Trading Market

It's tied in with seeing how the strengths that move the market collaborate each and every trading day. It's tied in with knowing who moves the market and how. When you comprehend the DNA of trading, you will comprehend when, where, how and why the market moves as it does. Try not to give anybody a chance to trick you into trusting the business sector's change. Markets don't change, individuals change! In the event that anybody tries to let you know that the "business sectors change," flee as quickly as possible. It's code for 'we upgrade and change our strategies all the time, since we don't realise what we are doing.' When somebody turns out each other week with another trading model or are back trying another time allotment or have another pointer, you KNOW you are conversing with the WRONG individuals. The DNA of trading has stood the trial of time for a long time, and we will never say, or surmise, in any capacity, that the market has 'changed'! Neither have our strategies! For most, a market is a place where, on the off chance that you are sufficiently fortunate, an epiphany happens once in your trading profession. By and large, it is discovered that your cerebrum is not made for trading. The component that is driving such ruinous conduct is called "Subjective Dissonance," and it is an interior assurance instrument that we people have created to make an agreeable reality around our day to day lives. Intellectual Dissonance is so profoundly established in our DNA that it controls a number of our activities and the greater part of our life. When you comprehend the DNA of trading, every single day will be an epiphany. Intellectual discord implies that we are encountering clashing and discomforting encounters, considerations and feelings that emerge from our own particular activities. A well-known case is smokers who are confronted with the perils of getting disease. It's anything but difficult to perceive any reason why smokers don't prefer to consider growth 20 times each day each time they light a cigarette. At the point when individuals experience such negative feelings, they begin to change their conduct or potentially their contemplations to decrease the distress.

Acknowledge Innovation in Trading

As trade choices are made, give yourself an undertaking that will expel you from the distressing circumstance. Many trading stages are furnished with perceptible alarms and even email or SMS cautions. Utilise this innovation to leave the system to get a crisp viewpoint and to involve your brain somewhere else. Along these lines, when you come back to discover the trade result, it is known quickly and in this manner, not a consistent weight on your shoulders. In doing as such, you are finding a way to reduce the dread of losing money. Individuals just notice data that seems to assert a packed course. All of a sudden, people just read affirming articles or converse with individuals who share their thoughts all together lessen the cacophony. In trading, individuals search for articles or utilise markers that legitimise remaining in a losing trade. On the other hand, when you are in a losing long trade, you give excessive weight to each uptick and you disregard the way that value continues going further and further down. Hazard administration is absolutely critical for every last trade. Having a trading plan to distinguish huge reward with generally safe is an incredible approach to acknowledge a little loss when it happens. Losing is a piece of trading and ought to be made arrangements for ahead of time. On the off chance that we are assuming an immense loss, we will most likely be unable to recoup both rationally and monetarily. Little loss takes into consideration life span and helps to diminish the dread, particularly when you see a substantial winning trade. The DNA of trading is the diagram of the market. It is the way to recognising particular occasions in the market that enable educated traders to benefit on a reliable premise. Understanding the DNA, the building pieces of the market give traders the capacity to perceive what the powers that move the market are routinely doing each trading day and benefit from those powers.

Demonstration Is Recommended Before Implementation

90% of all traders come up short since they all have been customised to trade in light of deception. Appropriate information and comprehension of how the business sectors function, the DNA, is the main way we know to wind up plainly as one of the 10% that benefit reliably. It additionally takes something other than a comprehension of how the business sectors function. It takes the correct outlook, the correct point of view and the right 'propensities for progress' to go too far from attempting to be a winning trader. It takes tolerance, determination, teachers and responsibility. It takes the REAL psychology of trading, and it is fixing intently to have a demonstrated approach to trade. Traders are regularly discovered supporting activities, keeping in mind the end goal to adhere to a unique course. As it's been said, "Everybody does that, so why not me?" It is a term frequently used to legitimise terrible conduct. This defending begins as early as kindergarten, we do it all through school and college. It's normal in work environments and furthermore, in our family lives. In trading, individuals attempt to think of reasons why adding to a failure is great or why they should break their entrance governs this time. Intellectual disharmony drives all our conduct and day by day activities, as a rule, without us knowing it.

Without subjective cacophony, we would feel awful and stressed all the time, since we'd need to confront the cool hard certainties and impacts that our own choices are bringing us. Keeping in mind the end goal to dodge those repulsive feelings, individuals put forth an admirable attempt to abstain from conceding the badly arranged truth with the "buy support" we persuade ourselves that something we purchased isn't "that terrible, all things considered," despite the fact that we most likely needn't bother with it and spent excessive money. The DNA of trading is the diagram of the market. It is the way to distinguishing particular occasions in the market that enable educated traders to benefit on a predictable premise. Understanding the DNA, the building squares of the market, gives traders the capacity to perceive what the powers that move the market are routinely doing each trading day and exploit those strengths.

Market Investigation Required Before Market Penetration

Intellectual disharmony has many structures in trading and it impacts all layers of our basic leadership as traders. At the point when traders make an uneven market investigation, they are excessively persuaded that they 'know' where the cost will go. At that point, they won't see in the data that they are incorrect. When you transparently talk about trades and positions, you will probably legitimise awful trades and safeguard your loss and remain in them longer. When you are losing money following 5, 6 or 7 years, you record it under 'taking in process' or 'market educational cost.' At its embodiment, the brain research of trading is basically how we as people handle and respond to "Hazard, Loss and Gain!" It's the practices that we have come to respond with most reliably to each of those things that decide how we will reasonable in the trading field and frequently, in many others parts of our life. The psychology of trading manages our own modified reactions to the instability in the market while trading every day. Dread is simply the conviction that we are not prepared to adequately deal with whatever comes to our direction. What's more, with regards to the value activity you see on your diagrams, intellectual discord is regularly the main impetus behind fake breakouts, fake-outs and absurdly unstable market tops where beginners are deceived into taking all the more losing trades and are then constrained out of their enormous loss. It's the REAL brain science of trading and why it's critical! Achievement and disappointment occur for some reasons. See how to make a triumphant mentality and take your trading to another level through straightforward systems that advance achievement!

Maintain Trade Diary Contained with Reasons of Failure

Each triumphant trade is an incredible feeling and delivers a feeling of energy. Nonetheless, we have a tendency to gain considerably more from our loss. Anything that damages makes us invest more energy on the issue, rather than simply proceeding onward. Utilise this opportunity to examine the activities that were executed accurately versus the ones that were executed erroneously. By taking note of this in a trading diary, it enables us to survey and ensure that we make each endeavour to not give the inaccurate events a chance to happen once more. There is no 'simple trap' that will, all of a sudden, kill the issues that accompanied subjective cacophony. We have built up this system for more than a large number of years, yet there are a couple of particular things and methods for believing that a trader needs to embrace, keeping in mind the end goal to settle on better trading choices, while making an trading plan, dependable thought of long and short trading situations. Stay away from uneven analysis to keep your psyche and eyes open to the two sides of the market. Keep a trading diary to bring issues to light for your trading conduct. A trader who tracks his conduct can perceive the amount he is losing by rehashing similar oversights and is then more inclined to change his conduct. Envision a trading business where everything runs easily and where you are never again compelled to freeze all through trades, settling on choices that with insight into the past, you wouldn't have ordinarily made. Rather, you can focus on bringing just those trades with the most elevated likelihood of accomplishment and stay with them when they are gainful or simply leave when the market doesn't do what you anticipated. Be modest! Acknowledge that you don't know everything and that you will, as often as possible, experience loss. A trader who can't assume a loss has no possibility of turning into an expert full-time trader. Prospects trading can be a superb approach to win a section or full-time income or it can be an outright bad dream on the off chance that you fail to understand the situation. The use fates give you is a two edged sword, you can make or lose your underlying edge, and you can do it rapidly if the market moves quickly one way or the other.

The Psychology Behind "Harmonic" Trading

There is a sort of music psychology of group basis the symphonious examples. Symphonious examples are shaped by the joint conduct of a huge number of dealers, swarm psychology, playing out dread and ravenousness, supply and request situations. Symphonious trading designs are an entirely organised group of Fibonacci-based outline designs that are utilised to gauge inversions in monetary markets with a high level of exactness. Dissimilar to the greater part of the traditional graph designs, the consonant examples must have a progression of particular Fibonacci connections between the fundamental parts of the example, keeping in mind the end goal to be substantial and precisely decide very plausible inversion focuses in the market. The brilliant Fibonacci proportion as the essential constituent and the other going with Fibonacci proportions are the foundations of the symphonious trading strategy and the consonant diagram designs. Twelve of the symphonious examples have been produced throughout the years, yet strikingly, every one of them is established upon one essential example – the ABCD design. In this book, we'll take a gander at the ABCD design and talk about how to trade it. In later articles, we'll likewise portray the other staying consonant diagram designs.

Understand Laws of Worldly Nature

To start with, to comprehend the consonant examples, we have to establish the frameworks by arranging the particular Fibonacci proportions that are utilised as a part of symphonious trading. It's likewise a smart thought to now include these Fibonacci levels into your Fibonacci device. This law is the advancement and relates to how cycles develop. Inside this law are sub laws relating to timing, adjustment and human recognition. At last, all sub laws likewise are guided by the laws of pushes, which are communicated through advancement. The occasions we see playing out in our lives and on the diagrams are basically advancement customised and individualised. This is the astounding endlessness of the universe which parts and differentiates itself into numerous types of appearances. The Bhagavad Gita depicts this delightfully. The idea is genuinely cunning in its perplexing straightforwardness. It is intended to keep us intrigued and speculating, tricked into the conviction of the failing to know humble human presence. While you work transcendently from the straight personality, you can't ever get to this profound comprehension and build up that inward realising that makes for good trading. The need to compartmentalise prevents you from applying a general law that relates to the presence in your trading rather you work in a robotic manner of compartments for various resources. Trading your psyche is a personnel that is represented by various laws, the laws of the intelligent personality. Your Elliott wave consider is just great as your elucidation of it. There are times when it works just effortlessly in light of the fact that your legitimate personality sees designs it can perceive. The same is valid for music trading and GANN.

Three Drive Structure Carries Unbearable Pressure of Trade

Amicability is about adjustment. Equalisation is not static, it relies upon development. The vitality that offers articulation to all living things is development. Without development, there is no life. When something gets "out of adjusting," the procedure is as characteristic and congruous as the move that paves the way to that state. The Three Drives Structure: When a three drives design develops, it is an inversion motion for traders to start considering contrarian "purchase" positions in a downtrend or "offer" positions in a prevailing uptrend. The example structure is one of the uncommon situations where symmetry in both cost and time turns into a basic identifier, expanding the likelihood that a pattern is achieving finish and that an inversion is unavoidable. For new consonant traders, the example can be hard to spot, yet with a little practice, the Three Drives structure turns out to be significantly simpler to find. In particular, the Three Drives design is made out of a progression of three back to back value crests (in an uptrend) or troughs (in a downtrend), making two interconnected ABCD designs. Each drive is trailed by a remedial leg and the third fulfilment drive makes a butterfly symphonious example (which will be talked about later). The introduction of a Three Drives design proposes that solid bull or bear markets are getting to be noticeably finished broadened and a valued remedy will be required, so costs trade more in accordance with recorded midpoints. One of the key points of interest of the example is that it tends to offer better hazard than compensate proportions, as stop loss levels are kept amazingly tight in the inversion zone. Disappointments in the example have a tendency to recommend more grounded continuation the beforehand predominant way.

ABCD Design for Legitimate Trade

There are times when the best of trading techniques seem to quit working. Has it, at any point, struck you that this is only one of the numerous figments your direct personality has been suckered into? The ABCD Pattern: The ABCD design is shaped by 3 showcase swings or legs, the AB leg, the BC leg and the CD leg, as appeared in the accompanying realistic. The CD leg will, as a rule, be of an indistinguishable size from the AB leg along these lines, this example is otherwise called the AB = CD design. In any case, the example is as yet legitimate if the CD leg expands and is bigger than the AB leg. The ABCD example ought to likewise have a generally symmetrical appearance, in spite of the fact that that is not completely vital. The bearish ABCD design shows up after an uptrend and demonstrates that a bearish inversion is likely at a particular value level. Correspondingly, the bullish ABCD design shows up toward the finish of downtrends, flagging a bullish inversion. The bullish ABCD designs are an identical representation of the bearish ABCD, in this way, every one of the standards and strategies applies similarly to the two examples. With the end goal of clarifying the tenets and strategies to trade the examples, we will utilise the bearish ABCD. You can apply similar standards to the bullish partner in the turnaround heading.

Build Instincts to Confront Unavoidable Trends

Move periods are a test on the grounds that the sensible person does not remember them in the time, since it doesn't comprehend the all-inclusive laws that make them. The conundrum is that traders trust that they can create trading frameworks that will deliver returns everlastingly, in light of a static law, not on bio dynamic laws. The universe is a bio dynamic place in which everything interfaces with each other, inside the law of development. Equalisation is not static, adjust determines its examples through the development of particles. There is request to the state of this development. The request gives off an impression of being arbitrary on the grounds that no state of the development ever rehashes in a similar shape. When you find out about the structure of the universe, you consequently build up a more profound comprehension of examples. The Heisenberg rule exhibits obviously how the individual impacts design through perception. Seeing how this rule functions in your trading ought to be foundational preparing for each trader. The Buddhists comprehended this foundational truth and transformed it into the craft of self-dominance. There is one basic motivation behind why I instruct brokers to look past the cloak of appearances and find out about general laws of advancement and how to peruse and decipher cycles: When you have these abilities, you build up a considerably more intense feeling of timing, together with an inactive valuation for how vitality streams in the business sectors and in life. You build up an instinct for unavoidable market moves you can't have when your trading choices are driven by an unthinking methodology. Intellectualising these ideas in articles isn't simple. I can just endeavour to give you an essence of what it resembles to trade from this higher vantage point and clarify a tad bit of what you need to do keeping in mind the end goal to get to this place.

Make Breathing Room for Stop Loss

The stop-loss request ought to be set a couple of pips behind the symphonious inversion zone (above it in a bearish ABCD and beneath it in a bullish ABCD). Cost may trade the symphonious inversion zone for a delayed timeframe. It's imperative to adhere to the trade. Cost may somewhat overshoot the inversion zone, subsequently it's prescribed to leave a couple of pips of breathing room with the stop loss (this will likewise rely upon the time period – a couple of pips on the 1-hour outline may mean 40 – 50 pips for the week by week graph). It is imperative at the cost to not close past the symphonious resistance zone (the 2 Fib levels in the ABCD design). A dismissal, with long shadows, is a decent sign that the symphonious ABCD example will work. Quick value activity after the inversion demonstrates that the principal benefit focus at 0.382 Fib will probably be surpassed and for this situation, it's sensible to focus on the 0.618 Fib as the primary focus for a more noteworthy benefit. When one leaves on another experience, the drive to do as such never originated from your legitimate, direct personality. It comes from the greater place inside you that is prepared to develop and extend. Try not to commit the error to enable your straight personality to be the ace of your (trading) universe. It will trick you into many trading blunders which could be maintained a strategic distance from.

Trading Psychology: Coping with Losing Trades

Losing money in the money related markets is an extreme pill to swallow for general traders. A major loss may influence your ledger as well as your trading brain science in general. Be that as it may, by letting your dread of losing control, you essentially ensure you'll never turn into a fruitful trader. While torment repugnance is an effective component of the human personality, it has antagonistic outcomes when connected to trading. Traders who let their dread of losing direct their trading technique experience the ill effects of loss repugnance. An expression initially began and exhibited by therapists Amos Tversky and Daniel Kahneman, loss abhorrence is a choice hypothesis that portrays individuals' dread of losing things. More often than not, individuals emphatically favour keeping away from a loss over making picks up. At the point when money is hanging in the balance, as on account of budgetary trading, this focal propensity can be all the more effective. Trading is a standout amongst the most sincerely turbulent vocations you could pick. Your point is to profit and losing money is the correct inverse of what you set out to accomplish, yet it is inescapable. Each trader will encounter losing trades. Some, more than others. When you lose on a trade, you may encounter sentiments of nervousness, stretch, weakness, disappointment, outrage, mistrust, fear and the yearning for exact retribution or a distress to do whatever you can to get your money back. All of these emotions are characteristic and ordinary. Be that as it may, you have to build up an approach to overcome or control these feelings to go ahead to improve trades.

Aspirant Traders Focus on Trading Psychology

One of the initial steps to turning into a fruitful trader is to ace your trading psychology. This implies dealing with your loss abhorrence. As per Tversky and Kahneman, our cerebrum, for the most part, relegates more than two times the heaviness of a loss as it does to a pickup. Loads of confirmation proposes people are so hardwired to abstain from losing that the dominant part of us would even fall back on betting, just to evade a loss. In spite of this heartbreaking reality, there are steps you can take to limit your dread of losing. The initial step is to perceive that loss will undoubtedly occur in money related trading. Regardless of the possibility that you take after a successful trading technique without deviation, you may, at present, capitulate to the laws of likelihood. As indicated by an American agent and financial specialist Peter Lynch, "around here, in case you're great. You're correct six times out of ten. You're never going to be correct nine times out of ten." If you think there's something other than the law of likelihood making you lose, such as awful conduct or poor system, enjoy a reprieve from trading by and large. This will give you an opportunity to prepare for what happened and recognise the wellspring of your failings. This is the ideal time to refocus and refine your trading technique. The second means to limiting your dread of losing is learning as much as you can about the instruments and markets you are trading. An educated trader is a surer trader, one who is less inclined to lose. This incorporates, yet is not constrained to, understanding specialised and essential investigation, setting up a successful hazard administration system and dealing with your desires. Hazard administration is completely basic to turning into an effective trader. By characterising your entrance and leave positions, utilising stop-loss and plainly characterising your satisfactory level of drawdown, you might be better situated to limit your loss consequently. The third means to beating loss abhorrence is to remain propelled by continually reminding yourself why you turned into a trader in any case. Trading is a long procedure that, when done accurately, should yield you better outcomes after some time. Extraordinary compared to other solutions for loss aversion is the achievement. By profiting as a trader, you will be propelled by benefit and reward instead of by fear.

Learn Economic Fundamentals Critically

On the off chance that you took after your Forex trading plan, the trade turned sour, note down in a trading journal what the economic situations were and the reasons why you made this trade. At that point, concentrate your brain on something else, it is essential to be completely discharged from this loss and rationally prepared to trade with a crisp viewpoint. After the business sectors have shut, you can survey this specific trade. Your trading framework won't be ideal for all economic situations. In the event that this is valid, you should recognise the economic situations that best suit your framework. In the event that you didn't take after the guidelines of your Forex trading plan, you should re-examine your approach and discover what isn't right. The issue isn't your strategy. The issue is you, since you didn't take after your strict rules. Recognise your misstep with the goal that you don't rehash it. The most widely recognised issues confronted by traders are mental issues. "Reprisal" is a negative perspective which regularly happens after you've endured a loss. Rash acts, uncalculated chance taking, sentiments of being almighty and so on are the consequence of a vindictive outlook. Rather than helping you escape a groove, it can add to your monetary decrease. Dread is frequently a motivation for vindicating. As a result of this dread, you can wind up going out on a limb. This is frequently unfavourable and not simply on account of Forex trading. Amid the recuperation of money related loss, it is vital that you go for broke and think practically. It requires the investment to recoup a substantial loss. Try not to make huge trades amid a condition of frenzy. Working at a relentless pace and keeping your trading positions stable will enable you to keep negative feelings from influencing your trading.

Keep Irrational Desires in Control
A section to sore losing in trading is loss abhorrence. This is a piece of human instinct and trading truly brings it out in all its wonderfulness. When we have a decent trading methodology and it takes a progression of losing trades, it's simple for this to turn out. Not exclusively does loss aversion tend to make us not have any desire to lose what we have, it likewise makes us not have any desire to acknowledge loss we've effectively taken. This specifically turns out to be more terrible on the off chance that we don't comprehend the idea of trading likelihood that a trading system will lose, and begin to trust the market should simply be 'off-base.' Trading isn't generally about doing 'x' and getting result 'y.' At that point, obviously, the following stage is relinquishing the trading plan as "unmistakably" it's futile. It completely should be comprehended that notwithstanding when you execute a decent arrangement well, there will be times when you should take a losing trade. Presently, I'd jump at the chance to bring up at that being a sore failure and detesting losing are not really a similar thing. Sore washouts, more often than not, loathe losing as well, yet despising losing is something to develop on the off chance that you can turn into a decent failure. I hear all the time that individuals say "figure out how to love little loss." For a great many people, loss aversion is a

manifestation of being human. As a trader, you should figure out how to limit it as much as you could so you can concentrate on making picks up instead of staying away from the loss. With a legitimate hazard administration procedure set up, you won't need to invest the greater part of your energy contemplating loss evasion. There is no space for foreswearing in the trading world. Every effective trader achieved the best through ponders activity and inspiration, not by keeping away from the loss. By driving with compensating rather than torment, you will be en route to acing your own particular brain science. The impacts of sore losing are obviously very negative, maybe more colossal than many would anticipate.

Be Categorical between Small and Big Losses

It's ideal to despise huge loss and hence take little ones. Likewise, it's imperative to characterise "little" as it drives the brain to think taking the loss of just a couple of ticks will enable you to be fruitful. This can be the total turnaround of reality. Little truly implies escaping a terrible trade when you can. That implies you may have an arrangement of criteria or are seeing some sort of value activity which will get you out of a trade before it hits your stop-loss arrange. It likewise implies not carelessly sticking on to a trade when it's well past your stop, in the expectation that it will return for you. Giving a trade a chance to keep running past your foreordained stop loss is terrible money administration and will make you assume a loss considerably bigger than you made arrangements for. Loathing losing can likewise be a major help as well. An incredible arrangement has been said in regards to utilising our regular feelings to accomplish craved reactions. On the off chance that you can utilise it to persuade you to get ready appropriately, to ensure you're rationally prepared to trade, engaged and free from diversion, at that point that is a positive reaction to the compelling feeling. Survey the trade after a short break. Comprehend why it turned into a losing trade. Were there any signs showing you shouldn't have entered the trade? How might you gain from it? What will you do any other way next time? Was it a player in your system? Positive proclamations intended to support new conviction frameworks, positive considering and conduct change. Losing trades are a piece of the pathway to my trading achievement. Attempt to utilise losing trades as a chance to develop and learn as a trader. Traders are constantly prescribed to welcome the achievement that accompanies losing trades and try to avoid panicking on that 'I am a fruitful trader whether I make a benefit or a loss.' Imagine an obstruction amongst yourself and the trade that shields you candidly from what is occurring while trading. Do not concentrate on this one trade. Take a gander at your profile through the span of half a month and months. Keep in mind, trading is a venture. For whatever length of time that you are transcendently going up, littler losing trades are only chances to learn. In the event that you think that it is difficult to envision, maybe pick a protest or thing that you can rationally envision handling feelings for.

Knowledge Estimation for Better Trades

On the off chance that a decent trading arrangement comes up short and you begin to trust there's some kind of problem with it, you're far more averse to stick to it. Be that as it may, considering all the exertion you've put into making, back testing and getting ready to trade your arrangement, it can act to make you feel unfit and less eager to put a similar exertion in once more. Estranging can be truly dangerous and push you into taking rash, vindicate sort trades and a position estimate you would not regularly take. Accepting at the time that the market must not be right and being irritated that it has the daringness to take money off you, you go on an individual campaign to bring it down. The market couldn't care less. With your head turning with the feelings of outrage, disillusionment, deficiency and whatever else, the genuine type of the market is probably going to end up plainly quite obscured. You may think, at the time, it's completely clear. However, that is most likely not the situation. Sincerely destabilising every one of the feelings which you feel, the high points and low points of every last trade can begin to be felt 100 fold. Each tick against you resembles an announcement of how awful you are at trading or how inept the market must be and at last drives you towards losing control. The first step to rectifying the problem clearly is recognition. This is the reason individuals strike into about keeping a diary. Regardless of the possibility that you think you know you have certain issues and what they are, a diary for a supported time frame can be an eye-opener with respect to why they happen and to what degree. Feeling terrible about losing trades doesn't mean you need to be controlled by untrained reactions to the feeling.

18 BIASES THAT EXPLAIN WHY TRADERS MAKE MISTAKES

Many entrepreneurs and rising stock traders charge full throttle into the business sectors with high-benefit desires. However, discover decently fast that profiting reliably isn't as simple as they anticipated. For a few, this acknowledgment can be very demoralising, especially in light of the fact that there are a couple of interests that fuel human feeling as essentially as trading. The possibilities of profiting regularly bait individuals into the trading field, yet the truth of losing cash can be a fast hindrance. In truth, most expert Wall Street traders have committed many trading errors, as indicated by trading specialists. The way to their possible achievement, nonetheless, is that the experts consider their oversights and figure out how to limit them going ahead. Dealers by and large purchase and offer securities all the more often and hold positions for considerably shorter periods than speculators. Such continuous trading and shorter holding periods can bring about mix-ups that can wipe out another broker's contributing capital rapidly. Committing errors is not terrible at all, and it is a piece of the procedure. However, when botches are made more than once, awful and unbeneficial propensities are shaped. The more terrible conduct you can dispose of from your trading, the better. It's good to commit errors. In the event that you aren't committing errors, you aren't learning. Be that as it may, it's totally inadmissible to rehash those missteps. The great thing about the share trading system is that you generally know when you're correct or off-base. In case you're losing cash, you've presumably accomplished something incorrectly. In the long run, if you learn not to rehash making similar mistakes, you'll begin coming up short on them. Here are the 18 most exclusive inclinations made by amateur brokers:

1. Little Readiness or Preparation

When you enter the market region, you would do well to be ready. Nonetheless, a couple of dealers play out the fundamental due persistence before moving quickly into the business sectors. It is said that in the event that you swim with the sharks, you better gain from the sharks. Hardly any books show you all that you have to think about trading stocks, so he suggests stacking the chances to support you by perusing however many as could be allowed. "You shouldn't disparage the time, devotion and duty it takes to be a fruitful dealer." You can't simply stroll into the market with a modest bunch of cash and hope to remove cash from the experts. In the event that that is the situation, you're betting, not trading.

2. Changing Trading Procedure after Consecutive Loss

Losing is unavoidable, and even the best traders will frequently acknowledge the loss. Changing your approach after a couple of losing trades sets you on the way to success. Adhering to your approach, each losing streak will end. A sudden market crumble, a surprising news discharge or the loss of your web association can occur at any moment. Be set up by having a settled stop loss set up. On the off chance that a solitary trade could wipe out your trading account, you have not gotten your work done as a trader.

3. Discouraging the Winner in You Too Early

This is an extremely great mix-up. Youthful dealers rush to take a little benefit when a position begins to go their direction and miss the huge move. Be understanding with winning trades. Apple is an extraordinary case. On the off chance that you had made a Rs. 10,000 interest in Apple in July 2002, nine months after the arrival of the main iPod, you would be a tycoon today. In any case, what number of individuals do you know who ended up becoming moguls trading Apple? Apple is a case of an organisation that everybody thinks about; its blast was before everybody's eyes, except it stayed under possessed by people in general.

4. Being Too Emotional about Money

As indicated by experts, the reason many rising traders neglect to reliably gain benefits is because of their view of cash. Dealers are required to portray, in a single word, what cash intends to them. Nine times out of 10, the appropriate responses are 'well-being,' "security" or 'power.' Excessively numerous brokers get so candidly included in their trades, long or short. In the event that trade conflicts with them, many feel they are losing security. That is the reason they have a tendency to respond so inwardly. Nobody can legitimately set up a broker for the enthusiastic exciting ride of the share trading system. Many fear being marked a failure.

5. Giving Loss a Chance to Mount

One of the characterising attributes of effective brokers is their capacity to assume a little less rapidly if a trade is not working out and proceed onward to the following trade thought. Unsuccessful brokers, then again, get deadened if trade conflicts with them. As opposed to making the speedy move to top a loss, they may clutch a losing position with the expectation that the trade will, in the end, work out. Notwithstanding tying up trading capital for an excessive time frame in a losing trade, such inaction may bring about mounting loss and serious exhaustion of capital.

6. Not Being Adaptive of Changes
Do you simply start up your PC, begin your trading programming and jump into the diagrams? Just as a plane pilot doesn't simply ask his co-pilot after the take-off where they are heading, a trader needs a point by point trading plan for the forthcoming trading session.

7. Giving Failures a Chance to Run
This is another great error. Youthful brokers become hopelessly enamoured with washouts and never get out. Be eager with losing trades! The way to losing trades is to set hard stop loss and proceed onward. Beginner traders search for pardons on why the market isn't right and clutch these fleabags. Keep in mind, the market is constantly right! You will hear pardons like "The stock is down so much, it can't go lower." Perhaps, unpractised brokers wavering to cut failures come from the way that it is conceding out.

8. Doing the Agreement Trades
One error youthful dealers make is becoming hopelessly enamoured with agreement trades. On the off chance that everyone adores the trade, it must be great, right? Agreement trades generally imply that all the news is estimated in. At that point, what happens is that assumption switches and unpractised traders never respond rapidly enough. They have a tendency to get halted out, even from a pessimistic standpoint conceivable time, lose all the cash they made and assert the diversion is fixed.

9. Suspecting Profits
Most traders would prefer not to recognise that a trade could betray them. They enter the market expecting they'll be effective, declining to

look in the rearview mirror. It's additional basis for developing brokers to utilise a minicomputer to foresee the amount they'll make and how they'll spend the undiscovered benefits! It is perilous to suspect the amount you'll make ahead of time. "Give the market a chance to disclose to you what you will make."

10. Not Completely Learning One of a Kind Technique

The reliable losing retail broker hops from starting with one technique then onto the next, wanting to falter over the Holy Grail. You need to acknowledge that there is no predominant trading technique and that it descends to your capacities to make a trading system work. Most trading specialists propose that if you need to trade effectively, you require an edge. What do you realise will give you some level of conviction?

11. Indiscriminately Following Mechanical Frameworks

A vast rate of traders utilise innovation, as web based trading stages that give graphing, investigate and back testing apparatuses to enable them to refine their procedures. A system and programming can give critical data about the specialised and key attributes about stocks. Be that as it may, numerous traders commit the normal error of depending excessively on these devices without a full comprehension of their abilities.

12. Not Figuring out How to Short

In the event that you neglect to figure out how to use short trading methodologies, you have removed yourself from various beneficial trades, specialists say. Many individuals believe that shorting is un-American or excessively dangerous. In any case, by not learning know how to go short, you're setting up a detour to one of the potential trading roads you need to acquire benefits, especially amid a declining market.

13. Awful Time-Administration Propensities

There are a huge number of stocks in the U.S. alone. There are securities trades in each significant nation, along with security markets, monetary standards, products and so on. With so much data, each great trader buckles down however they need to work shrewdly. Time administration likewise implies disregarding past trades. What's to come is before you. Agonising over what you could or should do is time squandered. What's more, time implies cash.

14. Giving Insight into the past to Assess Impact of Your Trading

Novice brokers watch a trade after they have left it and beat themselves up on the off chance that they have entered too soon. Different circumstances they attempt to discover reasons why a trade was a failure to change their entire trading approach on the spot. The expert broker gathers information and settles on taught trading choices in light of a sufficiently extensive specimen measure.

15. Inability to Execute Stop-Loss Orders

Stop-loss orders are critical for trading achievement and inability to execute them is one of the most exceedingly bad errors that can be made by a learner trader. Tight stop loss, for the most part, guarantee that loss is topped before they wind up noticeably sizeable. While there is a hazard that a stop arranged on long positions might be executed at levels well underneath those predetermined if the security holes lower, the advantages of such requests exceed this hazard. A conclusion to this basic trading botch is the point at which a dealer drops a stop arrange on a losing trade, just before it can be activated in light of the fact that he or she trusts that the security is getting to a point where it will switch course inescapably and empower the trade to even now be effective.

16. Not Concentrating on Your Qualities

A typical slip-up most inability dealers make is trading outside their customary range of familiarity. I frequently observe youthful traders have little achievement trading U.S. stocks, at that point they can choose likewise trade Brent unrefined lucks. Stick to what works. Work truly hard at what you are great at. That is the manner by which you end up plainly extraordinary at something. You could never observe an awesome stock financial specialist like Peter Lynch stop mid-profession to go trade here and now Greek obligation. Much the same as you wouldn't see Michael Jordan quit ball mid-vacation to go play baseball, you can't be incredible until you are great. That is the way you fabricate a long haul profession at this. Concentrate on your qualities.

17. Not Having a Trading Plan or Adhering to One

Experienced traders get into a trade with an all-around characterised design. They know their correct passage and leave focuses, the measure of money to be put resources into the trade and the most extreme loss they will take and so on. Novice brokers might probably not be going to have a trading plan set up before they initiate trading. Regardless of the possibility that they have an arrangement, they might be more inclined to relinquish it than prepared dealers if things are not going their direction. Then again, they may turn around course out and out 'whipsawed.'

18. Following the Herd

Another regular error made by new brokers is that they indiscriminately take after the crowd, and therefore, they may either wind up paying excessively for hot stocks or may start short positions in securities that have just dove and might be nearly pivoting. While experienced brokers take after the decree of "the pattern is your companion," they are used to leaving trades when they get excessively swarmed. New brokers may remain in a trade long after the savvy cash has moved out of it. Tenderfoot dealers may likewise not have the certainty to adopt a contrarian strategy when required.

It's the same trading stocks. Best dealers are always examining their specialty, searching for an extra edge that may enable them to settle on more-educated choices, given that they have kept their inclinations aside.

4 Trading Metrics to Boost Your Trading Performance

Trades, once in a while, work out as arranged. To start with, you need to pick your entrance and find sensible levels for your stop loss and benefit arrange which enables you to trade with a not too bad reward-hazard proportion. At that point, your trade is presented to advertise instability, the vulnerability of money related markets and your own passionate reactions and driving forces. Regardless of the possibility that trade begins with an inspirational standpoint and great conditions, things typically change. Stops get hit, orders are moved around, and benefits are taken too soon or past the point of no return or instability grabs your requests. There are four trading measurements which can enable brokers to assess their trades a superior way. Trading execution is something that I have by and by been examining for more than 15 years. It's one of those subjects that numerous traders either stay away from or invest little energy investigating. Most traders essentially consider execution regarding rupees made and lost. The main issue, as far as rupees, is dependably a definitive score. Be that as it may, alongside your trading venture, successfully measuring your day trading execution is the way to steady long haul picks up. In an alternate article, we have a couple of tips that can help you discover approaches to wind up a more beneficial dealer. In the accompanying article, we demonstrate to you how you can build your execution by breaking down your trading execution information in a productive way.

1. Trading Behaviour Impacts

Most traders only concentrate on the hazard remunerate proportion after entering a trade. Be that as it may, simply consider each one of those circumstances when you move around stops loss and take benefit arranges or shut a trade in front of your take benefit. To comprehend your trading conduct, it is critical that you track and assess both. The hazard remunerates proportion when you enter the trade and when you leave your trade. Monitoring how your choices affect your trading execution can help you effortlessly spot negative examples in your trading. Trading practices can be communicated in many structures and complex calculations. However, it's basically the instrument used to assess a broker's arrival and hazard resistance or deficiency in that department. A wide range of brokers can be measured, from informal investors to swing traders and everything in the middle. Tried and true way of thinking would disclose to you that with such a variety of numbers introduced on a page, you ought to have the capacity to zone in on your concern. The discussions with traders have demonstrated to me the inverse. Brokers wind up plainly embittered with every one of the proportions and recipes on the grounds that the larger part of us are not analysts on the most fundamental level. Most traders measure their reward-chance proportion. You get the reward-chance proportion by looking at the separation of your entrance and stop cost, to the separation of your entrance to your objective. Accordingly, the proportion looks at the potential hazard and the benefit capability of your trade. The reward-chance proportion is an imperative measure, since it breaks down if a trade merits taking in any case. In any case, numerous brokers picked extensive reward-hazard proportion by utilising stops that are too tight or benefit target which is excessively hopeful. On the other hand, they legitimise taking average trades by arbitrarily picking an expanded reward-chance proportion. Most dynamic brokers and informal investors are visual students. Why else would we feel totally open to sitting before glimmering screens for quite a long time at any given moment? What is good performance? This is an interminable burn that traders experience where they feel that if no one but they could be as better as the following broker, some way or another, everything in their expert trading vocation would mystically adjust. The primary outcome of putting the market in a 50/50 suggestion does not know whether you will wind up winning, by any stretch of the imagination and that one is a bummer. You will have decreased your future to what might as well be called a solitary flip of a coin. Has anybody seen that there is no individual here and now traders that have gone on for a considerable length of time? It was then proposed to separate tradable data from all the accessible information with an eye on n since it included so much the last yield of a trading system.

2. Strong Price Behaviour and Improving Orders

By contrasting your underlying prize hazard proportion with the ultimate result of your trade, you can get new experiences into your trading, regardless of whether your request situation was right or not. The idea of R-different (R remains for hazard) measures the result of your trade terms of the hazard. For instance, a long trade from Rs. 100, with a stop at Rs. 90 and the last leave value level at Rs. 120 has the result of +2R – the result was double the span of the hazard. Had the trader shut his trade for a loss at Rs. 90, the result would be - 1R. Another vital measurement, with regards to understanding your trading execution, is following the value run amid the length of your trades. How frequently have you been in benefits in a trade but it didn't make it to your take benefit arrange? In the event that you constantly observe this transpiring, setting your take benefit arranges somewhat nearer can fundamentally build your trading execution. Then again, on the off chance that you set your stop loss arranges too far away, you are reducing your hazard compensate proportion. Thus, reducing the entire hope of your trading technique. In the event that you see that cost, once in a while, approaches your stop loss arrange, you can build your execution effortlessly by utilising littler stop loss orders. Despite the fact that numerous brokers know about those two measurements, they don't look at them definitively. A dealer who can see that his last R-various is generally substantially littler than his underlying prize hazard proportion may see that he is having issues with giving victors a chance to run or that his benefit targets are excessively hopeful. Most extreme draw down speaks to how much cash you lose from a current record high before making another high on your record. For instance, in the event that you simply had a high of Rs. 100,000 and after that, draw back to Rs. 85,000 before surpassing Rs. 100,000, you would have a most extreme draw down of 15% (Rs. 85,000/100,000). The greatest draw down is presumably the most profitable key execution pointer you should screen with regards to trading execution. As I have talked about in past articles, the line between traders that explore their records and the main 10% of traders is the capacity to limit your draw downs. Numbers don't lie and once a broker can evaluate that his trade administration and additionally arrange situation does not function admirably with the market he is trading, he can make changes particular and focused on alterations.

3. Customised and Quantifiable Data

Indeed, now it's a great opportunity to take the discussion to the next level. Keeping in mind the end goal to gauge your execution, you have to first decide what number of trades you require in a cycle. Next, we have to begin following your R and most extreme draw down finished your favoured trading cycle. Toward the finish of each cycle, you will need to report the estimation of R and the greatest draw down qualities. At the point when traders break down their execution, they more often than not toss every one of their information together and after that, attempt to comprehend it. Frequently, brokers trade diverse setups, blends of markers or utilise distinctive trading devices to settle on trading choices. Besides, traders manage interesting issues and face singular issues in their day by day trading. What you will see is, you will start to set up your benchmark as a broker after your initial 5 to 10 cycles. In your first cycle, you may have a. 35 for R and a 25% for draw down. Try not to think about the numbers as great or terrible, recollect that it's all relative and novel to your trading venture. As you keep on establishing your gauge, several things will happen. One, you are moulding your psyche to think in shorter spans. As traders, we have a tendency to lose ourselves in a trade, wanting to become famous, we turn out to be candidly stuck. This is a side-effect of losing a grasp on the idea of time, which means we have huge amounts of it. It's truly basic when you separate it. Do you regularly extend stop loss orders, add to losing trades, close trades too soon, enter past the point of no return, take trades that are not in your trading plan or move stops excessively close? These are only a couple of the remarkable issues that brokers manage and understanding what makes you do certain things and how they affect your execution is vital in the event that you need to bring an end to negative behaviour patterns. These reproductions just serve to state that there is something there worth something other than a look. Particularly, in the event that it depends on such an extended numerical scenery. As said somewhere else: an equivalent sign is an intense proclamation. Additionally, a straightforward perception, if there was nothing there. At that point, the re-enactments would have demonstrated it. They, as a rule, are without kindness on such things.

No matter what we look like at the market diversion, it remains a CAGR (Compound Annual Growth Rate) amusement, and we must plan the best trading techniques we can. Yet, that does not imply that we will have the capacity to get away from the math of the diversion.

4. Future Performance Projection

Regardless of whether traders need to acknowledge it or not, with the end goal for you to make a benefit, another person must be on the flip side of the trade. Since it doesn't mean they will lose at last, yet think about having demonstrated that 85% - 90% of informal investors fizzle at turning a steady benefit. In this way, rather than running another person's race and agonising over their profits, be content with you. Quit asking how much cash you ought to be making or what a practical return is, begin characterising that in view of your capacities. When you know your execution insights and trading conduct, you can extend your execution into the future to comprehend hazard parameters much better. You would then be able to assess what's in store and how likely certain situations are. Moreover, anticipating your execution and conceivable situations into the future can enable you to improve your hazard and cash administration to maintain a strategic distance from the enormous draw down or different difficulties. The MAE is the biggest experienced loss amid a trade. It gauges how far cost conflicted with you. For instance, for a long trade with a section at Rs. 100 and the most minimal cost of Rs. 94 amid the length of that trade, you had a Rs. 10 MAE – with a stop at Rs. 90, the MAE (Maximum Adverse Excursion) could be communicated as 60%. The MAE estimation can be utilised to break down the adequacy of stop situation. A dealer with a low general MAE could conceivably expand his hope and the measure of his champs by utilising a more tightly stop. In any case, altering stop-estimate must be finished with mind, since a more tightly stop, as a rule, prompts a higher loss rate. The MFE (Maximum Favourable Excursion) is the inverse of the MAE and it gauges the biggest watched benefit amid a trade. A high MFE on losing trades demonstrates that cost went near the benefit taking a level, before transforming and running into the stop loss. A dealer could, at that point, conceivably enhance his approach by utilising benefit focuses on those that are somewhat more preservationist. Once more, changing request arrangement must be finished with the mind. A more tightly benefit adopting strategy prompts a lessened hope. A dealer, along these lines, needs to locate the correct harmony between utilising a little take benefit level to abstain from giving back benefits and not decreasing his general hope in the meantime.

Quit fixating on the many trading execution markers and reports. You have to set up an essential trading execution measurement revolved around gainfulness and measure these in short dashes. Past execution is not characteristic of future outcomes. The situation of unforeseen requests by you or specialist or trading consultant, for example, a "stop-loss" or "stop-restrain" arrange, won't really confine your loss to the expected sums, since economic situations may make it difficult to execute such requests.

Goals: Improve Profitability by Setting Goals

A business profitability objective decides the measure of income you have to create your business to meet your costs and turn a benefit. If you intend to maintain your business effectively, you require clear, particular objectives set up. That isn't generally an objective, since it's not particular, and it does exclude a progression of ventures to make it a reality. The benefit objective is the measure of cash you have to meet various foreordained responsibilities that are essential to both you and to the fate of your business. The financial plan or vital arrangement incorporates monetary execution objectives or some likeness thereof. As a rule, regardless of whether an organisation meets its objectives for development or profitability is the measuring stick for measuring achievement or disappointment, the premise whereupon budgetary motivating forces are paid out to chiefs and a strategic driver of shareholder returns.

Considering Financial Strategy Enhances Chances Profitability

A typical business objective is to run a beneficial operation, which normally implies expanding income while restricting costs.

Income objectives could comprise of expanding yearly deals by 10% or landing three new records every month. Cost objectives could include finding another working office that reduce your lease by Rs. 200 a month or cut month to month service charges by 15%. Monetary goals concentrate on accomplishing adequate gainfulness in an organisation's quest for its main goal/vision, long haul wellbeing and extreme survival. Budgetary destinations flag sense of duty regarding such results as great income, financial soundness and profit development, an adequate rate of profitability, profit development and stock value appreciation. You have to choose how much benefit you need your business to produce throughout the year. This could be a set dollar sum or a rate increment over the earlier year's deals. In the event that this figure isn't a particular sum, you won't know whether you have achieved your objective or not. The particular money related destinations organisations set for they can matter an awesome arrangement. Setting focuses on that are excessively forceful can imply that even the best endeavours go unrewarded, leaving individuals crippled. At long last, defining the correct objective for the wrong objective, say, concentrating on expanding deals when the issue is discouraged profitability can leave an association battling, even when its objectives have been met.

Strategic Implementation Improve Profitability

Strategic market objectives concentrate on the organisation's plan to support and enhance their aggressive quality and long haul showcase position through making client esteem. Cases of client benefit objectives are to build up discernment that your organisation is anything but difficult to work with or to enhance your reaction time to client dissensions. Objectives to help meet these objectives could be expanding your client benefit staff for one to three labourers, before the year's over or executing an arrangement where clients are ensured to get an arrival telephone call before the finish of the business day. Strategic goals concentrate on winning an extra piece of the pie, overwhelming strategic contenders on item quality or client administration or item development, accomplishing lower general expenses than rivals, boosting the organisation's notoriety with clients, winning a more grounded decent footing in worldwide markets, practicing innovative initiative, picking up a maintainable upper hand and catching alluring development openings. There is an approach to gauge an organisation's relative execution, set objectives and gauge the likelihood of accomplishing determined focuses over various eras that enable supervisors to oppose the draw of techniques that are regularly generally utilised, yet can be hazardously deceptive. Counting this approach as a feature of an organisation's objective setting procedure can prompt more reasonable objectives.

Employee Retention and Customer Satisfaction for Profitability

In case you have encountered an issue with employee turnover, your general objective could be to enhance maintenance. To accomplish this objective, your goal may be to create and execute a preparation program that subtle elements new-contract exercises for the initial 90 days at work. You additionally could execute one-on-one gatherings with your workers, with an end goal to assemble affinity and discover what is at the forefront of their thoughts. Another objective could be to end up noticeably more effective in your business operation, as an approach to expand profitability. To enhance profitability, you could challenge your business people to enhance their end proportion from 30% to 45%. In the event that you disperse an item, you should seriously mull over actualising another transportation technique that enhances your conveyance time from four days to two. Maybe you will likely develop your business operation. On the off chance that you possess an establishment unit, for instance, your goal may be to open three more units inside a five-year time frame. On the off chance that you work at a retail location, your goal may be to expand your offering space by 25%, by finishing an expansion to your working inside a year. Strategic goals should be contender centred and fortify the organisation's long haul aggressive position. An organisation shows vital aim when it seeks after driven strategic objectives and focuses its aggressive activities and energies on accomplishing that goal.

Sustainable Approach for Organisational Profitability

An elaborate plan must be produced in the event that you want to achieve your benefit objective. When you have a specific figure at the top of the priority list, you and your staff need to decide every one of the means important to achieve that objective and follow up on them. Audit your organisation's advance at general interims, so you can proceed with the techniques that function admirably and change or dispose of the ones that don't give the outcomes you are searching for. There is no reason for proceeding with a system or an approach that is not adding to your business incomes after you have given them a decent opportunity to pay off for you. By then, it's an ideal opportunity to have a go at something else. Come back to future development is the sum you have to contribute to future development and advancement of your business. You may need to extend your premises following a couple of years, build up an inventive approach to give an administration or new items or build up developed promotional strategy.

Luck vs. Skill for Trade Success

In the business sectors, luck and skill are hard to unwind. A considerable measure of value activity is usually commotion, prompting semi-arbitrary returns over a ton of time allotments. Our win rate with any contributing methodology will never be 100%, so we need to battle with the disappointment of putting on positions and regularly losing cash. Indeed, even the best brokers will encounter drawdown. However, that shouldn't deflect us from the quest for certified skill and authority. Fence investments trader, Bruce Bower, discloses how to deal with this. What's more, he will examine the head approach to winding up noticeably reliably gainful, by means of concentrating as much on understanding and enhancing the procedure, as opposed to putting excessive weight on single trades. Ordinarily, great brokers make the correct trade yet lose. However, it is alright in light of the fact that they will win in the long haul on the grounds that their strategy is tried, their hazard is overseen and their attitude is appropriate for long haul trading achievement. They have built up the skills of a fruitful dealer. In different circumstances, another dealer without any skills makes a trade in view of a hunch and wins enormous, the peril is that the new broker will mistake luck for ability.

Strategy Is Inevitable to Utilise Skill

There appears to be no end of stories about amateur speculators who hit the big stake instantly, producing restores that would make even masters jealous. So what is it about these venture chiefs and informal investors that they can finish this? Is it being great or being fortunate? Dealers with expertise have expansive increases after 100 trades and are moderately tranquil, brokers that were fortunate have tremendous increases after a couple of trades and are boisterous, at that point calm for the following couple of trades that generally convey their record to zero. Dealers with expertise hazard 1% to 2% of their trading capital per trade and win in the long haul, merchants that are quite recently fortunate hazard the larger part of their record for a couple of huge wins for the time being. However, they lose in the long haul when their luck runs out. Traders with skill utilise an effective strategy with various stocks, monetary forms, wares and future markets, while brokers with just luck are just fruitful with one fortunate pick in one of those business sectors and when it is up drift closes their triumphant streak closes. Brokers with ability have winning track records over numerous years. Traders with just luck just have winning track records measured in months. Brokers with ability have a chance administration as a top need. Merchants with just luck don't comprehend why the chance administration is critical, yet.

Luck and Skill Blends Success

It is helpful to make a stride back to consider why wagering on proceeding with progress doesn't work in contributing. It positively works in numerous different fields. For example, you can rely on the best chess players, sprinters or piano players to keep on performing at an abnormal state for their next match, race or show. In these exercises, comes about relate very with skill and luck assumes almost no part. Be that as it may, luck assumes an enormous part in deciding outcomes in contributing, particularly for the time being. Luck is additionally noticeable in the business system and card amusements, including blackjack and poker. One approach to consider the contrast between the outcomes for musicians and poker players is to imagine a continuum with all luck toward one side and all ability on the other side. At that point, put exercises along that continuum. Roulette haggles are on the luck side and swim and group races are on the skill side. The vast majority of the activity in life sits between those extremes. Brokers with skill are trading like it is a business. Traders working with luck are trading like they are a speculator in a gambling club. Merchants with ability utilise a trading plan and back tried the strategy. Traders with luck make surmises and are, once in a while, right. Dealers with expertise have gotten their work done. Merchants with luck think they are normally more quick-witted than the market.

Diagnosing System Is Recommended Ever

Regardless of what procedure you take in and from whom, you all must dependably make it a propensity to test it on a demo represent some time before you go live. The demo account is one of the ideal routes for a broker to try out a procedure. Initially, you can do a back testing on the system for no less than 3 months and then do a live testing on the methodology for an additional 2 months, and you will know how viable the technique is. Backtesting implies that you simply need to pull the graph back a while and gradually experience the diagram to see the section and the result. You will then need to record it down. From that point forward, you will do a live testing, which implies that you will trade the system on the demo itself to see the viability. Once the system figures out how to create benefits for the greater part of the months or for me, it must be each month, I will then trade it live on a live record. Dealers with ability are trained and adhere to their framework. Traders with luck make wagers in view of opinions. To locate a decent venture supervisor, take a gander at the measure of use that is being utilised to get a clearer examination between administrators. On the off chance that somebody has 10 times use, they may get 20% returns as a result of that use, rather than the 2% that every other person is gets and not on account of their splendid technique.

Use Luck as Educated Skill

Financial specialists ought to know about what sort of profits they need to see to discover the venture director that fits their style best, he includes. A few people incline toward outright execution, where they might want to get, for instance, a 5% restore each year, while others like relative execution, which includes beating a record. How regularly have we heard the articulation 'preferred fortunate over great'? In some ways, it's very interesting. We expect that luck can't be educated and skills can, so we'd like to have luck and take in the ability part later. We think that it is intriguing in a trade setting, on the grounds that most would like to have the recently genuine skill or far better, ability and good luck. In the business sectors, luck and expertise are hard to unravel. A great deal of value activity is frequently commotion, prompting semi-arbitrary returns over a considerable measure of time spans. Our win rate with any contributing methodology will never be 100%, so we need to battle with the disappointment of putting on positions and regularly losing cash. Dealing with the commitments of luck and skill is not generally simple. Be that as it may, even an essential feeling of where a movement lies on the good luck ability continuum can offer a significant contribution to the choices that you make – in contributing and past.

Neuroeconomics: Losing Money? Here's Why

A noteworthy point in the field of financial aspects is to utilise monetary ideal models with the apparatuses of neuroscience to pick up a comprehension of how people decide. By opening the "black box" and picturing what is going on inside the mind, the hidden intentions and the inactive procedures that drive basic leadership can be uncovered and fill in as an informative system for why people go astray from the sanctioned self-intrigue demonstrate. In this section, we audit the surviving neuroeconomics writing to pick up bits of knowledge about the diverse neural pathways that prompt pro-social choices. From this writing audit, we distinguish three mind frameworks that give off an impression of being reliably selected when individuals are confronting social quandaries. To be specific, the neural systems devoted to preparing reward, intellectual control and social discernment. Any individual who has been excessively frightened, making it impossible to offer a falling stock ("But I'll lose money!") or too offended to acknowledge Rs. 3 from somebody who means to keep the other Rs. 7 in free money given out in an investigation ("Why should he get far beyond me?" players of the Ultimatum Game think over and over) realises that feelings assume a part in our budgetary choices. Frequently, that is to our disservice, as the blossoming field of neuroeconomics suggests. In no less than one case, giving feelings a chance to direct us pays off for all concerned, a fascinating new examination finishes up and may clarify the "show proactive kindness" marvel, in which being the recipient of a kind or liberal deed motivates you to act out the kindness toward a third individual.

Traders Often Lack Profitable Framework

When we begin trading, regardless of whether it is a demo or genuine money account, we spend a few hours finding out about the craft of trading. We figure out how to decipher diagrams, news and pointers. I think most of the traders realise what are support and resistance lines, drift lines, overbought and oversold conditions, designs like twofold tops and bottoms, candle designs and other specialised devices and how to trade those, we take in these things in our initial 2 weeks or month. We get included in trading, that's true. Be that as it may, as time passes by we endeavour to take in everything that we heard around and we expect that more information will improve us as traders. That certification is valid, yet we miss the genuine setting around it. A few traders examine them and numerous others for quite a long time, despite the fact that they are not gainful traders. The reward framework, which incorporates areas of the striatum and the ventromedial prefrontal cortex, produces the thought process to collaborate by figuring typical money of unique reward sorts that accompany diverse choice results. Intellectual control, depending on districts of the parallel prefrontal cortex, empowers a leader to separate between settings with and without extraneous helpful motivating forces. Social cognisance includes an appropriated organisation, including the dorsomedial prefrontal cortex, temporoparietal intersection and amygdala and give individuals the ability to process trust signals from certain unobtrusive expressive gestures, (for example, facial components and motions) and also unequivocal social data. We propose a model to indicate the states of pro-social basic leadership. At the neural level, the choice to coordinate (or not) is the consequence of the modulator impact of psychological control and social discernment on the mind's reward framework. We talk about various neuroeconomics analyses to substantiate that the subjective control arrangement of the mind encourages financially level-headed, motivating force based participation, while social insight makes socially normal, trust-based collaboration conceivable.

Considering Reasonable Monetary Trades

Financial specialists have long held that we treat other individuals reasonably in monetary trades, since we think we should be thinking that in the event that we don't, the swindled gathering will correct requital on us down the line or if nothing else, demolish our great name, giving us notoriety for being an egotistical swindle. (Alright, this requirement didn't work too well when it came to offering lethal subsidiaries and other monetary items that sunk the worldwide economy a year ago.) Psychologist David DeSteno of Northeastern University presumes that we act respectably in light of the fact that we believe we ought to, not on account of what we think we should. For a certain something, feelings are considerably more established, developmentally, than the capacity to strategize about the future and about how your conduct will influence that of others. "We contend that feelings must exist that cultivate agreeably, long haul sees in monetary trade," DeSteno let me know. "To echo the perspectives of Adam Smith, people must have some 'ethical slants' which lead them to indicate worry" for individuals they work with. In any case, as of recently, he notes, "minimal experimental confirmation has been advanced to affirm." The possibility that feelings underlie whatever reason, even liberal, financial conduct we show. Despite what might be expected: a recent report found that inclination glad did not really encourage monetary collaboration. Trading includes pressure about everything said earlier and that's only the tip of the iceberg. Thus, the traders need to take this concern into their account in order to achieve the desired success from their approached trades. In this regard, it is also mentionable that a sufficient knowledge of trading economics keeps the traders ahead of the others. In any case, what the greater part of the general population disregards and scarcely anybody cautioned you before getting in this market is the trouble of basic leadership when you trade. Yet, to begin with, before going ahead, I have an inquiry: Would you give an unreasonable individual a chance to deal with your trading account, not making a difference in the event that he or she considered each and every part of the trading investigation?

Diversion in Trading

In an investigation upheld by the National Science Foundation and booked to be distributed in the diary Emotion, DeSteno and partners had 85 volunteers play a diversion in which half were made to feel thankful. More or less, the volunteers completed one long and irritating errand just to be advised they need to do everything over in light of the fact that the computed answers were smashed. However, a kindred volunteer (really one of the scientists) settles the computer, at some cost to herself in time and exertion, yet sparing the genuine volunteers from redoing the test. Presto! The volunteers feel quick appreciation. (The other portion of the volunteers didn't endure the fake PC crash, so they didn't feel a specific feeling after this piece of the trial.) All the volunteers at that point played one round of 'give a few' issue amusement. Each got four tokens that were worth Rs. 1 each to them and Rs. 2 to an accomplice. They could pick what number to keep and what number to provide for the accomplice, whom they accepted was settling on a comparable choice, in another room. The best joint result is for every player to give every one of the four tokens to the next, leaving each with Rs. 8 for a "shared" benefit of Rs. 16. Unadulterated self-intrigue, in any case, says to give away few or zero, guaranteeing that you get a few or the majority of your underlying Rs. 4, in addition to up to Rs. 8 increasingly, if the other player gives all of you four of his tokens (abandoning him with nothing, for a common benefit of Rs. 12). A large portion of the volunteers trusted they were playing the diversion with the individual who had quite recently helped them; the other half trusted they were playing with an outsider.

Behavioural Finance and Neuroeconomics

When we begin to consider how shrewd we will be, we immediately consider the accomplishments that the mankind has made. We have created inconceivable complex situations (monetary markets are the most complex of them). However, we ceased to commit similar errors again and again. Demonstration of this are the few times money related markets have pounded and the few times you lose a trade for similar reasons you guaranteed won't occur again only a couple of trades prior. However, this could not be totally our blame, I'm alluding that similar oversights about our choices can have further roots. A well-known analysis exhibits this, the examination made by Laurie R. Santos and M. Keith Chen demonstrates how the silly conduct lives with us for no less than 35 million years. The analysis included Brown capuchin monkeys as subjects; the hypothesis clarifies that even such far off relative as monkeys can mirror our conduct when we make choices. They reproduced the essential financial framework, educating the monkeys to utilise a kind of money (trust it or not, they say that it wasn't as troublesome as they thought, I urge you to scan for the consequences of this analysis), the monkeys began trade sustenance for money. The noteworthy outcomes came when they apply the behavioural choice hypothesis to the monkeys. Also, prepare to have your mind blown. They respond precisely as people, nonsensically. Two predispositions result from this analysis:

1. We scarcely think in outright terms, we have a tendency to associate the parameters of the conditions.
2. We have profound loss repugnance. Loss frightens us.

Numerous examinations were made about this field, incorporating the well-known research in the mid 60's that endeavoured to discover scientific clarifications for showcase developments. This flopped, yet something was found. The development of money related markets has a human component, something that can scarcely be foreseen in a recipe or an impeccable hypothesis. I'm not saying this can't be conceivable, just difficult to do so. As I comprehend, we may not change our approach to make choices over the time. However, we work inside business sectors that have an excessive number of changing factors, and they respond as erratically as the human conduct.

Assess and Flourish Trading Connection

Individuals who felt appreciation in light of their involvement in the initial segment of the examination gave away 25 percent, a larger number of tokens than controlled volunteers, whose feelings were not controlled. This held whether the accomplice was the individual of whom they felt appreciative or a more peculiar reason, demonstrating that their helpfulness, representing more prominent benefit, as opposed to out of unadulterated self-intrigue, was not driven by a feeling of correspondence. Rather, says DeSteno, "the more thankful one felt because of getting help, all the more agreeable one acted gratitude capacities to improve agreeable rather than narrow-minded monetary conduct." He hypothesises that regular choice supported the development of appreciation, which some of our gorilla cousins additionally appear to feel, since it helped our precursors shape stable "trade connections"— "you imparted your mammoth to me; here, have some of my berries." But appreciation, this examination appears, triggers agreeable, for-the-benefit of all conduct to the detriment of narrow-mindedness notwithstanding when the beneficiary of that participation is not the one you feel thankful to. Appreciation may, therefore, "increment the chances for collaboration" with loads of other individuals. Furthermore, along these lines was conceived "show proactive kindness."

Neuroeconomics, we contend, has additionally connected the once divergent fields of financial matters and brain research. Notwithstanding, this merging is only owing to changes in financial aspects. Neuroeconomics includes enlivened more change inside financial matters than inside brain science in light of the fact that the most imperative discoveries in neuroeconomics have postured all the more a test to the standard monetary point of view, than to overwhelming viewpoints inside brain research. For instance, a great part of the examination in neuroscience and in neuroeconomics challenges the bedrock presumption inside financial matters that basic leadership is a unitary procedure - a straightforward matter of coordinated and rational utility boost. A standout amongst the most vital bits of knowledge of neuroscience is that the cerebrum is not a homogeneous processor, but instead includes a merging of assorted specific procedures that are coordinated into various ways when the mind faces diverse sorts of issues. Particularly, a few financial analysts have come to value a refinement between program forms, which generally relate to what Tugwell called the "hardware for the old life" and controlled procedures, which compare what exactly Tugwell alluded to as the "energy of reflecting."

Intertemporal Option

Another focal point in financial aspects is intertemporal decision, choices including options whose expenses and advantages are dispersed after some time. Demonstrate is the prevailing model of the intertemporal decision in financial matters. In spite of the fact that the DU show, similar to the EU DU, reduced utility model can be gotten from an arrangement of primitive, instinctively convincing sayings, a few oddities have been distinguished that raise doubt about the model's graphic legitimacy. A standout amongst the most essential and regularly assessed suspicions of DU is the supposition of exponential reducing, which suggests that a given time postpone prompts a similar measure of markdown, paying little respect to when it happens. Deferring the conveyance of a decent by one day, for instance, apparently prompts a similar level of time marking down, whether that postpone has the effect of expanding the great tomorrow instead of today or in a year and a day as opposed to in a year. In any case, there is solid proof that individuals (and additionally creatures) don't rebate the future exponentially. Or maybe, individuals think more about a similar time delay on the off chance that it is proximal, instead of distal. A general example that has been alluded to as "hyperbolic time marking down." For example, deferring utilisation of a pleasurable descent from today to tomorrow is more upsetting than postponing utilisation from in twelve months to a year and a day from the present. Despite the fact that there are broadly acknowledged regularising benchmarks for hazardous basic leadership and intertemporal decision, no such benchmarks exist for how individuals ought to act toward others. Some hard-line business analysts have expected that unadulterated self-intrigue is, or ought to be, the standard, yet this is most likely a minority position. To stick to the conviction that individuals are simply childish would not just require that one overlooks boundless exploratory outcomes demonstrating the opposite. However, it would conflict with typical perceptions of conduct. The trial inquires about on "other-with respect to" conduct not just exhibits that individuals think about the welfare of others, yet additionally challenges the legitimacy of a portion of the more primitive models of social inclinations.

As you may comprehend the primary thing you should chip away at is your trading psychology, begin to consider your own particular conduct and how you will respond to some settling on choice circumstances. Set aside your opportunity to discover how you candidly react to the boost of trading, it will be hard, but in the event that you accomplish that, you will have something you can't get in any online class, book, supernatural occurrence framework or whatever another hypothesis you could buy at the 'right cost.'

Why 95% of Traders Lack Self Awareness

This may astonish you since the very actuality that you are ignorant of it demonstrates that you too are likely among the 95%. Most traders and most financial specialists "know" that trading is a session of brain research and is either won or lost relying upon your disposition. A little learning is a hazardous thing. It pushes you into a misguided sensation that all is well and good and causes numerous wrong choices. Having the scholarly comprehension is a certain something, yet applying this comprehension in a way that it is normal in your trading and contributing technique is something else. One reason why traders and speculators neglect to coordinate the information is that they basically do not have the comprehension of how their cerebrum functions, setting up barriers which could be maintained a strategic distance from with mindfulness and preparing. Keeping in mind the end goal to part from the crowd, there is a considerable measure of things that must be thought about you, human propensities and how these join to frame societal developments.

Loss in Trade Is Indispensable – Take It Easy Straight
Most traders have heard the insights, "95% of traders lose money," "Just 5% of brokers can bring home the bacon at it," or "Just 1%

of brokers truly profit." Whatever the specific number is from late examinations, the truth of the matter is, numerous traders will lose money and it basically can't be kept away from (for some hard numbers, see The Day Trading Success Rate, The Thorough Answer). A more profound reason in the matter of why most traders will lose paying little mind to what techniques they utilise. I indicate that regardless of the possibility that all traders knew how (remember knowing, and doing are two altogether different things) to trade effectively in view of current conditions, most traders would still lose as time goes on. Preparing is, obviously, something traders and speculators alike don't care for excessively. They accept as long as they have a procedure that has appeared to work and that is sufficient. Each games mentor will reveal to you that chipping away at their psychological distraction is the mystery edge of every single best entertainer. It is truly intriguing that while a support stock investment may make a normal of 20%/year in the course of the most recent 20 years, the normal financial specialist in that store has a high penchant to make far not as much as that. Why? Since they contribute and haul out their assets at the wrong focuses, as they do in the market.

Consider Market as Aggregate of Activities

80% of the informal investors stopped inside the initial two years. Among the informal investors, about 40%-day trade for just a single month. Inside three years, just 13% keep on a day trade. Following five years, just 7% remain. Traders offer victors at a half higher rate than failures. 60% of offers are victors, while 40% of offers are washouts. The normal individual financial specialist fails to meet expectations of a market record by 1.5% every year. Dynamic traders fail to meet expectations by 6.5% every year. Traders kept on saying that they wouldn't see any problems with doing anything as long as it yielded the high money related prizes they have been getting from trading. Why most brokers lose money and what traders regularly neglect to acknowledge is that the market is the aggregate development of their activities and responses to their own behaviour and to other individuals' activities. Sounds confounding. Consider this: You tee up a trade, close your eyes and hit "enter" (open the trade). You have no clue what the market is doing (your eyes are still shut). However, you start to respond to your action. You think about whether you settled on the correct choice, on the off chance that you ought to change your stop loss or in the event that you ought to have gotten in before or later. That keeps on happening after you open your eyes and perceive how your activity (trade) is acting in connection with other individuals' activities and responses. Indeed, even prepared traders can experience these feelings on occasion. At the end of the day, the market is a monster criticism circle, demonstrating brokers (and any individual who sees the market) a thermometer perusing of the social inclination under which traders and by expansion, society are working.

Coordination and Collectiveness for Profitable Trading

Most traders assume that the market is something that has some outer incentive outside of the value credited to it by traders. I like to consider it a continuous gaze of the general public's perspective of their own gainful limit or just social state of mind. At the point when markets are comprehended, the possibility that everybody can profit is off base as well as outlandish and ludicrous. Everybody profiting implies there is no market, since who might be taking the opposite side of the trade? Also, most traders feel they can move with the group to make a (paper) benefit and after that, get out before the group, transforming that trade into a genuine benefit. In principle, this is sound, yet recollect, every other person is embarking on doing a similar thing. It is this group development which enables traders to profit now and again. Without an expansive bit of traders going to a similar choice, markets basically would not move. It takes conviction by numerous traders to make a pattern, at that point it takes euphoric acknowledgment that as the new standard to end it and 'twist it.' It takes mass disappointment to crash it the other way. In all honesty, I was flabbergasted by the reaction, not by any means shocked. Things change, and we should change with them. As the world is experiencing an aggregate rising procedure where everybody is being compelled to take a gander at what they are doing from the viewpoint of new mindfulness, regardless of where they live on the transformative scale, this stances numerous a test the same number of traders are confronting up to the way that their cognisance is changing how they feel about numerous things in life, trading and contributing included.

Comparable Techniques Market Development

The cerebrum dislikes change. It works from known parameters alone. Known parameters just exist before. When one is confronting monstrous changes as the world is confronting today, the minor idea of investigating an obscure future is overwhelming. Individuals return to old propensities and look to the past for answers for what's to come. Trading and contributing choices are made in light of results usually frequently prompting enormous loss. Consider for a minute if each trader took after the management of not gambling over 1% of their record for every trade and utilised comparable techniques toted by experts. Stop loss requests would trigger everywhere and costs would blow up and empty. Similarly, as they do now with individuals holding fast to their own (and diverse sorts of) systems! At the end of the day, everybody attempting to do the same "right" thing makes a similar market development as everybody doing their own "wrong" thing. Informal investors with solid past execution go ahead to procure solid returns later on, despite the fact that around 1% of the informal investors can typically benefit net of expenses. This recommends informal investors even keep on trading when they get a negative flag with respect to their capacity. Beneficial informal investors make up a little extent of all traders – 1.6% in the normal year. However, these informal investors are extremely dynamic – representing 12% of throughout the day trading movement.

Recognising Social Inclination for Market Growth

With encounter, traders can figure out how to move with the group and furthermore, understand the group's flighty nature (and their own whimsical nature too). Traders may likewise, at last, discover that social inclination directs the business sectors and the news. This is straightforwardly restricted to the regularly held view that the news and the market manage the social inclination. Effective traders discover something that works and stick to it, not giving others a chance to pull them far from their system. This is the place most traders turn out badly and why the group loses money. Regardless of a great many people's earnest attempts, they can't pull themselves far from the group when it truly checks. Among all traders, beneficial brokers increment their trading more than unrewarding informal investors. Poor people have a tendency to spend a more noteworthy extent of their wage on lottery buys and their interest in lottery increments with a decrease in their pay. Speculators with an extensive differential between their current financial conditions and their desire levels hold less secure stocks in their portfolios. As a rule, trading choices are not in view of sound research or tried trading strategies, however, on feelings, the requirement for stimulation and the plan to make a million rupees in your clothing. Figuring out how to perceive when one's discernment is changing is a major thing. Achievement is from being in arrangement with what you do. Do you truly know what it feels like to be completely adjusted? A great many people don't.

Why Your Mind Will Forever Keep You a Losing Trader

Before the diagrams, you are the cause of all your own problems. Giving 100 individuals a similar system will have 2 of them proven to be the best as productive dealers and the other 98 will blow their records eventually. This is the interminable truth of trading and furthermore, the motivation behind why there is no widespread sacred vessel that holds recovery for everybody that beverages out of it. Truly, there isn't. You need to, at last, get this in your mind, help yourself out, please. You are the sacred vessel. What's more, in the meantime, you are the one that shields yourself from turning into your own sacred chalice. In trading, the vast majority of us are underweight when a trade is opened. Most individuals encounter comparable intuition examples and feelings as they trade the business sectors, and we can take in numerous imperative things from the distinctions in the way losing brokers think and the way winning dealers think. A significant number of us are even underweight before they put a trade on the grounds that they need to make a million rupees appropriate here, at this moment. Clearly, this mindset will keep you from perpetually making a single penny in trading.

Never Give up Gainfulness and Objective Trading

'Improbable Expectations' and 'No Work-Life-Balance' are thought to be the two moms of every single mental issue you have in your trading – fretfulness, outrage, dissatisfaction, dread, nervousness and ravenousness. They all originate from unlikely desires and being in an awful mentality from the get-go. Clearly, far-fetched desires come from false advertising and claims of individuals saying that they transformed Rs. 1000 into a million rupees and that you can do it, as well. No, you can't. Regardless of the possibility that their cases were valid, they are exceptions! Why do you think you would be the next anomaly? Is it true that you are that extraordinary? I wager not. To start with, you need to achieve gainfulness in any capacity. At that point, you can consider how to adapt that gainfulness. Be that as it may, you can't begin trading with the objective to make a fortune out of nothing, no. Once beneficial, you have a ton of decisions – flag administrations, tutoring, overseeing cash. This is the way the genuine cash in this industry is made, NOT in some other way. So, your objective ought to be to wind up plainly beneficial. 10% ROI per year and you are world class. That ought to be your definitive objective. In any case, before that, your first objective ought to be to secure your cash, no matter what. A more intensive look at the feelings that harm us will uncover that they are, for the most part, our own special manifestations, as all feelings seem to be, incidentally. In any case, most Forex sites attempting to offer some marker or the robot-based trading framework won't reveal to you this, since they need you to trust that you can profit in the business sectors essentially by purchasing their trading item.

Enthusiasm for Positive Trading

You have presumably heard that the vast majority who endeavour Forex trading wind up losing cash. There's a justifiable reason purpose behind this and the reason is fundamental that the vast majority consider trading the wrong light. The vast majority come from the business sectors with improbable desires, for example, supposing they will stop their employments following a time of trading or supposing they will transform Rs. 1,000 into Rs. 100,000 in a couple of months. These impossible desires work to cultivate a record pulverising trading mentality in many brokers, since they feel excessive weight or "need" to profit in the business sectors. When you start trading with this "need" or weight to profit, you will unbelievably wind up trading inwardly, which is the speediest approach to lose your cash. To be a smidgen more particular about 'enthusiastic trading,' we should go over the absolute most basic passionate trading botches that dealers make.

Voracity: Traders are insatiable when they don't take benefits, since they think a trade will always to support them.

Dread: Traders end up plainly frightful of entering the market more often than not when they are new to trading and have not yet faced a powerful trading technique like value activity trading.

Tension: It will strike after a triumphant streak. You feel that some way or another you, at long last, "made it" and that the following trade could be a failure and wreck your fantasies by and by.

Reprisal: Traders encounter a sentiment needing "exact retribution" available when they endure a losing trade that they were "certain" would work out. The key thing here is that there is no "certain" thing in trading.

Elation: While feeling euphoric is normally something to be thankful for, it can really do a great deal of harm to a broker's record after he or she hits a major champ or an expansive series of vectors.

Eagerness: It emerges in light of the fact that you need it all and you need it now. In the event that you need to make at least 20% every month, just to take care of your expenses or to achieve your improbable desires, this will lead you to overtrading, over-sizing your positions and driving trades.

Outrage: It is an aftereffect of both unreasonable desires and no work-life adjust. On the off chance that your entire fulfilment or your self-valuation as a person is received from your outcomes in trading, you will be on a consistent thrill ride set out straight toward hellfire.

Disappointment: It will get you when you are productive, despite the fact that you are now superior to 99% of dealers. You are forever discontent since you can't achieve your fiscal objectives which are set far too high.

Never Stay Away from Reality – Believe You Survive

Numerous dealers go into a spiral of passionate trading and losing cash after they hit a series of champs. The reason this happens is that they feel certain and euphoric and disregard the genuine threat of the market and that any trade can lose. The way to recall here is that trading is a long-haul round of probabilities, on the off chance that you have a high-likelihood trading edge, you will, in the end, profit over the long haul accepting you take after your trading edge with the train. Be that as it may, regardless of the possibility that your edge is 70% effective after some time, you could even now hit 30 losing trades a column out of 100. So, remember this reality and forget you never know which trade will be a "failure" and which will be a 'champ.' Acquiring and keeping up a viable Forex trading attitude is the consequence of doing a ton of things right and it requires a needful exertion for the dealer's benefit to fulfil this. It's not really hard to accomplish, but in the event that you need to build up a viable trading attitude, you need to acknowledge certain actualities about trading and then trade the market in light of these certainties. You have to realise what your a trading methodology (trading edge) is, and you have to face it. You need to wind up noticeably an "expert rifleman" in the market, rather than a "heavy weapons specialist." This includes knowing your trading methodology all around and having positively NO inquiries concerning what the market needs to look like before you hazard your well-deserved cash in it. You have to dependably deal with your hazard appropriately. On the off chance that you don't control your hazard on each and every trade, you open the entryway for enthusiastic trading to grab hold of your psyche. You can, to a great extent, dispose of the likelihood of turning into an excessively passionate dealer by just taking a chance with a measure of cash for each trade that you are 100% satisfied with losing.

Control Self-psyche and Know Self-psyche for Success

The thing with our psyche is that the vast majority are controlled by it. It reveals to us what to think, when to eat, when to rest, when to be cheerful and when to be pitiful. We are a play ball of our intuitive. In any case, we do have the ability to control our considerations and our feelings. We have the ability to make our mind work for us, rather than against us. However, this requires a ton of mental quality and many essentially don't have that quality or don't know about how they are controlling themselves. You should not over-trade. Most traders trade an abundant excess. You have to realise what your trading edge is with 100% assurance and after that, lone trade when it's available. You commence an exciting ride of enthusiastic trading that can be difficult to stop. Try not to begin trading and you will probably not turn into a passionate Forex broker. You additionally need to end up a composed trade. In the event that there is something that is the 'paste' that holds the majority of the focuses I've talked about in this part together, it is being a sorted-out trade. By sorting out, I mean having a trading plan and a trading diary and really utilising them reliably. At whatever point you wind up in an unpleasant spot, don't give your mind a chance to bamboozle you, since it is the cause of all your own problems.

Trading Behaviour – Emotion vs. Logic

One of the longest-running level headed discussions in promoting is whether to utilise a balanced or passionate publicising approach in marketing, but intellectual science says that contention is silly. While emotions overwhelmingly drive conduct, it is confused to trust that reasoning and emotion are by one means or another fundamentally unrelated. Emotion and logic are entwined. Everyone has inclinations. We make judgments about individuals, openings, Washington strategies and obviously, the business sectors. When we break down our reality without thinking about these inclinations, we put our perceptions through various channels produced by our encounters. At the point when a trader's mind is dissected, it is the same as a normal human cerebrum! Do you trade inwardly? On the other hand, do you see yourself as to be a coherent trader? Traders' psychology, irrespective of their trading strategies, can be followed along a range of outright emotionless legitimate scholars to a passionate trader who constructs his/her trades light of emotions. Striking a harmony between the two is the thing that most traders battle with. In the 1970s, two college behavioural science analysts, Daniel Kahneman and Amos Tversky, distributed a progression of articles on judgment and basic leadership. Their examination tested what market analysts thought to be valid a while ago: that individuals demonstration reasonably when profiting and funds. They found that individuals regularly settle on irrational choices when endeavouring to oversee hazard. Their discoveries opened up another zone of study, behavioural back, it looks at the brain science of trading and the role emotions, contemplations and practices play on our money related choices.

Focus on Basic Framework of Trade Plan

Behavioural science is presently revealing to us that we don't generally have 'choice.' We can offer into the instinctive motivations that drive us or apply the brakes of objective limitation. While we can't pick our emotions, since they start unwittingly, we can pick our conscious reaction to our sentiments. This is basically what cognisance is, an arrangement of basic reflections and understandings about how we are emotional. Seeing how passionate responses show themselves, to what degree and how they can influence choices is a vital stride in taking control of your trading execution. There are two distinct parts of our mind utilised when settling on a choice. Our prefrontal cortex, or external cerebrum, is the piece of the mind that makes us interestingly human. It controls our capacity to compose data, figure probabilities and plan for what's to come. The external cerebrum's capacity is to decipher emotions; "sensibly" evaluate a circumstance and deliver a choice. Our limbic framework, or internal mind, is the primal piece of our cerebrum, like that of different warm-blooded creatures. It controls emotions such as fear and fervour. It drives our senses of searching out charming and helpful things like crisp sustenance and clean water and guiding us far from repulsive or unsafe things like harmful plants or the edge of a sharp object. This piece of the cerebrum viablly holds alternate routes to choices, bypassing extra data or setting. Conscious intuition requires exertion. Around 20–25% of our caloric admission is expected to just keep our brains running. To monitor vitality, we abstain from connecting with our external cerebrum at whatever point conceivable. Subsequently, our reflexive internal mind is the first to survey a circumstance or process data and can frequently trump logic. Specialists found that the expectation of budgetary reward illuminates a similar delight focus in the inward mind as encountering other pleasurable exercises like eating a decent feast. It's this experience which may supersede logic and reason.

Develop Trading Conviction

At the point when our enthusiastic cravings start to move toward a forthcoming brand, we adjust our motivations to be steady to that aim. Our basic personality is continually searching for confirmation to help our convictions. The more grounded the emotion, the more grounded the conviction and the more noteworthy the propensity is to search for supporting confirmation. We are not normal, we are logical. This inclination is profoundly instilled in our regular encounters. In one investigation that Harvard teacher Ellen Langer led, specialists moved toward individuals in the demonstration of utilising replicating machines and inquired as to whether they could cut into the line and make photocopies. The trial subjects were given diverse explanations behind the demand running from the sensible to the apparently silly. For example, "since I'm in a surge" and "in light of the fact that I have to make duplicates." The analysts discovered that consistency was higher when they gave a reason, any reason inside points of confinement. As Langer clarified, "on the grounds that an elephant is after me" didn't cut it. An installed battle or flight reaction is a piece of our identity as people. In the contributing scene, this sentiment of fear or ravenousness is known as a hunch or a trader's sense. A trader may have a specific notion, regardless of a free trip or a relationship supervisor's recommendation that the stock that she/he has put resources into will take off or drop, that is a piece of enthusiastic trading. Numerous enthusiastic reactions can be obvious and simple to spot. They can likewise be unobtrusive, obfuscating our conduct and considering. As a trader, adjusting alert with certainty and going for broke is basic to a fruitful trading plan. In any case, your involvement with that arrangement, great or awful, may slide you abruptly or slowly to the other side of the range. Alert can possibly wind into fear or certainly transform into covetousness or power. At the point when the enthusiastic adjust is skewed, it can greatly affect trading choices in a not so ideal way.

Considering Trade with Behavioural Finance

Emotions are not just constrained to a person when we discuss the share trading system conduct. Every one of the business sectors is administered by aggregate emotions of traders as a gathering. There is a school of imagined that views the whole securities trade as a pattern of human emotions. This conviction depends on behavioural financial aspects i.e., a field of concentrate that represents considerable authority in investigating the effect of human conduct and emotions on the business sectors. At the point when traders feel that the business sectors are doing great, individuals begin purchasing while there is a sentiment of eagerness or doubt later on, for the market there is a hurry to offer, regardless of the possibility that the costs are too low. Think about a psychological inclination as a dependable guideline that might possibly be authentic. We've all observed films where a criminal wears a police uniform to go through a security checkpoint. The genuine cops expect that because the individual is wearing a uniform like theirs, he should be a genuine cop. That is a case of a psychological inclination. What does a fake cop have to do with your speculation decisions? You make similar sorts of suspicions that aren't really valid. Research demonstrates that we regularly don't think regarding riches as far as potential increases and losses are concerned. We feel the torment of a loss around twice as much as the delight of a pickup. We likewise tend to go out on a limb while picking amongst loss and go for broke while picking between picks up. The accompanying examination investigates individuals' propensity to look for more hazard when confronted with a loss.

Elucidation of Emotion and Logic

Traders are frequently discovered responding to coherent translations to the detriment of emotions. This propensity makes issues when individuals in overview research and centre gatherings search out motivations to clarify their sentiments about new items, ideas and advertisements. Self-announced research focuses on their sensible elucidation of emotion, instead of the helpers of conduct, the emotions themselves. Respondents and advertisers frequently wind up creating defences, rather than huge thoughts. Inventiveness endures and ideas kick the bucket rashly as advertisers endeavour to respond to the occasionally discretionary reasons individuals make up. Have you seen that you put more weight into the emotions of the individuals who concur with you? Financial specialists do this as well. How regularly have you broken down a stock and later explored reports that bolstered your proposal, as opposed to searching out data that may jab openings, as you would like to think? People are animals of propensity. Imperviousness to change overflows to speculation portfolios through the demonstration of more than once returning to similar stocks and ETFs, as opposed to inquiring about new thoughts. In spite of the fact that putting resources into organisations you comprehend is a sound venture system, having a short rundown of go-to items may constrain your benefit potential. The positively trending market is fit as a fiddle, yet numerous financial specialists have missed the rally as a result of the fear that it will turn around the course. Pessimism inclination makes financial specialists put more weight on awful news than on great news. Some may call this risk management. However, this predisposition can make the impacts of hazard hold more weight than the likelihood of reward. Warren Buffett wound up plainly a standout amongst the best speculators on the planet by opposing the temporary fad impact. His acclaimed exhortation to be eager when others are frightful and fearful when others are insatiable is a denouncement of this predisposition. Backpedalling to affirmation inclination, financial specialists feel better when they are contributing alongside the group. Be that as it may, as Buffett has demonstrated, an inverse mindset, after thorough research, may demonstrate more beneficial.

Building Balance in Trade

Fulfil the basic personality. On the off chance that you need individuals to purchase what you're offering, you need to give them consistent consent to purchase. Dyson put his interests into his items, not the promoting. An innovator and mechanical architect, Dyson established his organisation on twin item columns, a balance of building and plan. Not at all like numerous advertisers, had he really manufactured a superior mousetrap. Also, the appeal of the brand originated from the item itself, as he transformed an ordinary family unit machine into a form explanation. Made of delightful polycarbonate plastic with spotted aluminium and a reflexive splendid shaded sheen reminiscent of a Jeff Koons mould, they were sold even by garments producer and productive form architect Paul Smith, in his London store. You may see some cover amongst subjective and enthusiastic predisposition. However, consider this: One reason referred to by showcase watchers for mistrust that the present positively trending market is feasible is an attention on the past. "I bought a home in 2007 and got signed. Why might now be any unique?" That's a case of an enthusiastic predisposition. Basically, it is making a move in view of emotions, rather than truth. Dyson never faltered from the certainties about how his smash hit vacuum became. From the persevering final result of 5,127 models to an unmistakable item exhibit, from innovation that moves the air inside the vacuum at 924 miles for each hour to a savvy sounding, mechanically progressed name–G-Force Dual Cyclone, Dyson knew the minimum hot parts of his vacuum would offer the hotness of its plan. The final product is a noteworthy recognition that the vacuum cleaner is justified, regardless of each penny of its top-notch cost. Dyson now possesses a brand picture that is head and shoulders over the opposition.

Acknowledge Highs and Lows for Trade Success

Markets experience swings, they have their highs and lows. Having the capacity to foresee that or expect how the business sectors would carry on is the place a perfect trader is fruitful in light of the fact that knowing the market emotions goes far. At the point when a coherent trader thinks about market trends, she or he is fundamentally driving profound into human emotions and conduct. Brain research and trading are not fundamentally unrelated. Very regularly, advertisers hand off an undifferentiated item to their promotion organisation and anticipate that the publicising will make up for that absence of a passionate force. This approach is destined for disappointment, since we now live in an ocean of both equality items and promoting messages. So, whenever you consider what way to deal with use in advertising, ensure the two personalities, consistent and enthusiastic, are fulfilled some place in the blend. In the event that you truly need to expand your income, put your advancement and enthusiasm into what you're offering, not exactly on how you're offering it. Because you think about individuals' emotions, it makes you an intelligent trader. Intelligent trading fundamentally implies that you approach your budgetary choices through a perspective of down to earth thinking, which depends on exploring, comprehension of the market patterns, measurable models and specialised examination. At the point when experts say that there is no place for emotions, they're distorting the circumstance, since it's difficult to overlook your emotions.

Not taking money related choices when you are overwhelmed with emotions of insatiability or fear is a legitimate point. In any case, being candidly mindful is a piece of legitimate trading! Inside and out, an investigation of the business sectors and a general comprehension of components that impact diverse areas help in settling on quality choices as long as possible.

Say 'No' to Overtrade and Overestimation

Individuals regularly overestimate their insight, even on points for which they are commonplace. Specialists, researching how presumptuousness was adding to steady and exorbitant issues in different enterprises, made a certainty test to enable measurements to individuals' comprehension of known constraints. The members were posed inquiries particular to their industry. They were told to give an answering run, where they were 90 to 95% certain the right answer was contained inside the range. They found that even among exceedingly gifted, profoundly instructed experts, none of them approached the perfect rate decided at the start of the test. Having a comprehension and gratefulness for what you don't know and investigating it, instead of overlooking it, could help hold your arrogance under control. A man with presumptuousness predisposition trusts that his/her expertise as a financial specialist is superior to others' aptitudes. Take, for instance, the individual who works in the pharmaceutical business. He/she may put stock in being able to trade inside that segment at a more elevated amount than different traders. The market has tricked the most regarded traders. It can do the same to you. Reliably effective traders comprehend that emotions are a potential obstacle to overcome, as opposed to an impossible hindrance. They're mindful of their emotions by constantly asking themselves what is making them need to begin or stop an activity. Markets are controlled by emotions. Following human conduct and reckoning individuals' emotions give a trader an edge in the market. In the event that each trader disregards their impulse and trusts logic at all times, he will be distant from the market assumption, which may do him more mischief than great over the long haul. Overlooking one's intuition in the midst of the commotion of individuals requesting that you remain totally emotionless is inconceivable. Rather, understanding that individuals' sentiments run the market can enable you to settle on coherent choices in view of these emotions.

How to Remove Doubts, Uncertainty, and Fears

Brokers doubt their trading strategies, the way they oversee trades and their own capacities as dealers. They are indeterminate about how to approach the business sectors, how to oversee trades, when to leave trades or how to set a stop misfortune accurately. And this vulnerability and ceaseless doubting lead to fear, the dread that they are accomplishing something incorrectly or the dread that they are passing up a major opportunity. We have all accomplished dread instability and uncertainty on occasion in our lives. For the most part, we get over it and proceed onward. On the other hand, maybe we don't have hard-line political affiliations, so we waver before throwing our votes in decisions. Or maybe we don't put stock in our capacities and are not the speediest of the stamp at work when advancement chances call. A dealer who does not have full trust in his framework can't trade taking care of business, since he generally feels that he could (or even should) be accomplishing something else. This prompts settling on hasty choices, smaller scale overseeing trades erroneously or evidently trading sincerely without an arrangement. Such an approach prompts conflicting outcomes and numerous brokers commit similar errors over and over, which strengthens the convictions that they are accomplishing something incorrectly and more doubts, addressing and fear enter their psyche.

Never Rely on Foggiest Ideas

In any case, you ought to never get some information about such vital, individual and technique particular inquiries. To start with, you don't have the foggiest idea about his complaints and above all, the other dealer has no clue how you trade, he doesn't know your full approach, how you execute your trades and what your battles are. Best case scenario, the appropriate responses you get are then absolutely negligible and dangerous, in the most pessimistic scenario. By posing the inquiries above, traders plan to pick up clearness and expel the doubts they have. In any case, when the appropriate responses you get are not right and you begin rolling out improvements to your trading that result in more loss, you will wind up with more regret. You falsely made expectation and sureness by asking arbitrary traders and your expectations got pounded once you saw that your outcomes didn't enhance your execution. At that point, you are starting over from the beginning and numerous dealers wind up trading with a Frankenstein-like framework, where the individual ideas don't fit and it makes terrible trading comes about in light of the fact that a trader doesn't know how to work it. Instability, dread and uncertainty are steady pals of a business person. They are the ever uninvited companions of each living business visionary. As I put down these words, I am, as of now, experiencing a hard time managing these 3 musketeers myself. As I have gained from life, all things, both great and terrible, are generally valuable. The inquiry in the most case is whether we'll sufficiently understand to search out the helpfulness amid disagreeable circumstances. So, the unavoidable issue is this, what great does instability, dread and uncertainty bring?

Consistent Enquiry Removes Doubts

Fortunately, you can answer every one of your inquiries yourself. An organised trading routine and a decent trading diary are worked in a way that enables a trader to look over an assortment of factors and measurements to analyse his trading. By noting your inquiries yourself through your own confirmed information, you won't just have the capacity to expel the voices in your mind for good. The appropriate responses you get are likewise going to be the correct ones, no doubt. Trading is a business, and each great business monitors where the cash goes, it breaks down consumptions, thinks about the rates of profit for particular tasks and keeps extremely itemised records. On the off chance that a business does not know how much cash it spends, where it creates the most benefits, where it loses cash and what works, it won't be good to go for too long. Traders approach trading from a languid point of view where whatever they do is punching in trades while never glancing back at what they did. Instability, Fear and Doubt are the 3 terrifying companions of our own that assist business visionaries to place things in clearer viewpoint. They simply make a decent showing with regards to clearing the haze. They enable us to see better those things such as positive thinking and energy occasionally escapes us. The triple play of instability, dread and uncertainty abandons us in an intelligent state. Abruptly, all the good faith will vanish; the adrenaline surge that frequently accompanies the origination of another thought vanishes. All that is left is the sharp reality that encompasses you. Let's be honest, business does truly have a dim side.

Visionaries Removes Obstacles and Vulnerabilities

Try not to feel pitiful, a rude awakening is great. We business people are regularly visionaries. It is a piece of what makes us mindful. In any case, it can get into our head now and again that we have a tendency to overlook actualities or the truth of our present circumstance. Genuine men don't contend with actualities, neither do they deny its reality. They contemplate it and attempt to figure out how to incorporate their discoveries into whatever they are attempting to fulfil. Just tricks contend with realities. Here's the thing, you can't change your existence by denying or contending with it, you can just change your world by tolerating that it exists. That is the sharp pill vulnerability dread and uncertainty pass on for us to swallow. Like it or not, there are endless difficulties on the entrepreneurial way, tolerating this hard certainty are what vulnerability, dread and uncertainty help us to accomplish. You can just deny them at your own hazard. Do you recollect your last 5, 10 or 20 trades? Would you be able to review what functions admirably for you, where you lose the most cash and under which conditions? Most brokers have no clue and that is the reason they will continue battling.

Track Distinctive Measures and Times for Planning

The way of a business person surely is unverifiable, dreadful and suspicious. Our assignment as business visionaries is to acknowledge them, comprehend their source and innovatively discover answers to the inquiries they provoke. We are to look at them ideally without flinching and proffer answers to every one of the vulnerabilities, our feelings of trepidation and our doubts. They exist for one reason, to enable us to consider our consequences, to know better what we are up against, with the goal that we can be better arranged to defeat the ceaseless difficulties of business enterprise. So, quit battling instability, dread and uncertainty. Grasp them, for they are your partners on this strange adventure. Track the distinctive time spans that your trade depended on and see which one has the best execution. You can do that effortlessly and simply set up another Custom Statistic and label the trades. You can dole out each trade with an alternate setup, and you can undoubtedly think about two distinct frameworks or diverse methods for entering trade. You have a smart cerebrum and your own particular experience on which to draw. Get off the fence and have the fearlessness to hop one way or the other. Business visionaries can be egocentric. This is regularly because of our achievements. Thus, we, at times, escape by winding up so loaded with ourselves. Instability, dread and uncertainty advise us that we are not superior to others, simply just favoured. Instability, dread and uncertainty advise us that past victories are no assurance for future ones. They advise us that what got us here may not take us there. They help us to remember our blemishes as mortals.

Never Carry Misfortunes for Long

Numerous traders regularly think about whether they ought to take after an alternate stop loss or take benefit methodology. We realise that and that is the reason we have included the Alternative Strategies in our diary. Basically, record the potential result of other trade administration techniques and let Edgework demonstrate to you which works best. The main certain thing in life is change. Which is only a superior method for saying that nothing is sure. All that you thought you had in order will turn out wrong 99% of the time. So where does that abandon us? Humble. At the end of the day, we are just nature's instrument for the progression of humankind. All that we make was made through us. We are not the makers as such, we are instruments of creation. It is not up to us to choose the result of what is being done to us. It is up to nature and the entire mankind. Our own job is to submit ourselves to the more prominent innovative compel inside and permit the creation inside to spring up. Achievement breeds solace and solace prompts lack of concern. You realise that moment that you don't see the need to accomplish increasingly and you simply need to sit on your butt and appreciate the ride. So, when next vulnerability, dread and uncertainty fly up their revolting head, go have a re-look, revaluate and re-shape your thought, pruning out the wheat from the pole. You should know when to take a stand and dispatch, regardless of the vulnerability, dread and uncertainty.

Risk Intelligence: The Dirty Little Secret at The Heart of All Successful Trading

In all actuality, no methodology comes without loss and gaining from losing trades and making alterations is the way to long haul benefit. Here are four losing trades and enduring lessons from each. Fruitful traders and venture experts come in all shapes and sizes. They have numerous, regularly immensely contrasting, identities and attributes. They have generally varying ways to deal with discovering quality, and they embrace an expansive exhibit of various approaches to adapt that esteem. In my part as an execution mentor, I have been favoured to approach numerous remarkable traders and investment supervisors. One inquiry I get asked more than some others is, 'What could it be that separates the best traders from those numerous exceedingly competent people who don't exactly measure up?' What are the qualities and attributes they have which those others don't? What is their scandalous little titbit? Amid a current discussion with a training customer, the customer commented to me that he couldn't perceive any rationale or soundness in anything in the market. He needed my sentiment on this and how he ought to deal with this. I clarified how frequently the rationale we apply to the market is full grown or finished. On the off chance that we sit tight for finishing of the rationale, the market has typically moved to mark down it. Along these lines, we should settle on a choice in light of deficient data. This is trying for some, yet it is the best time to trade. At this stage, the market has completely moved to cost in new 'esteem factors,' accordingly the hazard compensate is significantly higher. Similarly, there is a hazard that the photo we see shaping might be false. This is the reason, as I would like to think, incredible traders, are regularly 'Experts of the Best Guess.'

Flourishing Uncertainty and Complexity

Individuals may surmise that it is propelled news, better information or more prominent frameworks or on the other hand, maybe predominant intellectual abilities, extraordinary astuteness or an exorbitant profundity of learning. Profitable as every one of these things seems to be, they are not the key differentiators. For me, the key contrast is that these people have or have built up the capacity to flourish in uncertainty and complexity. On the other hand, more distinctly, they have created unrivalled 'Hazard Intelligence.' Hazard Intelligence, as an idea, is still rising. Early developments of it concentrated on hazard in the authoritative setting. However, British savant Dylan Evans got it to the individual idea in his splendid book 'Hazard Intelligence: How to Live with Uncertainty.' In the book, Evans characterises it as "an extraordinary sort of knowledge for considering danger and vulnerability," which at the centre concentrates on enhancing the capacity to gauge probabilities all the more precisely. Making this one stride further and applying it in an investment and trading setting, I see risk insight as, 'the capacity to have the capacity to decide, survey and assess dangers with more noteworthy precision and afterward to adapt these dangers all the more successfully.' How might you separate between bona fide venture openings and pitches that are recently expected to part you from your capital? Everybody has heard the term 'Ponzi conspire.' However, do you know what the commencement of that reference is? Charles Ponzi thought of offers to speculators in the 1920s that guaranteed a half return for ventures over just a 45-day time span and an overpowering 100% for more than 90 days. As everybody soon discovered, the skeleton in the closet was that Ponzi was essentially paying off introductory speculators with money from new financial specialists, keeping the rest for himself. Clearly, this "speculation" will make up for lost time with both the maker and the members inevitably bringing about the grievous loss for the financial specialists and ideally critical prison sentences for people like Ponzi or the late Bernie Madoff. The lesson of the story is that if any speculation opportunity sounds like a pipe dream, it likely is. There are constantly corrupt "traders" conveying mail requesting and with innovation, it's regular to be deluged with messages and web sees showing speculation openings that "can't miss" or will make you rich beyond anything you could ever imagine.

Hazard Intelligence for Trading

'Hazard Intelligence' is a quality particularly unique in relation to what we would call 'Intellectual Intelligence,' as measured by IQ. Warren Buffett once stated, "You don't need to be a scientific genius. Contributing is not an amusement where the person with the 160 IQ beats the person with 130 IQ." The revered Mr. Buffett positively knows this 'scandalous little titbit.' Hazard Intelligence works over all areas and is not quite recently shown by contributing bosses. For example, a Warren Buffett or a George Soros. I see traders and speculators of all hues who are high 'Hazard Intelligent.' From informal investors to energy and value activity traders, from relative esteem traders to longer-term large-scale support chiefs. I additionally observe numerous methodical traders and venture a supervisor, whose frameworks and the way they run and oversee them, mirror their hazard insight. The subject of 'Hazard Intelligence' is something I have touched upon in a large number of my articles, without making it so direct. Specialised Analysis is a case of a reflection, instead of a rationale based account. The account which I developed depended on the full scale financial principal case, this built story was totally wrong, in any case, and left me with an inaccurate crucial evaluation of the market which thought up to undermine that trade (a greater amount of which I will clarify later). Truth be known, contributing effectively is difficult and it's not for the black out of the heart. Day trading and dealing with your hazard takes to explore, consistent perception and no less than a fundamental comprehension of venture vehicles and procedures that assistance you constrain loss. Nobody is 100% impeccable at choosing winning speculations, regardless of the possibility that you're Warren Buffet. There will be failures in your history. You simply require victors that outpace them. From one perspective, it reminds us to take a look at ourselves and not generally over think matters, as I had done above. Then again, this is really what we do. We can't help but over think things since we are made so. In this way, trading 'What we see' and 'What we think we see' are one and the same. To add to the test, especially in business sectors, what we see is once in a while, if at any time, a genuine finished picture or view. We see a pieced complex picture, with our comprehension of this in light of layouts as a matter of fact. This is how the cerebrum works. It doesn't see things in their actual shape. However, it develops a picture in view of what we hope to see.

Scholarly Approach Is Useful

You will discover numerous cases of 'exceptionally keen' individuals who need 'Hazard Intelligence' and numerous other people who need 'scholarly insight,' which is so esteemed in our reality, yet who decidedly emanates 'Hazard Intelligence. These individuals who need 'Hazard Intelligence' may have many fine qualities and capacities, they may even be virtuosos in different spaces. However, without 'Hazard Intelligence,' they are regularly destined to flop in exercises which require going out on a limb. An extraordinary case is the Nobel Prize victors behind 'Long haul Capital Management.' The deadly defect in this virtuoso's model was due to their absence of 'Hazard Intelligence.' They were a firm, who as far as anyone knows, contracted the brightest and the best, but on what measure? It absolutely wasn't 'Hazard Intelligence.' You will discover individuals who are 'Hazard Intelligent' in all kinds of different backgrounds, business people and effective specialists, poker players, military pioneers, surgeons and sportspeople. In specific ranges and fields, it is difficult to get to the best and remain there reliably, without creating 'Hazard Intelligence,' trading and speculation are one of them. In trading and speculation, the 'Hazard Intelligent' individual is cognisant that they won't generally win. They will endure or relinquish loss, yet limitedly, in the quest for winning enormously in the long haul. Fully trusted, this may appear to be confusing. However, 'losing great' is the key. There is an idiom: 'In trading, the best failure is frequently the long haul victor.' Markets never demonstrate to us an unmistakable and consistently developed picture. There are recently excessively numerous factors, diverse perspectives, vistas and potential outcomes. We are accordingly left making 'best suppositions,' in any case.

Empowering Market Promotions and Hazard Control

Your job, as a trader, is to wind up the ace of playing the 'best figure's diversion' and this is an expert, an aptitude which needs steady improvement and sustaining. We need to keep an eye on our practices, on our idealism and negativity, egotism and on our levels of certainty, both over and under. It is the reason we require some kind of process and structure to our trading, our progressing investigation and the juxtaposition of the two. A solid procedure and structure guards us, also empowering ourselves to take part in advertising chance. It is the reason we require a solid hazard administration rehearse and a procedure for situating. Hence, traders are constantly prescribed to practices to minimize investment losses. There are various essential approaches to shield you from amazing loss and to appreciate productive trades. Secure your increases when you have effectively picked a victor, ensure the benefits that you've understood. Your procedure ought to incorporate a left point for the offering. When you achieve that point, take after your pre-decided choice and abstain from being covetous. This guarantees you keep the additions you had sought after. Utilise stop loss alternatives. Utilise the stop loss's capacity on your trade to restrain the effect to your record when your trade goes south. You will never be correct 100% of the time, so get used to that reality and proceed onward. Stop loss activities will, at any rate, shield you from an aggregate loss of your capital. Let feelings alone for your trades. Talking about feelings, when you aren't feeling especially mindful or mentally arranged for a trading session, should be held off until you are. Trading requires clear idea and brisk choices to be productive. Make educated trades. If you can't distinguish a reasonable picture or pattern, it shows that it's a great opportunity to purchase. Hold up until one drops by, it will. Purchasing on "gut feel" or only on an enthusiastic hunch is not the best approach to succeed. Utilise the diagrams. There are a wide assortment of lists and outlines accessible to traders continuously that give you a minute-by-minute perspective of general market patterns and points of interest of a specific stock, ETF, item or money that you need to take after. Figure out how to utilise them and which ones relate to your specific trade system.

In trading, the Best Washout Is frequently the Long Haul Champ:

Another reason individuals find this so difficult is that our Western sensibilities have prepped us all of our lives to win. We are raised to become best of the class, to collect information, to have answers, to get the best grades, to win places in the best colleges. In the Western talk, disappointment is not quickened or endured. Losing is not simply 'terrible' but also very 'awful,' conceivably even 'existentially awful.' We don't lose, we don't come up short, and we don't acknowledge being overwhelmed. The very 'Hazard Intelligent' have built up a capacity to move beyond these states of mind. They usurp regular considering. This is the thing that the best traders and speculators do. They will acknowledge vanquishing, as a vital malevolence, while in transit to triumph. They will concede they don't have the foggiest idea about the responses to complex issues, which unexpectedly permits 'the best responses' to emerge. Utilise an online trader you trust. There are various online intermediaries who can deal with your trade movement. Assess their accessible alternatives, hours of accessibility, charge structures and bolster offerings to enable you to decide the one that meets your trade prerequisites generally viable. It was pivotal to stay away from a paper trail that may enable the specialists to detect an association between a US citizen and a mystery account. For an additional quarterly expense, the bank would allude to customers just by a code name on all archives identifying with their Swiss records. During a time of gravity, nonconformists had railed against monetary structures that they accepted kept the rich well off to the detriment of different citizens. Presently, here was what may have felt to them like a counterpunch against 'the 1%.' It was as though Thomas Piketty, the financial analyst whose book on imbalance had been a runaway hit, was distributing equity.

Guarding Against Investment Losses

Your online agent can give you the apparatuses expected to use your trade technique for gainful sessions. At the point when a man's hazard states of mind are in a consonant position in connection to their hazard sort, there will be practically zero weight on the chain amongst stay and vessel, and the pontoon itself won't go under strain. In this piece of the similarity, the individual is more equipped for settling on educated and ideal choices and are less inclined to be influenced naturally by choices and elements which hinder basic leadership. For example, behavioural inclinations. In these circumstances, they will probably be profitable and execution will probably be ideal. At the point when hazard mentalities are not helpful and not in amicability with chance sort, there will be stress and pressure on the chain. A man's hazard state of mind might be in a struggle with their hazard sort. In this piece of the similarity, they are in threat of settling on more problematic decisions and disabling trustworthy basic leadership. Subsequently, they will be helpless against crashing practices. For example, passionate seize or self-image based decisions and more vulnerable to oblivious behavioural predispositions and other default practices. In these circumstances, they might be far less beneficial and obligated to below average execution. The 'Hazard Type Compass' created by PCL (Psychological Consultancy Limited) enables individuals to see more about their hazard identity and how this comes to affect their basic leadership in high-chance circumstances. This basic effective instrument distinguishes individuals as one of 8 diverse hazard sorts, each with their own specific attributes, upside characteristics (we mark them Bright-side Behaviours) and drawback qualities (Dark-side Behaviours). We can't help ourselves as people in applying rationale and defences to fill holes in information or to attempt to clarify information or occasions. It enables us to understand things. This is both our approval and revile. For me, more prominent mindfulness is what is expected to enable us to catch the upside abilities of ourselves and to restrain the drawback which comes about because of these. More noteworthy mindfulness implies understanding the fundamental drivers of your basic leadership and practices, building up a comprehension of your identity from a 'third individual' viewpoint and being aware of how your raising circumstance impacts your practices and activities.

Neuroplasticity: Your Brain and Your Trading

Psychology is the logical investigation of the sensory system (how it builds up, its structure and action), including the cerebrum, the spinal string and the systems of nerve cells called 'neurons' and their impact on cognisance, conduct and psychological capacities. What we think about the mind is changing at an amazing pace. When you rest, the mind is dynamic. It is more dynamic during waking hours. It is not genuine that your mind crumbles with age. Each time you take in another aptitude, you change your cerebrum. All practices change the mind, and this is not restricted by age. Brains can adjust to ailment and damage by having one a player in the cerebrum assume control over the elements of another piece of the mind that has been bargained. For instance, impairing wounds to the discourse focuses of the left cerebrum can be "educated" by the correct mind as a compensatory measure. Neuroplasticity picked up a decent measure of unmistakable quality amid the last 50% of the twentieth century. Analysts could demonstrate that various parts of the human cerebrum stay plastic or alterable as a man propels into adulthood.

Cerebral Needs of Trade Strategies

For the last time, this exploration demonstrates that the cerebrum, once generally thought of as permanent and unchangeable after a specific age, is, indeed, a dynamic organ that progressions continually over the span of our lives, as we increase new learning and encounters. This capacity to change is alluded to as neuroplasticity, from the words 'neuron' (nerve cells in the cerebrum connected by neurotransmitters) and 'plasticity' (the ability to be formed, shaped or changed). Neuroplasticity is the mind's capability to make neural pathways and to rearrange itself as indicated by how it's being utilised or not being utilised. The mind's capacity to revamp itself by framing new neural associations all through life is called 'neuroplasticity.' Each individual neural cell is comprised of an axon, dendrites and is connected to each other by a little space called the neurotransmitters. The word plastic means to shape or adjust. Neuroplasticity alludes to the potential that the cerebrum has to redesign by making new neural pathways to adjust as it needs. At the end of the day, it is the limit of neurons and neural systems in the cerebrum to change their associations and conduct in light of new data, tangible incitement, advancement, harm or brokenness. Albeit neural system, they show particularity (how much a framework's segments might be isolated and recombined) and do particular capacities. They hold the ability to go amiss from their typical capacities and to revamp themselves.

Ways to Define Changes in Trade

There are three courses in which your cerebrum changes. The first is concoction change. Concoction change underpins here and now a memory. The second change is the association between neurons. This procedure is associated with long haul memory. Like figuring out how to exchange or play the piano. While the synthetic response changes your transient encounters, it has no enduring effect on your conduct or learning. What you find in the here and now does not reflect long haul learning. The third way the mind changes is to modify its capacity. When you utilise a specific cerebrum district, it turns out to be increasingly volatile. The piece of the cerebrum winds up noticeably less demanding to invigorate and enact. For instance, this is our main thing when we utilise guided contemplation. It is intended to animate certain parts of the mind, which after some time makes the cerebrum go to that inclination, thought or feeling increasingly regularly. The impact is enduring change after some time in light of the fact that specific parts of the mind that evoke an idea or feeling drilled in reflection wind up noticeably less demanding to get to and inspire. Territories of the cerebrum that you utilise regularly are fortified as they wind up plainly greater and more grounded, while parts that are utilised less habitually turned out to be little and less successful. For example, each time you feel irritated and baffled with misfortunes, the neural systems and the regions of the cerebrum in charge of the experience are strengthened, and the structures that create the experience of being 'quiet and calm' gradually fall by the wayside. Rehashed activity underpins certain parts of the mind. For instance, a London taxicab driver who needs to recall expansive parts of London delineates bigger mind areas alluding to exceptional memory.

Neuroplasticity Prepare Traders for Trade Changes

Neuroplasticity is upheld by substance, basic and utilitarian changes in the entire mind. These progressions happen constantly, for the most part, unknowingly. Individuals neglect to roll out enduring improvements since they don't know how to intentionally re-prepare their brains to learn. A great many people don't see the amount it takes to inspire enduring change. In the event that you are not kidding about making an enduring positive change, it is not a shoddy wander, either in cash terms or time responsibility. Oh dear, it should be possible. The regions and structures of the mind that are dynamic in psychological capacities (all parts of thinking, considering, assessing, judging, recalling and feeling) are dynamic when we exchange. Thus, the mental procedures that occur amid this action (counting your musings, judgments, feelings and states of mind) are fortified. Along these lines, coincidentally, you exchange (regardless of whether you act incautiously, let your failures leave hand, cut your champs off, take exchanges outside of your procedure) you are fundamentally preparing your brain for that sort of conduct. Not every person is the same. Neuron versatility changes from individual to individual. For example, some brokers conform to changing economic situations quicker than others. Too bad, all can figure out how to roll out improvements. Numerous exercises we take part in today don't energise neuroplasticity, but diminish it. Sitting before the PC diminishes neuroplasticity, prompting other behavioural issues like dyslexia, mental imbalance, sadness and perpetual diseases, to give some examples. Your mind is moulded by the things you constantly do and the things you frequently don't do. To streamline results every individual requires singular evaluations and meditations.

Comparison for Defining Standards of Changes in Trade

For a long time, it was believed to be carved in stone in psychology that specific capacities were hard-wired in particular, confined areas of the mind and that any occurrences of cerebrum change or recuperation were minor exemptions to run the show. Be that as it may, since the 1970s and '80s, neuroplasticity has increased wide acknowledgment as a standard idea. As indicated by the hypothesis of neuroplasticity, considering, learning and acting change both the mind's practical life systems and its physical life systems. It is continually changing as it cooperates with nature. Whatever you think, see and feel (regardless of whether oblivious or purposeful) even when you're not exchanging, is preparing the cerebrum to think, see and feel in those same ways when you are exchanging. It's slippery. It likewise demonstrates exactly how genuine brain research is – your states of mind, judgments and inward discourse. This may be somewhat to a lesser degree a worry for those of you who exchange low maintenance as a leisure activity. In any case, on the off chance that you exchange as a profession, as I do, developing the correct brain science consistently is as critical as your market edge and your hazard administration strategy. Preparing is an imperative idea to grasp the thought of neuroplasticity. You realise that your body will react to the worry of reliable exercise that pushes your points of confinement, making the framework leave homeostasis and adjust in this way, building up the limit with respect to more noteworthy quality and continuance.

Being Reliable Is Being What You Can Afford

Screen what you are letting yourself know. A significant number of your musings are out of your mindfulness or oblivious to you. In this way, it is imperative to track your contemplations, and when you end up noticeably mindful that you are considering or saying negative, dangerous and downgrading things about the market or yourself, it is important that you change them from being unsupportive to positive and proactive. A Forex merchant should persistently search for roads on the most proficient method to better comprehend their point of view and how their reasoning influences their general exchanging. At the point when a Forex dealer audits their contemplations on a reliable premise, they are placing themselves in a triumphant exchanging circumstance. Stay at the time and in the now of the exchange, enabling you to place yourself into a place of the arrangement of the body, brain and feelings going a similar way and for similar objectives. When you are adjusted, it is more probable that you will have the capacity to successfully manage inside clash that originates from musings, convictions, predispositions and feelings that are in opposition to your destinations. At the point when a Forex dealer knows about systems, musings or other related exercises to exchanging, they ought to be recording the specifics and returning to these archives every now and then. What's more, a Forex dealer ought to know about their negative feelings in that they have significant data which can be related with them. Find out about your brain's inclinations and rehash the practices that are useful for your mind and drop those which are most certainly not. It is about customary work on learning is tied in with finding what and how your mind adapts best.

Intelligence, Overconfidence and Trading

Much consideration has been paid in the previous decade to how brokers' mental components influence advertises properties. Pomposity is a standout amongst the most imperative attributes of dealers. It is notable that present day money related monetary hypothesis depends vigorously on the supposition that the delegate operator in the market carries on judiciously and has balanced desires. Under this suspicion, it is demonstrated that benefit costs completely mirror all accessible data and dependably mirror their natural esteem. In this circumstance, future value developments can't be anticipated on the premise of past data. Any budgetary control force available ought to create no significant impacts. However, result in the postponed disclosure of the data. Milton Friedman is one of the most grounded advocates for supporting the discerning desires approach. Looking at the effectiveness of genuine monetary markets has been an intriguing theme in the previous three decades. Many investigations have scrutinised the legitimacy of the productive market speculation EMH in genuine money related markets and have given the hypothetical establishments or experimental confirmation to demonstrate the presence of market wastefulness. Intelligence is exaggerated. Training, persistence, learning, consideration regarding subtle elements and some innovativeness are significantly more critical than intelligence.

Disappointment – Enemy of Intelligence and Overconfidence

In case you're canny, you may turn out to be exceptionally sure. Genuine confidence is imperative, yet arrogance is deadly to your record. Combined with a major inner self that is a certain approach to budgetary destruction in the business sectors. On the off chance that you have no dread of disappointment, you will come up short. Obviously, the dread of disappointment can't incapacitate you, yet no dread of disappointment is as terrible. I trust carelessness is an awful character in trading. It will make you daze for hazard and improve you feel then you are. Fortunes and irregularity are substantially greater components than generally figuring it out. You must be modest. The inescapable outcome is that your interpretation of more hazard than you should. You need to realise that disappointment is plausible. An inclination to be careless increments if a man trusts insight is unchangeable and can prompt a false faith in their level of insightfulness. Dr. Joyce Ehrlinger, a right-hand educator of brain science at Washington State University, who drove the investigation, said that we additionally realised that being arrogant shielded individuals from learning. Individuals expected to comprehend and recognise what they didn't know with a specific end goal to really learn. Careless individuals attempt to keep up the high by continually focusing on the least demanding parts and dodging the harder errands. While individuals with a development mentality, who trust intelligence is an alterable quality, invest more energy concentrating on the testing errands, thus this gives a level of confidence that is in accordance with their capacities.

Assumption Becomes Exact with Intelligence

In the previous two decades, inquiry about examinations given to money related financial aspects have considered models that veer off from full discernment. One branch concentrates on the impacts of clamour traders. Their discoveries have shown that the nearness of commotion traders can create considerable impacts, which are not the same as those seen in the market populated by normal brokers alone. The other branch concentrates on the outcomes coming about because of brokers' mental inclinations. This line of research has been a critical issue in the field of the behavioral fund. Really, the significance of this exploration drift that considers the behavioural qualities has been taken note of. Maybe, the heartiest finding in the brain science of judgment is that individuals are arrogant. Brokers' presumptuousness might be expected to a 'tying down and alteration' prepare. The grapple has a noteworthy impact with the goal that the change is normally inadequate. Along these lines, dealers have tight subjective likelihood appropriations. This marvel is likewise proving in the exact writing on judgment under vulnerability. Choice and survivorship predispositions may likewise be wellsprings of carelessness and fruitful dealers, for the most part, overestimate their own commitment to their prosperity. Such a thinking is upheld by the attribution hypothesis, which depicts that people, for the most part, property results that help the legitimacy of their choices to high capacity and results that are conflicting with the choices to outside clamour. Be that as it may, hypothetical outcomes depend intensely on particular suspicions viewing the qualities of brokers, the market conditions and the data structures. Since many components are included and brokers' conduct may produce externalities on others, there would be a clearer and more solid picture with respect to the impacts of traders' mental predispositions if a heterogeneous-operator structure were to be utilised.

Sensation Seeking Is Overconfidence Rather Confidence

Sensation seeking is a steady identity attribute, contemplated in the brain science writing, which fluctuates crosswise over people. The individuals who are sensation searchers scan for the novel, extraordinary and fluctuated encounters, by and large connected with genuine or envisioned physical, social and budgetary dangers. The quality creates practices in numerous ranges that are less seen among those invested with bringing down degrees of the sensation looking for characteristic. These incorporate unsafe driving, hazardous sexual conduct, visit vocation changes, medication and liquor mishandling, support in specific sorts of games and recreation exercises (like bungee jumping or exciting rides) and betting. Sensation-chasing conduct crosses numerous areas. Consequently, a poker player or an activity violator may indicate sensation looking for conduct in different fields. Trading fits the meaning of a sensation looking for conduct. Support in money markets is seen to be fiscally dangerous. However, without trading, needs curiosity and assortment. Betting is unsafe, yet rehashed betting changes it up. A solitary wager may not be as fulfilling to the sensation searcher as a progression of littler and unmistakable wages (despite the fact that the last has less instability). It is the curiosity of the new stock in one's portfolio or the adjustment in one's position in a stock that gives immoderate utility to the sensation searcher. Along these lines, an expanded portfolio can be as invigorating to the sensation searcher as a non-diversified portfolio. In any case, a steady portfolio is not as energising as a new one.

Say 'No' to Solitary Trade

Already, arrogance had just been viewed as an issue for drivers, bungee jumpers, specialists and legal advisors. However, Ehrlinger and her group trust that this outlook can upset advancement and opportunity. Dr. Ehrlinger said that a smidgen of arrogance could be useful. However, bigger measures of carelessness can lead individuals to settle on terrible choices and to pass up a great opportunity to learn. One could contend that a progression of stock positions in a solitary stock is more fortifying to a sensation searcher than an expanded portfolio where one has minute changes to each position. This would imply that there are some stock speculation practices that can be driven either by sensation chasing or by specific hazard avoidance parameters. Our examination is centred on trading in essence, which (aside from immaterial rebalancing inspirations) is not driven by hazard avoidance parameters. Moreover, we control for the number of stocks in the speculator's portfolio. Among all financial specialists, with a similar level of broadening, the sensation searchers should trade more. Sensation searchers find trading engaging. However, that does not imply that the individuals who find trading engaging are sensation searchers. It is the assortment, oddity and the danger of trading that makes trading (and also other presumptuousness related exercises) engaging. Note, in any case, that if trading were just engaging, in a similar sense that TV or golf is engaging, there would be no distinction in the proclivity to trade between sensation searchers and the individuals who do not have the attribute. Rather, those inspired by a moderately more prominent utility from amusement (i.e., golfers and 'love seat potatoes') would trade the most, ceteris paribus. In the event that trading is roused by sensation chasing, the individuals who enjoy arrogant exercises such as hazardous driving, drugs, dangerous games, betting and so on, would trade the most.

Reality Check Is Intelligence

On the off chance that you have no dread of disappointment, you will fall flat. Obviously, the dread of disappointment can't deaden you. However, no dread of disappointment is just as awful. It is trusted that arrogance is an awful character in trading. It will make you dazzle for hazard and improve you feel then you are. Fortunes and irregularity are significantly greater variables than generally figure it out. You must be modest. The inescapable outcome is that you thought on more hazard than you should. You need to realise that disappointment is a probability. Carelessness is the propensity to put an unreasonably intemperate level of trust in one's capacities and convictions. This definition has developed into two distinct elucidations. The first is hubris or what is, once in a while, alluded to as the 'superior to anything normal impact.' One can think about this as an unreasonable move in the apparent mean. The other is 'mis-calibration.' This emerges when the confidence interim around the financial specialist's private flag is tighter than it is in reality. This can be thought of as a silly move in saw difference. This produces a bigger eagerness to trade than would be seen in a less certain financial specialist. The connection amongst arrogance and trading action has a current hypothetical and observational writing behind it.

The Journey of Self-Development

Traders start the voyage into trading with high expectations. They accept, with great preparing and enough screen time, they will have the capacity to ace trading and accomplish their fantasies through trading. They hone tirelessly in recreation, back-test their philosophy, as well as utilise a trading association's "close money" until the point when they unmistakably observe that they can win this diversion with their own particular money. Certain that their past experience of diligent work and aspiration has paid off, they expect this ethic will lead them to accomplishment in trading. Efficiently, they have prepared themselves to accomplish their fantasies. Everything starts with looking in the mirror. Achievement in general society runs as an inseparable unit with accomplishment in your private life. Viable authority streams from adequately driving yourself. Our accurately commanded culture puts all emphasis on the outer and physical world, blinding the significance of the interior and mental self. Self-authority is being responsible for the inner manners of thinking that guide your feelings, propensities and practices. It's the capacity to react instead of responding. The previous is finished with aim and mindfulness, the last is instinctive and without reason.

Right Expectation for Desired Success

There's a voice inside your head and that is totally typical. It's your interior trade, the internal discourse that endeavours to understand the world. The main critical stride in creating self-dominance is to wind up noticeably an onlooker of your considerations. To end up mindful and self-intelligent. All through history, therapists and thinkers have displayed hypotheses on the variety of the human personality. Plato isolated the mind into appetitive, coherent and cheerful. Freud sorted it into the Id, Ego and Superego. Current speculations keep on being exhibited and wrangled about. However, they all concur on the multi-dimensional angle. As peculiar as it sounds, there is by all accounts, more than one "you" within you. What's more, frequently, we're at odd with ourselves. Self-dominance is tied in with making inward harmoniousness, an assenting and peace between an outer jolt, our inside understanding and our enthusiastic reaction.

Control Excitement to Stay Focused

Any individual who has been around trading for some time knows the war stories. The stories of exploded records and the moderate seep of a thousand little cuts litter the scene of the trip into trading. After the loss, fear relocates to the trader's brain and self-question turns into the imperceptible accomplice riding crowd over the broker's psyche. When they have a triumphant streak, they wind up getting pompous and giving back every one of their benefits and then some. Some place the trader's brain gets captured by dread or happiness and a productive trading mind is never again accountable for the technique that (on paper) gave them the edge to be gainful. An absence of care will react to outside boost quickly with a passionate reaction. Self-dominance causes an example break and take into account an inner elucidation to occur. Stop to completely watch the feelings springing up inside you and the considerations that present themselves. When in a dealer's trip, they have pursued the Holy Grail through various approaches, the most recent trading master, the following "can't miss" pointer, new stages and mechanical trading frameworks that remove the feeling from trading. Be that as it may, they can't get through to the following level. By the procedure of disposal, some start to understand that they are looking in all the wrong places for the missing fixing to their prosperity; the Holy Grail is not to be found "out there" in new frameworks or approaches.

Trading Framework Required for Objectified Success

So, after you begin building up some kind of trading framework and reasoning and are immovably on the way of the authority of those, what are the different things you can do accelerate the procedure? Where can the potential barricades to advance and fascination of trading benefits originate from? One of the classifications is in self-improvement, also called Self-Help. I jump at the chance to call it individual change in light of the fact that if you go on the procedure, over a period of years, you develop and the following 5 or 10 years, you wind up noticeably unrecognisable from the earlier you. It is genuinely a wonderful change. Make peace with your past. While there's a fact in the announcement, where the whole of our encounters, self-authority remembers we're positively not restricted to them. It is difficult to do. Our encounters, specifically negatives, have a method for leaking profoundly into our spirit. In any case, though a few stains can't be evacuated, we can pick not to wear those garments once more. Making peace with your past permits you an untarnished and more targeted way to deal with the present, preferably bringing about a positive future. It's difficult to get anything new when your hands are full of troubles. It intends to give up, pardon and as humanly conceivable, to overlook. You have a few rules for realising what and when to purchase and offer some technique for position estimates and so on.

Study and Mindset for Trading Success

You are the most vital factor in your trading. You are the person who settles on the choices, and you are the person who chooses what happens once you open a trade. It is the thing that goes on inside your head that will represent the moment of truth of you as a broker. You have to create mindfulness and comprehend your thought processes in trading. Trading is not just about profit. It's tied in with turning into the best dealer you can be. Have a decent look at yourself and your identity drivers. See how your identity impacts the way you trade. Understand your qualities and shortcomings in the market and investigate methods for conquering your shortcomings. I suggest that you begin a trading journal and record your trading feelings every day as they happen and you remember them. A few people battle in trading in light of the fact that they don't have their mindset. They have all these negative voices inside them, playing out all these ghastly situations. They experience issues with calming and cantering the brain. So, they can produce some serenity and peace inside them, so they can go comprehend their difficulties in an ideal way and maybe even get to new thoughts that you would never have thought of. So, they don't attempt to take care of issues out of some unreasonable dread or terrorising or cover of nervousness that they are conveying with them amid the day, consistently for the duration of their lives. Evacuating the mental issues, false convictions and a cover of tension that a few people bear on them, consistently, is basically imperative.

Focus on Positive Approaches and Psychological Improvement

You are constantly required to make positive representations and a positive inward discourse. As a feature of becoming more acquainted with yourself, you will begin to wind up plainly mindful of the things you say noiselessly inside your head. I realise that I used to whip myself after leaving a losing trade. I put myself down and obsessed about what could have been. Despite the fact that I comprehended that losing was a piece of the session of trading and that I should gain from my encounters, it didn't prevent me from conversing with myself in this way. To conquer this, I took a few courses in self-improvement and enhancing my attitude, addressing the nuts and bolts of NLP (Neuro-linguistic programming). This helped me to put my life into the point of view, pick up control over my feelings and build up an uplifting state of mind and vision for myself. Keeping in mind the end goal to make progress, you have to figure out how to be your own particular best helper and have faith in yourself. Encircle yourself with constructive individuals who trust in you. It's a given that we are who we draw in. To stay persuaded and constructive, we should be with these sorts of individuals. Self-authority implies continually adopting a dynamic strategy in life, being an entertainer instead of an onlooker. Trading the share trading system is an extraordinary affair for self-improvement. You will go up against your own particular evil spirits, and you will hear that little voice inside your head that will put you down. When you can conquer these obstacles in your psyche and trade the share trading system discipline by following a sound trading plan, you will develop immensely.

Testosterone, Cortisol, Predict Risky Trading

It is generally realised that budgetary markets can turn out to be perilously flimsy, yet it is misty why. Late research has highlighted the likelihood that endogenous hormones, specifically, testosterone and cortisol, may basically impact brokers' budgetary basic leadership. Here, we demonstrate that cortisol, a hormone that balances the reaction to physical or mental anxiety, predicts insecurity in monetary markets. In particular, we recorded salivary levels of cortisol and testosterone in individuals taking an interest in a trial resource showcase (N = 142) and found that individual and total levels of endogenous cortisol anticipate ensuing danger taking and value flimsiness. We, at that point, administered either cortisol (single oral measurements of 100 mg hydrocortisone, N = 34) or testosterone (three dosages of 10 g transdermal 1% testosterone gel more than 48 hours, N = 41) to youthful guys before they played a benefit trading diversion. We found that both cortisol and testosterone moved venture towards less secure resources. Cortisol seems to influence hazard inclinations specifically, while testosterone works by initiating expanded idealism about future value changes. Our outcomes recommend that progressions in both cortisol and testosterone could assume a destabilising role in budgetary markets through expanded hazard taking conduct, acting by means of various behavioural pathways.

Never Promote Aggressive Workplaces

Raised levels of the hormones testosterone and cortisol can make traders go out on a limb, which could make unsteadiness in budgetary markets, an examination recommends. Specialists said upsetting and aggressive workplaces could be expanding hormone levels and affecting basic leadership. Volunteers played a securities trade diversion while hormones levels were measured. Specialists said it was vital to know how hormones influenced brokers. Both cortisol and testosterone occur naturally in the body. Levels of cortisol increment when we encounter mental or physical anxiety. This causes the glucose levels to rise and readies the body for a 'battle or flight' reaction. High testosterone levels in men have appeared to make them certain and fruitful in focused circumstances. Past research works have demonstrated that male traders make essentially higher benefits on days when their morning testosterone levels were over their day by day normal. Trading floors are profoundly distressing and have aggressive conditions. In the two people and non-human creatures, such conditions are known to be related with vacillations essentially in two endogenous steroid hormones: cortisol and testosterone. Cortisol is lifted because of physical or mental anxiety and is especially touchy to circumstances of curiosity, instability or risk. Intense increments in cortisol advance dread, physical excitement and sensation chasing. Testosterone has been found to both foresee achievement rates and trust in focused experiences with levels expanding in light of triumphs or testing circumstances, thought to be a piece of a positive input circle named the 'victor impact.' Testosterone has likewise been firmly connected with seen economic wellbeing. In men, hoisted levels of testosterone have been related with expanded animosity, sexual capacity and mindset.

Never Fly High with Success

The confirmation would appear to demonstrate that either hormone could assume a part in balancing singular inclinations for hazard taking and market insecurity, especially while taking part in a field as upsetting and focused as a cutting edge monetary market. This probability is upheld by information from field examinations analysing the hormone levels of expert traders. One investigation detailed that traders made fundamentally higher benefits on days when their morning testosterone levels were over their day by day normal and that expanded inconstancy in benefits and instability in the market was dependably connected with heights in their cortisol levels. A moment considers found that traders' second-to-fourth digit proportion, a hypothesised marker of prenatal presentation to testosterone was likewise connected with higher benefits and professional life span. Men who had more elevated amounts of cortisol will probably go for broke, which prompted unsteadiness in costs. Be that as it may, there did not seem to be a connection between cortisol and dangerous trading in the ladies who partook, which is reliable with other research demonstrating that ladies react to worry in various ways. In a moment explore, 75 young fellows were given one of the hormones before playing the diversion and after that, a fake treatment. The outcomes demonstrated that cortisol seemed to support more hazardous ventures while testosterone expanded the inclination that they were on a triumphant streak. The examination group said their work gave a superior comprehension of traders' conduct and how it may influence monetary markets.

Controlling Hormone is Anticipating Success

In the underlying investigation, 10 members traded and resourced out a mechanised trade. The "market" comprised of 15 diverse preparing periods at 2 minutes each and after every period, the advantages yielded an irregular profit that was certain or negative.

Members entered the market with 10 units of the benefit and a money advance of 28 pounds and after the last session, every advantage paid a development estimation of 1 pound. The creators composed that this setup kept the primary attributes of genuine budgetary markets in that few members traded stocks as purchasers and traders and were allowed to decide costs 'in an arrangement of reciprocal trades.' Analysts concentrated on the primary time frame when looking at how endogenous testosterone and cortisol levels influenced hazard taking, on the grounds that the subjects had constrained data about alternate traders and were less inclined to group like conduct. The scientists, at that point, broke down the connection between individual hormone levels from before, then after the fact, trading through every one of the sessions and looked at the connection between normal hormonal levels in the market and total value steadiness. For the initial segment of the examination with endogenous hormone levels, cortisol was unequivocally connected with more prominent trading movement, which remained in more hazardous trading conduct in the investigation in men ($t = 4.35$; $P = 0.001$, $R2 = 0.381$). Be that as it may, testosterone was adversely, and not fundamentally, associated with trading action ($P = 0.1$). By differentiation, the trading movement of ladies in the initial segment of the investigation demonstrated a negative, yet not noteworthy pattern toward a relationship with cortisol ($P = 0.08$) and an insignificant positive pattern related to testosterone ($P > 0.6$). "The outcomes so far demonstrate a positive relationship between pre-sell-off Endogenous Cortisol and early trading action in men, however not in ladies," closed the creators. What's more, neither one of the hormone's levels anticipated benefits.

Never Give Up in Uncertainty

Since the essential estimation of a benefit in money related market is a collection of the stochastic stream of future profits, trading at costs higher than the basic esteem is just beneficial when there is a broad conviction that different brokers will keep on buying at costs much further from basic esteems. Such theoretical and unsustainable trading procedures are dangerous and contribute towards value flimsiness. An expanded eagerness to go out on a limb makes these questionable ventures, everything else being equivalent, more attractive, and this, thus, makes value bubbles and money related market precariousness more probable. Neither testosterone nor cortisol was related with a general speculation. In any case, cortisol was related to more interests in more dangerous stocks contrasted and fake treatment (z = 2.17; P = 0.030), as was testosterone contrasted and fake treatment (z = 2.00; P = 0.046). Be that as it may, for the slightest unsafe stocks, the hormones seemed to have little impact. "The watched impacts are perfect with field perceptions in proficient traders and propose that these hormones may assume a destabilising part in monetary markets," composed the analysts. They likewise proposed that the worry of a focused domain may advance more elevated amounts of cortisol and testosterone. Guide confirmation to help a connection amongst hormones and speculation conduct is constrained, and it is uncertain whether any of these discoveries can be summed up to trading budgetary markets, where different factors, for example, certainty and capacity, are probably going to assume a vital part.

Keep Hormones in Control during Budget Plans

The instrument by which cortisol and testosterone influence advertise choices is obscure. Despite the fact that the discoveries recommend a part for both cortisol and testosterone in the shakiness of budgetary markets, recognising a neurobiological component from this information is all the more difficult, especially since the neural relates of market conduct have just started to be explored. A critical confinement of the investigation is the way that it was led in a simulated setting made to emulate a true one. It is difficult to envision that the outcomes wouldn't mean genuine budgetary markets. However, the little exploratory markets that the specialists set up fluctuate enormously from true ones. Endogenous levels of either cortisol or testosterone would foresee chance taking and value flimsiness in a surely known exploratory trading condition that mirrors the key components of a certifiable budgetary market. This analysis included no hormone organisation. Changes in subjects' hormonal levels must be actuated by the characteristic response to our test trading condition. The neurobiology of the mental reaction to testosterone is less surely known, however later work has demonstrated that organisation of testosterone in ladies is related with increments in the differential cerebrum reaction to jolts related with rewards and appetitive objective. Dependability in money related markets may be enhanced by considering how social, natural and procedural factors such as the arrival of imperative monetary data may affect.

Attribution and Cognitive Bias

Having bias can extremely disable our capacity to peruse the business sectors unbiased and settle on great trading choices. The initial step to beating these biases is to end up noticeably completely mindful of them. Underneath, you'll discover a rundown of five of the most widely recognised trading bias. Attribution predisposition alludes to the propensity of people to credit their triumphs to inborn angles. For example, ability or foreknowledge. As a rule, the faulting disappointments are needy for outside impacts. For example, loss. Self-attribution is a psychological wonder by which individuals credit disappointments to situational variables and victories to dispositional components. On the off chance that you inquire about the subject of intellectual inclination, you will discover many biases. You will likewise locate that a large portion of them are connected or are recently slight varieties of each other. It basically demonstrates that our brains are difficult to comprehend by any stretch of the imagination.

Self-attribution Poses Increase Speculation Loss
Self-attribution biases speculators to unwittingly go up against improper degrees of money related hazard and to trade too forcefully, enhancing individual market instability. Self-attribution bias regularly

drives cognitive bias to trade more than is reasonable. The idea of behavioural back encourages us to perceive our regular bias that leads us to settle on silly and frequently unreasonable choices with regards to ventures and funds. A prime case of this is the idea of prospect hypothesis, which is the possibility that as people, our enthusiastic reaction to saw loss is unique in relation to that of saw picks up. As indicated by prospect hypothesis, a loss for a speculator feels twice as agonising as increases can rest easy. A few financial specialists stress more over the minimal rate change in their riches than they do about the measure of their riches. This manner of thinking is in reverse and can make speculators focus on the wrong issues. The intellectual inclination alludes to giving excessive weight to the stay when we settle on our choices.

As dealers utilising specialised examination, who or what offers us the most data? It is the market, obviously. The market continues offering us new data. Each value tick that comes in speaks to new data. We have to break down new information. Be that as it may, would we say we are tied down by the primary snippet of data?

Trade Rundowns from Cognitive Biases

Psychologists characterise cognitive biases as subjective mistakes in the way individuals figure out whom or what was in charge of an occasion or result. Say what?! In trading, attribution predisposition shows itself when you credit your own frantic aptitudes for winning trades and accuse losing trades on outside elements. For example, the flightiness of the business sectors or on your moderate web businesses. This is the place the significance of having a definite trade diary comes in. Run down the things that you did well, what you fouled up, what you expected and didn't expect and what you could've improved. As per Dr. Steenbarger, this will enable you to take responsibility for qualities and shortcomings, which would ideally make you turn out to be more aware of your trading forms.

For example, a trading session starts with a solid bullish push. Despite the fact that the market hinted at clear depletion, you kept up that it was bullish. A financial specialist whose reasoning is liable to subjective inclination would probably search for data that back his or her unique thought regarding a speculation, as opposed to searches for data that negates it. Working with a money related organiser can enable financial specialists to perceive and comprehend their own individual behavioural inclinations and inclinations and hence have the capacity to abstain from settling on venture choices construct altogether in light of those bias.

Biases Abandons Alternative Routes of Successes

The field of attribution and cognitive biases endeavours to comprehend and clarify choices by consolidating the points of brain science and contributing on a small-scale level (i.e. the choice procedure of people and gatherings) and a full-scale level (i.e. the part of money related markets). The basic leadership procedure of speculators fuses both a quantitative (objective) and the (subjective) perspective that depends on the components of the venture item or budgetary administration. Speculator conduct looks at the mental procedures and intense subject matters that people, money related specialists and dealers uncover amid the budgetary arranging and venture administration handle. By and by, people settle on judgments and choices that depend on past occasions, individual convictions and inclinations. They set up alternate routes or heuristics that can spare time, yet lead them far from sound, long haul considering. The lesson is one that cautions against tenacity. Perceive what the market is letting you know, now. Practically, it strikes adjustments. This is on account of specialised investigation expecting us to think back in time for help and imperviousness to outline the present market. In this sense, it expects us to be tied down to past data. However, we have to always look at new perceptions to take after the market stream. To keep up this fine exercise in careful control, examine chronicled information. However, it is recommended not to clutch authentic conclusions.

Financial Improvements in Trade Disapproves Biases

After a phenomenal trade with a pleasant benefit, you begin to feel like a virtuoso, believing that your trading abilities made it conceivable. After a losing trade, you accuse your handle, your PC and your seat. Assume praise for the correct things. Assume acknowledgment for following your principles and not for your beneficial trades. Assume praise for your predictable benefits over a vast specimen and not for a solitary gainful trade. Assume liability for everything, including your loss. As an autonomous broker, you don't move blame in light of the fact that it doesn't enable you to advance. Assuming liability to discover what turned out badly and doing what it takes to enhance does. Perceiving that we have no power over the market is the initial move towards dealing with our hazard. Try not to look for conviction and control. Look to be agreeable in unverifiable circumstances outside our ability to control. Henceforth, concentrate on controlling what we can control. Financial specialists tormented with self-attribution inclination may wind up noticeably presumptuous, which can prompt overtrading and underperformance. Monitoring individual oversights and victories and creating responsibility instruments. For example, looking for productive input from others can enable financial specialists to pick up the consciousness of self-attribution predisposition.

Optimistic Pessimism is Good for the Trader

Optimism/Pessimism is a mental attribute surely understood by money related professionals and clinicians. Improbable traders misperceive the normal returns of the hazardous resource or the past, make a judgmental mistake on both the unpredictability of the benefit returns and the difference of the commotion in his/her private flag. For the situation where the market producer is reasonable, hopeful traders buy progressively or offer littler amounts, though sceptical traders offer more or buy fewer amounts than if they were sensible. Hearing that the world is going to hell fire is, evidently, significantly more fascinating than foreseeing that things are on the up. Positive thinkers are expelled as credulous, best case scenario and offering a lie even under the least favourable conditions. While the worry wart looks bourgeois by examination, with sharp basic deduction abilities. Next time you go to the shops or to work, will you be making another stride towards a more joyful, more beneficial and naturally stable future by urging thoughts to affectionately reproduce? Or will you be assaulting the world? It relies upon who you inquire. Matt Ridley will guarantee you of the previous. Check Boyle is so persuaded of the latter that he has relinquished money inside and out and now lives in a troop in the forested areas outside Bristol. When each is taken alone, optimism and negativity are not advantageous to the fruitful trader, but when utilised as a part of conjunction, we have an alternate story. We should investigate what I mean when I say, "hopeful negativity is useful for the trader."

Effective Trading Acknowledge Both Optimism and Pessimism

Both optimism and pessimism can draw on realities, yet the worry wart can include a solid dosage of dread to the story, which urges us to prick up our ears and listen. Then we harp on those apprehensions for longer than we will over the uplifting news, passing those feelings of trepidation on to others. Pessimism is characterised as an inclination to push the negative or horrible or take the gloomiest conceivable view. Clearly, the effective trader is not critical. Provided that this is true, he could never trade the primary spot or if he did, he would just trade short; a "permaban" maybe. An absolutely critical trader would likewise question his edge, question any market bearing, just trade after the move has happened, stop his champs while enabling his washouts to run, over trade, under contribute and so on. At the end of the day, an absolutely sceptical trader would break every one of the principles. You'd have justifiable reason to feel cynical, isn't that so? Yet, that is not the full story. In the event that we look at worldwide tyke mortality, the survival rate for the initial 5 years of life for a kid has ascended since 1960 from 81.5% to 95.6%. Nations as poor and tormented as Haiti, Burma and the Congo have baby death rates today that are lower than those that any nation on the planet accomplished in 1900. Total populace development, which was an unsustainable 2% a year in the 1960s, has been falling consistently and is going to dip under 1 for each penny a year. This is uplifting news for the planet. In Western Europe, we're presently getting a charge out of the longest time of peace since Roman circumstances. In a previous couple of years, clashes have finished in Chad, Peru,

India, Sri Lanka, Angola and Columbia. Those appear like a lot of things to be merry about. What's more, how would you get that move from negativity to optimism? It's as straightforward as making a stride back and looking at a more extended time period. Naturalists notice warming world, diminishing water supply and nourishment and fuel frailty. This may make Boyle's course look like the more sensible one. The 31-year-old vegetarian lives on the sustenance he develops or finds in the forested areas around his parade, washes in waterway water, craps in a fertiliser latrine and brushes his teeth with ground cuttlefish bones and fennel.

Convert Pessimism into Fortune

The pessimist trader will be expecting the most noticeably bad news. That is not really an awful thing, since we ought to be set up for loss. An excessive number of traders indiscriminately expect that a losing run could never hit them. Be that as it may, in case you're continually expecting the most exceedingly awful, odds are that you won't put a trade. Why might you, if it will lose?! Furthermore, a negative trader (accepting they have opened a position) will just trade after the move has happened, and he'll stop his champs. The hopeful trader, then again, has his own arrangement of issues. He'll presumably have unreasonable desires of how quickly he can profit, he'll stake too high, he'll leave losing trades open, adding to them and he'll permit his affirmation predisposition to legitimise breaking the standards. The self-assured person and the worry wart are as terrible as each other! Yet, each can help the other. Good faith is characterised as the slant to suspect an ideal result, while trusting that most circumstances work out generally advantageous. The unsuccessful trader, particularly the starting trader, is hopeful about getting rich in the share trading system. Regardless of what each trade will, in the long run, profit, he reasons. The idealistic trader additionally stacks up on a "beyond any doubt thing," tries to legitimise each trade by means of affirmation inclination, adds to failures, gloats about champs while concealing washouts, declines to create as a trader and so on. Similarly, as with negativity, the hopeful trader breaks the guidelines. Many individuals are still attempting to process what occurred with NAFTA and the WTO (a considerable measure occurred in these two understandings, for example, financial specialist state, TRIPS and GATS), to check whether the outcomes require some refinement. It would be astonishing on the off chance that they were impeccable. Would they say anything is ever great? The slowing down of FTAs, as of late, is halfway hence.

Positive Thinking Drives Pessimism to Exit Way

Trader's hopeful negativity as decides based positive thinking that acknowledges a pickup or a loss as an ideal result while keeping up a sound dosage of pessimism in a market where anything can happen. There was a lot of trade struggle amid the Clinton years. Once in a while, the blemishes of the past are disregarded. We can face off regarding the explanations behind it. However, the Clinton years were truly great as far as monetary development is concerned, which clarifies why there was not the same number of huge trade cure activities. By differentiation, the Bush subsidence had the steel shields and the current money related emergency brought about the Obama tire taxes. Regardless of how great your investigation is, regardless of how ideal your set-up or example might be, regardless of what number of others may concur with your examination and regardless of what number of wins in succession you have had, once you enter a trade, anything can happen. Truth be told, you ought to be amazed each time you profit! A trader ought to be hopeful about his generally tried trade set-up or "edge," realising that when he takes after the guidelines as a plot by that edge, he has a high likelihood of profiting. In the meantime, the trader likewise knows and trusts no two trades are the same. That is quite recently the way it is (and will be)! As well as can be expected put on a trade without the scarcest piece of dithering or struggle and similarly, as openly and decisively or strife, letting it out isn't working. They can escape the trade even with a loss and doing as such doesn't reverberate the smallest piece of passionate uneasiness. As such, the dangers natural in trading don't make the best traders lose their education, centre or feeling of certainty. At the point when trade cures activities and other trade measures are taken, nations, for the most part, attempt to play by the principles. What's more, when the WTO chooses that the measures are in infringement, these nations, more often than not, attempt to bring them into consistency. That is as much as I anticipate from the framework, and I'm inspired that we have a multilateral trade framework that keeps on conveying this, even during a genuine monetary emergency.

Sense of Liberty Encourages Optimistic Pessimism

For as far back as 400 years ago in the West, bourgeois believing depended on positive thinking, illumination and advance. Oliver Cromwell and his supporters suspected that their Revolution had issued in the Kingdom of God on earth. The Founding Fathers of the United States have persuaded the nation they made would be superior to everything, offering natives life, freedom and the quest for joy. Amid the Great French Revolution, the bourgeoisie stimulated the semi-ordinary masses of Paris to battle against medieval oppression under the banner of Liberty, Equality, Fraternity and the Rule of Reason. In the meantime, in England, a significantly more prominent Revolution was starting. A modern transformation in light of steam power, apparatus and the processing plant framework. In those circumstances, the good faith of the bourgeoisie had a material premise, due to free enterprise, regardless of every one of its wrongdoings and horrifying severity, by and by assuming a dynamic part in toppling rotted and deteriorates feudalism and building up the beneficial powers. In the quest for the benefit, the industrialists created industry, agribusiness, science and innovation to an unfathomable degree. In this manner, unwittingly, they built up the material reason for a higher type of society – communism and the class that is bound to topple it. What is positively genuine is that there are clear periods of the improvement of free enterprise, and each period has a tendency to be distinctive to each other period. On the off chance that we contemplate the historical backdrop of free enterprise in the course of the most recent 150 years, we see, from one viewpoint, a consistent arrangement of blasts and drops (which bourgeois financial analysts used to call "the business cycle"). This has a fairly sporadic example that varies in various periods. In Marx's day, the ordinary cycle was around ten years, despite the fact that there is no unmistakable lead about the consistency of the monetary cycle, which can fluctuate for impressive periods. Well ordered, the deterioration of private enterprise set up the route for progressive advancements. The street to awesome social changes is set up by an entire arrangement of halfway battles. This is the essential preliminary stage in which we get ourselves.

Trusting Intuitions Often Help Capitalising Market

What necessities to endeavour to be are a long haul self-assured person and a transient pessimist? We ought to enter each trade arranged to lose it, that way we won't over-trade or stake too high. Rather, we'll deal with our hazard deliberately, constantly prepared for the following losing run. We'll not be tossed by the here and now lost, since we have an eye on the long-haul execution of our technique, which (insofar as you're utilising the correct one!) should give you a lot of motivations to be hopeful! Then again, I concede that I have a few questions once in a while. The inability to gain much ground in the Doha Round and the proceeded with concentrate on reciprocal/provincial trade understandings, are quite negative advancements, in my view. Furthermore, what some different nations have a tendency to do, is somewhat misleading. (In such manner, I was enjoyably shocked to see that the most recent U.S. trade activity is being alluded to as the "Trans-Pacific Partnership." I don't know this was an evident move in word decision, as it might have been constructing more in light of what the current gatherings to the understanding were calling it. However, it's a change in any case.) Still, even with the negative parts of such feeling and the reality they are, for the most part, slowed down in the U.S., there are sure advancements. For example, the effectiveness of the China-ASEAN FTA, which will be 'the world's third-biggest facilitated commerce territory.'

Dealing with Loss Aversion in Trade is Indispensable for Profit

There is an interesting wonder in the field of human brain research known as "loss aversion." Loss aversion is, to some degree, precisely what it sounds like. It is the propensity which we as a whole need to keep away from loss, yet it is somewhat more perplexing than that. When we encounter loss aversion, we will trade a shot at considerable increases for an opportunity to just stay away from a loss. Loss aversion is most likely affecting the way that you trade paired alternatives at this moment. Consider something you'd truly prefer not to lose, something of significant worth to you. For example, a cherished ownership. Presently, envision you're informed that on the off chance that you lay that protest on hold in a wager, you have a decent shot at multiplying its esteem, but on the other hand, there's plausibility you'll lose it. How low would the shot of loss be before you'd go out on a limb? May be 10%? Not as much as that? The appropriate response may lie in a behavioural monetary hypothesis called 'loss aversion.'

Considering Certain Period Is Recommended

Fundamentally, clinicians have discovered that loss has an altogether more intense effect on our minds than increases (some gauge that the impact could even be twice as capable). This data is utilised each day by financial experts, traders and advertisers who need to locate the most convincing approach to outline an arrangement. You may perceive a few cases of loss aversion in your own life. Consider a period in your life when you were offered a little raise, say Rs. 50 a month. You likely were very glad, yet not really blissful, isn't that so? Presently, think about a period when your compensation was cut by Rs. 50 a month. There is a decent shot you were level out angry. Consider a period when your insurance agency chose to allow you some breathing room on your rates, putting Rs. 5 a month back in your pocket. Decent, yet not astonishing, isn't that so? In any case, consider a period when your insurance agency chose to raise your rates by Rs. 5 a month. Despite the fact that it is a genuinely ostensible sum, you presumably were exceptionally despondent. You may even have gotten the telephone and called to whine. Specialist Maurice Schweitzer and Devin Pope look at more than 2,500,000 from the 2004–2009 PGA Tour. They were hoping to perceive what rate of golfers effectively finished birdie putts versus putts for the standard. On the off chance that you are not a golfer, a "birdie" is basically finishing a gap, a solitary stroke under the standard. A birdie is superior to standard. The discoveries of the examination were very striking. The analysts discovered that exclusive 28.3% of birdie putts were effectively finished versus 82.9% of putts for the standard. The suggestion is the golfers consistently and intentionally keep away from birdie putts, leaving the subject of why.

Conceptual Trading Framework Helps to Definite Goal

The dread of loss can make financial specialists pass up a great opportunity for open doors as well as take passionate activities.

For example, selling their benefits. That could run counter to their long-haul speculation objectives. Dread has a major influence in showcase brain science, and it can be an intense drive! Loss aversion isn't really a decent or awful thing all alone; the genuine inquiry is whether it makes you settle on great or awful trading choices. Truly, this all boils down to how hazard opposed you are. One fascinating case includes win rate and the sizes of your losses and wins. A lot of brokers contend about which measurement is an essential one. There is a typical attitude that your win rate is a definitive estimation, regardless of whether you have an effective or dependable trading framework. Loss aversion makes us need to limit the quantity of loss that we encounter on the grounds that each and every one of them is agonising, regardless of whether vast or little. There are circumstances where a dealer with a framework that wins 60% of the time really is beating a broker with the framework that wins 80% of the time. In the event that the merchant who encounters more losses is getting a significantly little loss and generously bigger wins, that dealer may really have the more beneficial framework.

Traders Need to Calculate Loss Always

The cost of saw 'well-being' is the thing that numerous speculators see as 'security' and it can include some significant downfalls: loss of potential return. You can envision how the yearning to attempt and maintain a strategic distance from showcase loss frequently makes speculators move their cash out of stocks and into money or settled salary vehicles, but instead of dodging loss, they regularly end up trading potential market loss for potential negative genuine returns, particularly once the effect of expansion is calculated in. What does this move into low-yielding instruments mean for financial specialists? It implies their speculations are basically at a halt, while their venture objectives such as purchasing a home, school, retirement, et cetera, are presumably keep on requiring some kind of capital appreciation.

You can perceive how loss aversion may make you disregard the framework with the 60%-win rate. 60% simply does not appear as mentally agreeable as 80%. The possibility of encountering loss 40% of the time may just be excessively overwhelming for a lot of traders to consider. In any case, it might, in any case, be the predominant approach impartially.

Controlling Predetermination Leads to Loss

The most hazardous part of loss aversion with regards to trading apparently has nothing to do with trading frameworks or cash administration. It needs to do with the all-encompassing brain research. The additional time you spend on gatherings in the trading group, the more you come to understand that a great many people who long for trading as a profession will never really move past the envisioning stage. There are many components impacting everything, starting with one individual then onto the next, yet loss aversion is certainly a typical guilty party. All ventures include dangers, including conceivable loss of central. Stock costs vary, at times quickly and significantly, because of elements influencing singular organisations, specific enterprises or segments or general economic situations. In the event that you fantasise about moving out of your normal everyday employment and into the world where you are allowed to control your predetermination through trading, you are putting a lot of enthusiastic eggs in one wicker container. In the event that you are in a pickle this way, the main thing that you can do is change your perspective. You need to put your feelings into an alternate point of view. You need to figure out how to begin allocating more importance to your positive feelings, despite the fact that you may feel them less strongly than your negative feelings. You ought to never toss yourself thoughtlessly into trivial dangers, yet you can't experience existence without going out on a limb. You will accomplish the most with an adjusted approach!

Trading Psychology Quotes:

"I take a Zen-like view. You have to be part of the market and be able to get into the market flow. Don't try to pick bottoms and tops; let the market determine where it's at and then go with it."

–**Lewis Borsellino**

"The big ones take the psychology out of the game. Have a game plan, and stick to it."

–**Tim Erber**

"I find that the percentage of successful traders is higher among women. They tend to be less arrogant, and arrogance is a deadly sin in trading."

–**Alexander Elder**

"Trade like you don't need the money. It takes so much pressure off you."

–**Martin Niemi**

"Our personal beliefs form the texture of our lives. When nourished with energy and action, our self-beliefs act as powerful for achieving our goals and dreams. They access resources deep within us and direct these resources to support and achieve desired outcomes."

–**Toni Turner**

"The male ego – that wonderful trait that has been bringing us wars, riots, and bloodshed since time immemorial – tends to get heavily caught up in trading. A guy studies his charts, decides to buy, and now his self-esteem is involved – he has to be right! If the market goes his way, he waits to be proven even more right – bigger is better. If the market goes against him, he is tough enough to stand the pain, and waits for the market to reverse and prove him right – while it grinds down his account."

–**Alexander Elder**

"The 'making money' part of trading is simply a by-product (end result) of a focused and precise utilisation of our trained psychological and mechanical resources to successfully find and manage trades. Under the most intense circumstances, the best results will be produced only with a deep concentration and focus on the task at hand."

–**Chris Lori**

"The ability to subordinate an impulse to a value is the essence of the proactive person. Reactive people are driven by feelings, by circumstances, by conditions, by their environment. Proactive people are driven by values – carefully thought about, selected and internalised values."

–**Stephen Covey**

"If there is such a thing as a secret to the nature of trading, this is it: At the very core of one's ability 1) to trade without fear or overconfidence, 2) perceive what the market is offering from its perspective, 3) stay completely focused in the 'now moment opportunity flow,' and 4) spontaneously enter the 'zone,' it is a strong virtually unshakeable belief in an uncertain outcome with an edge in your favour."

–**Mark Douglas**

"Success in investing doesn't correlate with I.Q. once you're above the level of 125. Once you have ordinary intelligence, what you need is the temperament to control the urges that get other people into trouble in investing."

–**Warren Buffett**

"We are what we repeatedly do. Excellence, then, is not an act, but a habit."

–**Aristotle**

"A habit is the intersection of knowledge, skill and desire. Knowledge is the theoretical paradigm, the what-to-do and the why. Skill is the how to do. And the desire is the motivation, the want to do. In order to make something a habit in our lives, we have to have all three."

–**Stephen Covey**

"The essential element is that the markets are ultimately based on human psychology, and by charting the markets you're merely converting human psychology into graphic representations. I believe that the human mind is more powerful than any computer in analysing the implications of this graph."

–**Al Weiss**

"For the past eight years I have been working with top-notch Wall Street traders unearthing specific psychological issues that interfere with the trading process. These include resistance, fear of failure, defensive behaviour, negative self-characterisations, and negative mindsets that become self-fulfilling prophesies."

–Ari Kiev

"To succeed as a trader, it is absolutely necessary to have an edge. You can't win without an edge, even with the world's greatest discipline and money management skills. If you don't have an edge, all that money management and discipline will do for you is to guarantee that you will gradually bleed to death. Incidentally, if you don't know what your edge is, you don't have one."

–Jack Schwager

"Environmental distractions and boredom cause a lack of focus – All of us have limits to our attention span and these are easily taxed during quiet times in the market."

–Brett Steenbarger

"I really like my life. I've arranged my life so that I can do what I want."

–Warren Buffett

"Those traders who have confidence in their own trades, who trust themselves to do what needs to be done without hesitation, are the ones who become successful. They no longer fear the erratic behaviour of the market. They learn to focus on the information that helps them spot opportunities to make a profit, rather than focusing on the information that reinforces their fears."

–Mark Douglas

"Fatigue and mental overload create a loss of concentration – The demands of watching the screen hour after hour make it difficult to be sharp, creating fatigue effects that are well-known to pilots, car drivers, and soldiers."

–**Brett Steenbarger**

"While this may sound complicated, it all boils down to learning to believe that: (1) you don't need to know what's going to happen next to make money; (2) anything can happen; and (3) every moment is unique, meaning every edge and outcome is truly a unique experience. The trade either works or it doesn't."

–**Mark Douglas**

"Therefore, my objective is to assist traders to change their behaviour so as to increase their profitability. Part of this process is urging traders to be more analytical about themselves and what they are doing."

–**Ari Kiev**

"It is very well documented that people get things wrong. They make errors of logic and reasoning with uncertainty."

–**Peter Donnelly**

"Trading is easy; anyone with a few bucks can do it. Making money, however, is a whole different ball game."

–**Marcel Link**

"The key is consistency and discipline. Almost anybody can make up a list of rules that are 80% as good as what we taught. What they can't do is give (people) the confidence to stick to those rules even when things are going bad."

–**Richard Dennis**

"We look for evidence to reinforce our models. Some folks are all too able to provide that evidence, or to create other barriers to understanding."

–Jonathan Drori

"An awful lot of people keep a stock too long because it gives them the warm fuzzies, particularly when a contrarian stance has been vindicated. If they sell it they lose bragging rights."

–John Neff

"The ability to change one's mind is probably a key characteristic of successful traders. Dogmatic and rigid personalities rarely succeed in markets. The markets are a dynamic process and sustained trading success requires the ability to modify and even change strategies as markets evolve. Successful traders have the ability to adapt to the changing dynamics of the market and in the process, maintain their consistency of performance."

–Gill Blake

"To be a successful trader, you have to be able to admit mistakes. People who are very bright don't make very many mistakes. In a sense, they generally are correct. In trading, however, the person who can easily admit to being wrong is the one who walks away a winner. Besides trading, there is probably no other profession where you have to admit you're wrong. In trading, you can't hide your failures. Your equity provides a daily reflection of your performance. The trader who tries to blame his losses on external events will never learn from his mistakes. For a trader, rationalisation is a guaranteed road to ultimate failure."

–Victor Sperandeo

"Overconfidence follows a string of successes – It is common for traders to attribute success to skill and failure to situational, external factors. As a result, a string of even random wins can lead traders to become overconfident and veer from trading plans – especially by trading too frequently and/or trading excessive size."

–**Brett Steenbarger**

"If you're going to panic, panic early."

–**Unknown**

"Fear of Regret – An inability to accept that you've made a wrong decision, which leads to holding onto losers too long or selling winners too soon."

–**Gavin McQuill**

"Quantum Wealth combines money with time, energy and desires. The desire generates income as desire and fulfilment become at least as, if not more, important as the money."

–**Gary Scott**

"There seems to be some perverse human characteristic that likes to make easy things difficult."

–**Warren Buffett**

"We typically trade our beliefs about the market and once we've made up our minds about those beliefs, we're not likely to change them. And when we play the markets, we assume that we are considering all of the available information. Instead, our beliefs, through selective perception, may have eliminated the most useful information."

–**Van K. Tharp**

"Myopic loss aversion (a.k.a. as 'short-sightedness') – A fear of losing money and the subsequent inability to withstand short-term events and maintain a long-term perspective."

–**Gavin McQuill**

"Unwillingness to accept losses – This leads traders to alter their trade plans after trades have gone into the red, turning what were meant to be short-term trades into longer-term holds and transforming trades with small size into large trades by adding to losers."

–**Brett Steenbarger**

"Cognitive dissonance – The inability to change your opinion after new evidence contradicts your baseline assumption."

–**Gavin McQuill**

"Most often, traders have four fears. There's the fear of being wrong, the fear of losing money, the fear of missing out and the fear of leaving money on the table. I found that basically, those four fears accounted for probably 90% to 95% of the trading errors that we make. Let's put it this way: If you can recognise opportunity, what's going to prevent you from executing your trades properly? Your fear. Your fears immobilise you. Your fears distort your perception of market information in ways that don't allow you to utilise what you know."

–**Mark Douglas**

"Traders who are not ready to accept responsibility for the outcomes of their interpretations and actions will find themselves in a dilemma: How does one participate in an activity that allows complete freedom of choice, and at the same time avoid taking responsibility if the outcome of one's choices are unexpected and not to one's liking?"

–**Mark Douglas**

"Overconfidence – People's tendency to overestimate their abilities relative to individuals possessing greater expertise."

–Gavin McQuill

"Loss of confidence in one's trading plan/strategy because it has not been adequately tested and battle-tested – It is difficult to tolerate even normal drawdowns unless you have confidence in your methods. This confidence does not come from mere positive self-talk. Rather, it is a function of testing your methods (historically and in real-time) and seeing in your own experience that they truly work."

–Brett Steenbarger

"Anchoring – People's tendency to give too much credence to their most recent experience and to show reluctance to adjust their current beliefs."

–Gavin McQuill

"There is no shame in making a mistake. Despite a great deal of research and analysis, I make plenty of them, and so does every other investor, because the future is inherently unpredictable. But there is shame in refusing to acknowledge a mistake and rectifying it."

–Warren Buffett

"Representativeness – The tendency of people to see patterns within random events."

–Gavin McQuill

"If your goal is to trade like a professional and be a consistent winner, then you must start from the premise that the solutions are in your mind and not in the market."

–Mark Douglas

"Situational performance pressures – These include trading slumps and increased personal expenses that change how traders trade and lead them to place P/L ahead of making good trades. By worrying too much about how much money they make, traders can no longer follow markets with a clear head."

–Brett Steenbarger

"Win or lose, everybody gets what they want out of the market. Some people seem to like to lose, so they win by losing money."

–Jack Schwager

"The hard reality of trading is that, if you want to create consistency, you have to start from the premise that no matter what the outcome, you are completely responsible. This is a level of responsibility few people have aspired to before they decide to become traders."

–Mark Douglas

"Trading positions that are excessive for the account size – This is much more common than is usually acknowledged. It creates exaggerated P/L swings and emotional reactions that interfere with cool, calm planned behaviour."

–Brett Steenbarger

"It should be clear that human patterns of-less-than-perfectly rational behaviour are central to financial market behaviour, even among investment professionals, while at the same time there is little outright foolishness among investors."

–Robert Shiller

"Trading presents us with a fundamental paradox: How do we remain disciplined, focused, and consistent in the face of constant uncertainty?"

–Mark Douglas

"Trading a time frame, style, or market that does not match your talents, skills, risk tolerance, and personality – All too often, traders veer from their plans because those plans are ones that they feel they *should* follow, but that don't truly come naturally to them. These departures from discipline are actually unconscious attempts to trade in a style that is more in tune with the trader's skills and talents."

–**Brett Steenbarger**

"Ninety-five percent of the trading errors you are likely to make – causing the money to just evaporate before your eyes – will stem from your attitudes about being wrong, losing money, missing out, and leaving money on the table. What I call the four primary trading fears."

–**Mark Douglas**

"There is one important caveat to the notion that we live in a new economy, and that is human psychology, which appears essentially immutable."

–**Alan Greenspan**

"Optimism means expecting the best, but confidence means knowing how to handle the worst."

–**Max Gunther**

"Chains of habit are too light to be felt until they are too heavy to be broken."

–**Warren Buffett**

"Want to trade successfully? Just choose the good positions and avoid the bad ones. Poor trade selection takes a heavy toll as it bleeds your confidence and wallet. You face many crossroads during each market day. Without a system of discipline for your decision-making, impulse and emotion will undermine skills as you chase the wrong stocks at the worst times."

–**Alan Farley**

"I think that if people look deeply enough into their trading patterns, they find that, on balance, including all their goals, they are really getting what they want, even though they may not understand it or want to admit it."

–**Jack Schwager**

"Personality traits that lead to impulsivity and low frustration tolerance in stressful situations – Psychological research suggests that some individuals are more impulsive than others and less conscientious about adhering to plans and intentions. These personality traits often are accompanied by stimulation seeking and a high degree of risk tolerance: a deadly combination."

–**Brett Steenbarger**

"Many short-term players view trading as a form of gambling. Without planning or discipline, they throw money at the market. The occasional big score reinforces this easy money attitude but sets them up for ultimate failure. Without defensive rules, insiders easily feed off these losers and send them off to other hobbies."

–**Alan Farley**

"You have to be very, very honest with yourself. You must not kid yourself. Whether you have a position that is underwater or you are sitting on a huge profit, you have to look at it in exactly the same way. That is the main reason why people lose money in the market. I am very glad that that's the case because if it wasn't the case, it would be very difficult for people like me to consistently make money in the market."

–Alpesh Patel

"Put another way, understanding and controlling your perception of market information is important only to the extent that you want to achieve consistent results."

–Mark Douglas

"As human beings, we are free to act however we see fit, but when presented with danger or opportunity, most people act with surprising predictability."

–Tom Williams

"One has to have an interest to understand what is going on in this market. That is a characteristic which very few people have. Most people feel bored. Even though they think it is exciting and they are going to have a good time, they get bored very quickly, because it takes a lot of energy to go out and dig for more – why the market is doing what it is doing, what is new, who is buying and selling, and why. It takes a lot of patience and energy and motivation to ask these questions all the time."

–Alpesh Patel

"Do your own thing (independence), and do the right thing (discipline)."

–Unknown

"Confidence replaces fear! Only trade when you have confidence in your trading plan. If you have any doubts about the market or your plan, don't trade. If you identify your profit and loss parameters BEFORE you enter a trade, set your stops and stick to your trading plan, you will trade with confidence. If you follow the plan, your confidence will not be shaken after a losing trade and you will still have your capital to enter a new position when the time is right."

–**Unknown**

"Never let your market decisions be restricted or influenced by concern over what others might think. Don't worry about looking stupid."

–**Unknown**

"Optimally, trading is process oriented in that you define what constitutes a winning trade, and when you identify that pattern, indicator combination, or setup, you take the trade. As a result, your confidence should make you feel good about the trade." **Unknown**
"The key to trading success is emotional discipline. If intelligence were the key, there would be a lot more people making money trading."

–**Victor Sperandeo**

"Interestingly, the behaviour of crowds is a paradoxical indicator when applied to stock markets. When most investors are in consensus and are driving the market in a particular direction, one naturally thinks that the consensus will continue ad infinitum and that the best trading decision is to follow the crowd. But history has proven exactly the opposite. When driven strongly by consensus, crowd behaviour is actually a contrary indicator."

–**Jason Van Bergen**

"You don't have to make money back the same way you lost it."

–**Warren Buffett**

"If you cannot execute when you identify that pattern, indicator combination, or setup, it is probably because you are experiencing fear from previous trading experiences. This fear is caused either because you do not have confidence in the reasons for taking the trade or you don't believe that you will act appropriately in the market."

–**Unknown**

"It's when you're winning that you are most susceptible to making a mistake, overtrading, putting on too large a position, violating your rules, or generally operating as if no prudent boundaries on your behaviour are necessary. You may even go to the extreme of thinking you are the market. However, the market rarely agrees, and when it disagrees, you'll get hurt. The loss and the emotional pain are usually significant."

–**Mark Douglas**

"When you are confused, it is best to do nothing. You are just going for a random walk and that is when you are liable to get mugged, because you don't have staying power. You are likely to be faked out by some stray fluctuations because you lack the courage of your convictions. As my friend, Victor Niederhoffer says, the market destroys the weak – that is, investors who don't have well founded convictions. You need some convictions to avoid getting faked out, but having the courage of your convictions could get you wiped out if your convictions are false. So, I prefer to take a stand only when I have well-founded convictions."

–**George Soros**

"To overcome your emotional barriers to trading, remember that winning at trading is conditional upon low risk relative to potential reward. Because you may be trading with substantial risk, it is imperative that you identify time and price levels where your potential risk is minimal compared to your potential reward."

—**Unknown**

"Most of traders lose because they don't have a winning strategy. Apart from this even among those traders who do, many don't follow their strategy. Trading puts pressure on weaker human traits and seems to seek out each individual's Achilles' heel."

—**Gill Blake**

"Traders who are consistently successful are consistent as a natural expression of who they are. They don't have to try to be consistent; they are consistent."

—**Mark Douglas**

"Fear of regret is when people tend to feel sorrow and grief after having made an error in judgement. For example, before selling a stock, investors can be emotionally affected by whether the security was bought for more or less than the current price. In this process, investors avoid selling stocks that have gone down to avoid the pain and regret of having made a bad investment."

—**Unknown**

"So if you are afraid of being wrong or losing money, it means you will never learn enough to compensate for the negative effects these fears will have on your ability to be objective and your ability to act without hesitation."

—**Mark Douglas**

"The embarrassment of having to report the loss to the IRS, accountants, and others may also contribute to the tendency not to sell losing investments. As a result, investors follow the crowd and conventional wisdom to avoid the feeling of regret that comes with being incorrect."

–Unknown

"Most important, by establishing a belief that anything can happen, he will be training his mind to think in probabilities."

–Mark Douglas

"When you understand the fear of regret, it is easy to see why so many investors find it easier to buy a popular stock and rationalise it going down. Buying a stock with a bad image is harder to rationalise if it goes down. It is for this reason that money managers and advisors may favour well known and popular companies because they are less likely to be fired if they underperform."

–Unknown

"I know it may sound strange to many readers, but there is an inverse relationship between analysis and trading results. More analysis or being able to make distinctions in the market's behaviour will not produce better trading results. There are many traders who find themselves caught in this exasperating loop, thinking that more or better analysis is going to give them the confidence they need to do what needs to be done to achieve success. It's what I call a trading paradox that most traders find difficult, if not impossible to reconcile, until they realise you can't use analysis to overcome fear of being wrong or losing money. It just doesn't work!"

–Mark Douglas

"Besides the money management and risk assessment issues, you must first learn to tackle the psychological problems common to all traders and especially troublesome to day traders and short-term traders: Analysis Paralysis; Gambling Tendencies; Fear; Greed; Reluctance to 'Pull the Trigger;' Self Discipline. Once you have mastered your mental state of mind, you will produce better results."

—Unknown

"Overcoming the propensity to play emotionally requires a conscious commitment to specific trading objectives. This entails choosing a target, developing a strategy, and finding a method for adhering to it. A goal enables you to keep a relatively even keel through good and bad periods, to sustain momentum, and to keep from becoming bored."

—Ari Kiev

"Have an opinion on what the market should do but don't decide what the market will do."

—Bernard Baruch

"Be happy with a percentage of the move."

—Bernard Baruch

"Fools say that they learn by experience. I prefer to profit by others' experience."

—Bismarck

"I'll be here until I die. Even if I had fifty million dollars, what else am I going to do? This is what I love to do. I think those people who come in and say that they want to make a million dollars, or ten million dollars, and then plan to quit are the people who never make that much money because they have the wrong focus. They have a focus on being done with it, so they'll become more aggressive than they need to be. They'll take stupid trades because they feel really rushed and don't want to be here. Whereas, my goal is that I always want to be here."

—Brandon Fredrickson

"Being wrong is acceptable. But staying wrong is totally unacceptable. Being wrong isn't a choice, but staying wrong is. To play any game successfully, you have to have some skill, an edge, but beyond that it is money management. Good traders manage the downside; they don't worry the upside."

–Mark Minnervini

"Most traders who are new to the markets will very easily become Weak Holders. These people are usually under-capitalised and cannot readily cope with losses, especially if most of their capital is rapidly disappearing, which will undoubtedly result in emotional decision-making. Weak holders are on a learning curve and tend to execute their trades on 'instinct.' Weak holders are those traders who have allowed themselves to be 'locked-in' as the market moves against them, and are hoping and praying that the market will soon move back to their price level. These traders are liable to be 'shaken out' on any sudden moves or bad news. Generally, weak holders will find that they are trading on the wrong side of the market, and are therefore immediately under pressure if prices turn against them."

–Tom Williams

"You can be successful at anything if you set a goal and take action. But you must acquire the knowledge to accomplish those goals."

–Brian Tracy

"Marcus, Michael taught me one other thing that is absolutely critical: You have to be willing to make mistakes regularly; there is nothing wrong with it. Michael taught me about making your best judgment, being wrong, making your next best judgment, being wrong, making your third best judgment, and then doubling your money."

–Bruce Kovner

"As long as you are susceptible to the kinds of errors that are the result of rationalising, justifying, hesitating, hoping, and jumping the gun, you will not be able to trust yourself. If you can't trust yourself to be objective and to always act in your own best interests, achieving consistent results will be next to impossible."

–Mark Douglas

"If you personalise losses, you can't trade."

–Bruce Kovner

"There is no such thing as means & ends. Everything that we do is an end, in itself, that we can never erase."

–Cesar Chavez

"Men, it has been well said, think in herds; it will be seen that they go mad in herds, while they recover their senses slowly, and one by one."

–Charles MacKay

"The 'herd' will panic after observing substantial falls in a market (usually on bad news) and will usually follow its instinct to sell. As a trader who is aware of crowd psychology, you must ask yourself, 'Are the trading syndicates and market-makers prepared to absorb the panic selling at these price levels?' If they are, then this is a good sign that indicates market strength."

–Tom Williams

"After substantial rises, the 'herd' will become annoyed at missing the up-move, and will rush in and buy, usually on good news. This includes traders who already have long positions, and want more. At this stage, you need to ask yourself, 'Are the trading syndicates selling into the buying?' If so, then this is a severe sign of weakness."

–**Tom Williams**

"I Hear, I Forget. I See, I Remember. I Do, I Understand."

–**Unknown**

"When you do what your emotions tell you to – on the spur of the moment – you are doing exactly what the 'masses' are doing, and this is not generally profitable."

–**Claude Rosenberg**

"Graham's observations that investors pay too much for trendy, fashionable stocks and too little for companies that are out-of-favour, was on the money…why does this profitability discrepancy persist? Because emotion favours the premium-priced stocks. They are fashionable. They are hot. They make great cocktail party chatter. There is an impressive and growing body of evidence demonstrating that investors and speculators don't necessarily learn from experience. Emotion overrides logic time after time."

–**David Dreman**

"However, knowledge becomes obsolete. Thus, the person who stops learning will slide backward. One bit of knowledge at a critical moment can change the course of your whole career. You must open up to a continuous stream of information that is constantly available to you."

–**Van K. Tharp**

"You will need to learn how to adjust your attitudes and beliefs about trading in such a way that you can trade without the slightest bit of fear, but at the same time keep a framework in place that does not allow you to become reckless."

–Mark Douglas

"It's possible for traders to tap into one of three general attitudes when they approach the market. The first attitude is one of pessimism; the second is one of randomness and/or neutrality; and the third is one of empowerment. The first attitude never works. The second attitude seldom brings much success, while the third attitude, when properly done, guarantees success."

–Van K. Tharp

"Dramatic and emotional trading experiences tend to be negative. Pride is a great banana peel, as are hope, fear, and greed. My biggest slip-ups occurred shortly after I got emotionally involved with positions."

–Ed Seykota

"Consistent success is difficult to achieve because the trading environment differs in almost every way from the environment in which we live our everyday lives. For example, in our everyday lives our fears help us avoid unpleasant or painful experiences. In the trading environment, fear colours our perception of market information thereby influencing our actions. As incredible it may sound, fear of making a mistake, losing money or missing an opportunity, will actually cause us to create the very experiences we are trying to avoid. Consistency as a trader does not depend upon your knowledge of market behaviour, but rather upon a very unique mind-set."

–Mark Douglas

"I prefer not to dwell on past situations. I tend to cut bad trades as soon as possible, forget them, and then move on to new opportunities."

–Ed Seykota

"You are responsible for what you have learned, as well as for everything you haven't learned yet that's waiting to be discovered by you."

–Mark Douglas

"Trying to trade during a losing streak is emotionally devastating. Trying to play 'catch up' is lethal."

–Ed Seykota

"The best traders stay in the flow because they don't try to get anything from the market; they simply make themselves available so they can take advantage of whatever the market is offering at any given moment."

–Mark Douglas

"Losing a position is aggravating, whereas losing your nerve is devastating."

–Ed Seykota

"Being right is more important than being a genius. I think one reason why so many people try to pick tops and bottoms is that they want to prove to the world how smart they are. Think about winning rather than being a hero. Forget trying to judge trading success by how close you can come to picking major tops and bottoms, but rather by how well you can pick individual trades with merit based on favourable risk/return situations and a good percentage of winners. Go for consistency on a trade-to-trade basis, not perfect trades."

–Jack Schwager

"Be sensitive to subtle differences between 'intuition' and 'into wishing.'"
—Ed Seykota

"If you're not afraid, you don't need courage."
—Mark Douglas

"Everybody gets what they want out of the market."
—Ed Seykota

"I believe that to be a good trader it's very important to be rational and have your emotions under control. I've been trying for years to get rid of anger completely when I completely lose money, and I've come to the conclusion that it is impossible. I can work towards that goal, but until the day I die, I don't think I'm ever going to be able to look a big loss in the face and not get angry."
—Monroe Trout

"When people are free to do as they please, they usually imitate each other."
—Eric Hoffer

"Of course, most investors enjoy the process of amassing profits, the satisfaction of adept trading, or simply outwitting the crowd. But it is not just the outcome that is important, it is also the process. The tension that accompanies being in the market is an integral part of the overall experience. For profit without risk, or loss without care drains much of the pleasure out of the investing process."
—F. J. Chu

"If a man will begin with certainties, he shall end in doubts, but if he will be content to begin with doubts, he shall end in certainties."
—Francis Bacon

"The traits of a successful trader: The most important is discipline – I am sure everyone says that. Second, you have to have patience; if you have a good trade on, you have to be able to stay with it. Third, you need courage to go into the market, and courage comes from adequate capitalisation. Fourth, you must have a willingness to lose; that is also related to adequate capitalisation. Fifth, you need a strong desire to win."

–Gary Bielfeldt

"You have to have the attitude that if a trade loses, you can handle it without any problem and come back to do the next trade. You can't let a losing trade get to you emotionally."

–Gary Bielfeldt

"If you don't know who you are, the stock market is an expensive place to find out."

–George Goodman

"Professionals don't perceive anything about the markets as painful; therefore, no threat exists for them. If there's no threat, there's nothing to defend against. As a result, there isn't any reason for their conscious or subconscious defense mechanisms to kick in. That's why professionals can see and do things that mystify everyone else. They're in the flow, because they're perceiving an endless stream of opportunities, and when they're not in the flow, the very best of the best can recognise that fact and then compensate by either scaling back or not trading at all."

–Mark Douglas

"The public's out there throwing darts at a board, sport. I don't throw darts at a board. I bet on sure things. Read Sun-Tzu The Art of War. Every battle is won before it's ever fought. Think about it."

–Gordon Gekko

"The most efficient path to discovering what you need to be successful is to develop a winning attitude, because it is an inherently creative process."

–**Mark Douglas**

"As reasonable as this may sound, it has been my experience that traders with losing attitudes pick the wrong trades regardless of how much they know the markets."

–**Mark Douglas**

"The crowd never thirsted for the truth."

–**Gustave Le Bon**

"Many short-term players view trading as a form of gambling. Without planning or discipline, they throw money at the market. The occasional big score reinforces this easy money attitude but sets them up for ultimate failure. Without defensive rules, insiders easily feed off these losers and send them off to other hobbies."

–**Unknown**

"Once we are in action, tactical aspects tend to be overriding, while the strategic framework tends to be forgotten."

–**Henry Kissinger**

"Many people commonly stereotype stocks, futures, and other investment instruments based on one specific event or experience, or sometimes based on recent activity. Basing decisions on a specific historical event or experience often causes traders to develop mental 'blocks,' which can be detrimental to their state of mind while trading. Blocks will narrow the trader's perspective, potentially shutting out considerations that might be critical to his or her decisions. This type of activity generally demonstrates that the trader doesn't have a good understanding of his own trading personality and isn't confident about his trading plan."

–Unknown

"Very few people who go into trading start out with the appropriate beliefs and attitudes about responsibility and risk."

–Mark Douglas

"Basing decisions on recent activity can also cause problems for the trader. Suppose a specific stock has been steadily rising and you've made quite a bit of profit by trading it. Because of this recent activity, you mentally label the stock as a 'good' one. The likelihood is that the stock is not going to maintain such a steady rise. In fact, it's likely that it will 'correct.' By virtue of mentally labelling the stock, you've formed a personal attachment to it, which will cause you to overlook potential reversals or corrections, have great difficulty in sticking to your stop losses, and therefore to give back most, if not all, of your prior gains. Such losses can lead to further issues about self-esteem and confidence."

–Unknown

"If there is such a thing as a secret to the nature of trading, this is it: At the very core of one's ability (1) to trade without fear or overconfidence, (2) perceive what the market is offering from its perspective, (3) stay completely focused in the 'now moment opportunity flow,' and (4) spontaneously enter the 'zone,' it is a strong virtually unshakeable belief in an uncertain outcome with an edge in your favour."

–Mark Douglas

"Stereotyping tends to be indicative of misplaced confidence. Any successful trader can tell you that if your confidence is coming from a stock's price patterns (over which you have no control), instead of from your trading plan and personality (over which you have the most control), you're headed for losses."

–Unknown

"The key to avoid stereotyping is to understand that trading instruments can't be 'good' or 'bad' – traders can be successful or unsuccessful. Avoid judging stocks, futures, or whatever you're trading, and focus on objectively evaluating the effectiveness of your trading plans and personality. Strive to hone your trading psychology and to develop a set of solid tested plans. The rest of it can't, and doesn't need to be determined."

–Unknown

"There are few things in life more frustrating than recognising the possibilities evident from a hunch, intuition, or an inspired idea, and not taking advantage of that potential because we talked ourselves out of it."

–Mark Douglas

"The problem is that overconfidence is not entirely a bad thing to have. It's heavily based on confidence, which is essential for success in the markets. But at a certain point, a normal level of confidence can develop into overconfidence, and that's a trait that can destroy you."

–Unknown

"If you are a trading and investing hobbyist and you love it, then more power to you. But if you want to be a wealth building trader or investor, make sure that you are spending your time on the process of trading and investing, not on the 'stuff' that is tangential to the process."

–D. R. Barton

"I think one of the most underestimated attributes of successful traders is patience. Patience is a factor in a number of different situations in trading from trade entry, to trade management and your expectations."

–Stuart McPhee

"One of the most important attributes (in anything in life really) is self-confidence. Self-confidence is a measure of your belief in yourself, and has a number of consequences in trading should you lack it. Essentially, being successful requires you to trust and follow your trading plan. If you lack self-confidence, then you are not likely to trust and follow something you have developed."

–Stuart McPhee

"The psychology behind overconfidence is both complex and insidious. It starts simply enough: The typical pattern is to know nothing when you first enter a new field or discipline, such as trading, and have very little or no confidence regarding your ability to do well. Over time, through hard work and study, you tend to increase your knowledge of the field, and as a result your confidence grows."

–Unknown

"But here's where the problem comes in because, for most people, your confidence grows much faster than your knowledge. For example, as a novice in trading, you have very little confidence. After a while, you know a small amount, and your confidence has grown to the point where begin to feel you're getting it. By the time you know a medium amount about trading, you're completely confident of your ability to make money in the markets. Within a year, you can be extremely knowledgeable about trading, and can even have made some very successful trades. It's at this point that your confidence level can easily accelerate way beyond what you know to make you think you're invincible, invulnerable, and capable of being right all the time."

–Unknown

"Once you've over-leveraged your knowledge of trading and become overconfident, it's only a matter of time until you start feeling the markets must come your way, even when they're moving against you, or that it's sensible to risk a large percentage of your account balance on a single uncertain position."

–Unknown

"Winning streaks lead to complacency, and complacency leads to sloppy trading."

–Jack Schwager

"You are today where your thoughts have brought you; you will be tomorrow where your thoughts take you."

–James Allen

"Never trade just to make a trade – even veteran traders can identify with this temptation. It takes tremendous discipline to stay away from frivolous trades due to boredom."

–Jea Yu

"The only time I really ever lost money was when I broke my own rules."

–Jesse Livermore

"In 1980, I researched the history of markets and saw these as classic signs from the heartland of America to the streets of Manhattan that in certain hard-money sectors, individuals believed the world had fundamentally changed to a new landscape. That's how humans react to long-term divergences. They begin to believe that what is happening now will go on forever. The fact is new landscapes emerge and they last longer than anyone can foresee, wiping out convergence traders. But they do not last forever. Another landscape emerges. That's why I'm a trend follower. Twenty years later diamonds are still roughly 80% cheaper than they were at that time. Farmland in the Midwest still does not sell for what it did when I sold my land in 1980."

–**John Henry**

"Even outside the field of finance, Americans are apt to be unduly interested in discovering what average opinion believes average opinion to be; and this national weakness finds its nemesis in the stock market."

–**John Maynard Keynes**

"I believe that the public wants to be lead, to be instructed, to be told what to do. They want reassurance. They will always move on masse, a mob, a herd, a group, because people want the safety of human company. They are afraid to stand alone because the pressure is to be safely included within the herd, not to be the lone calf standing on the desolate, dangerous wolf-patrolled prairie of contrary opinion."

–**Jesse Livermore**

"Reasonable people act unreasonably when they are afraid. And people become afraid when they start to lose money, their judgment becomes impaired. This is our human nature in this stage of our evolution. It cannot be denied. It must be understood."

–**Jesse Livermore**

"As we've seen the danger once you've ridden a good move is arrogance. You get to think you're smart, and all you need to do is trade to make money. The old cliché has it that it's much easier to make money than to keep it. And the cliché is dead right for this phase in the trading cycle. There is nothing easier than to give back in a consolidation all that you've made in a good move. You're thinking in terms of bigger stakes. You're careless. You're on a roller. You get reckless; and you fall to pieces. Very disciplined traders may be able to handle this phase, but for lesser mortals, the best discipline is to get out and wait for the market to tip its hand again, the way it did when you made your original play for the move."

–John Percival

"No man can always have adequate reasons for buying or selling stocks daily- or sufficient knowledge to make his play an intelligent play."

–Jesse Livermore

"It takes a man a long time to learn all the lessons of his mistakes. They say there are two sides to everything. But there is only one side to the stock market; and it is not the bull side or the bear side, but the right side."

–Jesse Livermore

"There is nothing like losing all you have in the world for teaching you what not to do. And when you know what not to do in order not to lose money, you begin to learn what to do in order to win. Did you get that? You begin to learn!"

–Jesse Livermore

"There are several major problems that result when fear becomes a motivation to do or not do something."

–Mark Douglas

"The loss of the money didn't bother me. Whenever I have lost money in the stock market I have always considered that I have learned something; that if I have lost money I have gained experience, so that the money really went for a tuition fee. A man has to have experience and he has to pay for it."

–Jesse Livermore

"Worldly wisdom teaches that it is better for reputation to fail conventionally than to succeed unconventionally."

–John Maynard Keynes

"There are men whose gait is far quicker than the mob's. They are bound to lead- no matter how much the mob changes."

–Jesse Livermore

"Fear and greed are emotions felt when you don't have specific rules in place. Follow your rules, and the only way to have confidence in them is to test them."

–Unknown

"The sucker has always tried to get something for nothing, and the appeal in all booms is always frankly to the gambling instinct aroused by cupidity and spurred by a pervasive prosperity. People who look for easy money invariably pay for the privilege of proving conclusively that it cannot be found on this sordid earth."

–Jesse Livermore

"The effects of fear on one's behaviour are obvious, limiting one to the point of complete immobility. If you can't execute your trades properly, even when you perceive the most perfect opportunity, it is because you have not released yourself from the pain contained in the memories of past trading experiences and because you still don't trust yourself to act appropriately in any given set of conditions. If you did, there would be no fear or immobility."

–Mark Douglas

"In a winning trade, the fear of losing will cause us to focus our attention on information that the market is going to take our profits away, compelling us to get out early. In a losing trade, we will focus our attention on just the opposite information – anything other than that which would indicate the trade is a loser."

–Mark Douglas

"We have only one sample of the past."

–Paul Samuelson

"Fear causes us to act without a perception of choice. When we are afraid to confront certain categories of market information, it drastically limits the choices that we perceive as available. Cutting a loss isn't a choice if we systematically block from our awareness any information that would indicate that we are in a losing trade. Staying in a winner isn't a choice if we are consumed with the fear that the market is going to take away our money… To prevent these blind spots in our perception, we have to learn to trade without fear."

–Mark Douglas

"Sometimes the noisy handful is right, sometimes wrong; but no matter, the crowd follows it."

–Mark Twain

"On the last trading day prior to the holiday, the market had an exceptional tendency to rise, no matter what holiday was involved."
—Martin Zweig

"In summary, people trade for both cognitive and emotional reasons. They trade because they think they have information when they have nothing but noise, and they trade because trading can bring the joy of pride. Trading brings pride when decisions turn out well, but it brings regret when decisions do not turn out well. Investors try to avoid the pain of regret by avoiding the realisation of losses, employing investment advisors as scapegoats, and avoiding stocks of companies with low reputations."
—Meir Statman

"The balance between confidence and humility is best learned through extensive experience and mistakes."
—Michael Steinhardt

"All great traders are seekers of truth."
—Michael Steinhardt

"The markets are always changing, and the successful trader needs to adapt to these changes."
—Michael Steinhardt

"The greater danger of most of us is not that our aim is too high and we miss it, but that it's too low and we reach it."
—Michelangelo

"The best time to buy is when blood is running in the streets."
—Nathan Rothschild

"I had to learn discipline and money management. I decided that I was going to become very disciplined and business-like about my trading."

–Paul Tudor Jones

"I spend my day trying to make myself as happy and relaxed as I can be. If I have positions going against me, I get right out; if they are going for me, I keep them."

–Paul Tudor Jones

"I am always thinking about losing money as opposed to making money."

–Paul Tudor Jones

"If I have positions going against me, I get right out; if they are going for me, I keep them… Risk control is the most important thing in trading. If you have a losing position that is making you uncomfortable, the solution is very simple: Get out, because you can always get back in. There is nothing better than a fresh start."

–Paul Tudor Jones

"Don't be a hero. Don't have an ego. Always question yourself and your ability. Don't ever feel that you are very good. The second you do, you are dead."

–Paul Tudor Jones

"I know that to be successful, I have to be frightened."

–Paul Tudor Jones

"It seems some Behavioural Finance traders try to find any market underreaction to a given event, to invest in its consequences before the other investors get used to the new situation, and to get out when those late investors overreact to the point of creating excessive market prices. They try to make a bridge between fundamental analysis and momentum trading, by trying to understand what makes investors tick."

–Peter Greenfinch

"When things go bad, traders shouldn't stick their head in the sand and just hope it gets better."

–Richard Dennis

"The worst mistake a trader can make is to miss a major profit opportunity. 95 percent of profits come from only 5 percent of the trades."

–Richard Dennis

"Your trading performance is a direct reflection of how you feel internally, not the other way around. When you feel good, you perform at high levels."

–Robert Koppel

"Emotions can be managed but not controlled."

–Scott Billington

"View each trade merely one in a series of probabilities."

–Scott Billington

"Know why you take a trade and what must happen for you to remain in it."

–Scott Billington

"It is not the 'system' that makes the trader, it is the trader that makes the 'system.'"

–Scott Billington

"Our brains are shaped for fitness not truth."

–Steve Pinker

"Going against the consensus is the way an analyst makes his or her mark."

–Steven Garmaise

"A lot of people do not recognise opportunity because it usually goes around wearing overalls and looking like hard work."

–Tom Edison

"Who can you trust? Yourself."

–Michael Covel

"If you have realistic confidence in your method and yourself, then temporary setbacks don't matter, because you will come out ahead in the long run."

–Michael Covel

"To further illustrate the point, consider a modern-day example: the blue-collar Joe v. the entrepreneur. The blue-collar Joe is paid the same lump sum every two weeks like clockwork (with the occasional miniscule raise paced to keep up with inflation). In terms of winning percentage, blue collar is king: his ratio of hours worked to hours paid is one to one, a perfect 100%. He has a steady job and a steady life. Of course, the security he feels is something of an illusion – his pay check comes at the whim of his local economy, his industry, and even the foreman of his plant. And the pay isn't exactly impressive. It gives him a solid, liveable life, but not much more. In contrast, consider the entrepreneur. His paydays are wildly irregular. He frequently goes for months, sometimes years, without seeing tangible reward for his sweat and toil. His winning percentage is, in a word, pathetic. For every ten big ideas he has, seven of them wind up in the circular file. Of the remaining three, two of those fizzle out within a year – another big chunk of time, money and effort down the drain. But we can't feel too sorry for the poor entrepreneur who spends so much time losing. He has a passion for life, he controls his own destiny and that last idea paid him off with an eight-figure check."

–**Michael Covel**

"Most people will never take the time or energy to learn how to trade properly since it is so much easier to be seduced by the ease and comfort of a free charting service that appears to be credible. But trading is zero-sum. For every winner, there is a loser. At Michael Covel we expect, we even hope that many people will continue to stay fixated on the likes of a CBS Market Watch (and others). That is fine with us since it makes it that much easier to win their losses."

–**Michael Covel**

"The hopes and desires of men and women are manifested in market trends."

–**Michael Covel**

"If you missed a trade, don't worry, there is always another."

–**Walter Downs**

"You have to be able to control yourself. You can't let emotions get in the way of your mind."

–**Warren Buffett**

"If your edge puts the odds in your favour, then every loss puts you that much closer to a win. When you really believe this, your response to a losing trade will no longer take on a negative emotional quality."

–Mark Douglas

"I know of a few millionaires who started trading with inherited wealth. In each case, they lost it all because they didn't feel the pain when they were losing. In those formative first years of trading, they felt they could afford to lose. You're much better off going into the market on a shoestring, feeling that you can't afford to lose. I'd rather bet on somebody starting out with a few thousand dollars than on somebody who came in with millions… This is one of the few industries where you can still engineer a rags-to-riches story. Richard Dennis started out with only hundreds of dollars and ended up making hundreds of millions in less than two decades – that's quite motivating."

–William Eckhardt

"Markets invariably move to undervalued and overvalued extremes because human nature falls victim to greed and/or fear."

–William Gross

"The majority of unskilled investors stubbornly hold onto their losses when the losses are small and reasonable. They could get out cheaply, but being emotionally involved and human, they keep waiting and hoping until their loss gets much bigger and costs them dearly.. . In a similar vein, investors cash in small, easy-to-take profits and hold their losers. This tactic is exactly the opposite of correct investment procedure. Investors will sell a stock with a profit before they will sell one with a loss."

–William O'Neil

"Markets offer unlimited opportunities for self-sabotage, as well as for self-fulfilment. Acting out your internal conflicts in the marketplace is an expensive proposition. Traders who are not at peace with themselves often try to fulfil their contradictory wishes in their market. If you do not know where you are going, you will wind up somewhere you never wanted to be. You can succeed in trading only if you can handle it as a serious intellectual pursuit. Emotional trading is lethal. To help ensure success, practice defensive money management. A good trader watches his or her capital as successfully as a professional scuba-diver watches his or her air supply."

–Alexander Elder

Previous Books by the Author

1. 1,000 Tips and Tricks for traders.

Available at Notionpress.com and other e commerce websites

2. Words to trade by

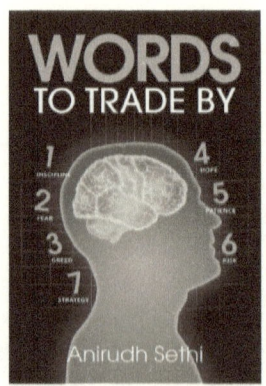

Available at Notionpress.com and other e commerce websites

www.ingramcontent.com/pod-product-compliance
Lightning Source LLC
Chambersburg PA
CBHW020625220526
45464CB00001B/22